A COMPLETE INDEX

TO

THE NAMES OF PERSONS, PLACES AND SUBJECTS MENTIONED IN LITTELL'S LAWS OF KENTUCKY

A GENEALOGICAL AND HISTORICAL GUIDE

PREPARED BY

W. T. SMITH
OF THE LEXINGTON, KY., BAR

CLEARFIELD

Originally published
Lexington, Kentucky, 1931

Reprinted for
Clearfield Company, Inc. by
Genealogical Publishing Co., Inc.
Baltimore, Maryland
1994, 1996

International Standard Book Number: 0-8063-4663-9

Made in the United States of America

PREFACE

The present work was undertaken at the suggestion of Judge Samuel M. Wilson, the noted lawyer, historian and genealogist of Lexington, Kentucky.

The plan of the work, as originally conceived, was to compile an index merely of the names of all persons, as they appear in the five volumes of Littell's Laws of Kentucky. However, as the work progressed, it developed that identical names from time to time appeared in the series of enactments collected by Littell, which the context showed often referred to entirely different persons. It seemed desirable, therefore, in order to avoid confusion, to show further, in the index, as concisely as possible, the connection in which mention of any name is made.

As the volumes of Littell's Laws furnish a fair view and exposition of the early development of the Commonwealth of Kentucky, it has, likewise, seemed desirable to include, in addition to the names of individuals, an index of schools, newspapers, and corporations formed for public purposes, such as those for the opening of streams to navigation, the building of roads, and the like, and of corporations engaged in manufacturing enterprises. As showing the growth and trend of the tobacco industry, there is appended an index of all inspection sites established by law. Much more, not here specified, will be found covered by the contents of the present index.

With the hope that it will be of interest and value to historians as well as genealogists, and not without use to the members of the legal profession, this work is respectfully dedicated to my friend and counsellor, Judge Samuel M. Wilson.

W. T. SMITH.

INTRODUCTION

As set forth in the preface by the author, Mr. W. T. Smith, of the Lexington Bar, this Index to "The Statute Law of Kentucky," as compiled and edited by the Honorable William Littell and published in five volumes, between the years 1809 and 1819, and commonly called "Littell's Laws," is the result of a suggestion offered by the undersigned several years ago. The suggestion, perhaps, owed its origin to the fact that a similar index of "Personal Names in Hening's Statutes at Large of Virginia and Shepherd's Continuation" was prepared and published in 1896 by Joseph J. Casey, Esq., and that work had been frequently consulted and found most useful by the present writer. "Littell's Laws" bears much the same relation to the early history of Kentucky that "Hening's Statutes" bears to the early history of Virginia. To the student of history and genealogy, no less than to the student of law, both of these works are indispensable. Approximately 5,000 proper names will be found listed in this compilation. Frequently it will occur that some name or the act from which it is taken furnishes little more than a bare clue to the identity, family or other social or business relationships, or the history of the individual mentioned, but it is by the aid of such frail clues that the genealogist or historical inquirer is oftentimes enabled to pursue his quest to a successful conclusion. Speaking from long personal experience, we feel safe in saying that "Littell's Laws" constitute a veritable storehouse of genealogical and historical lore, to be found nowhere else in any publication of which we have knowledge. But such lore must remain a sealed record without a key to unlock its treasures. Fortunately, at the expenditure of much time and labor and despite serious handicaps, Mr. Smith has carried out his voluntary undertaking to an eminently satisfactory and successful termination. The tedious and exacting task thus faithfully performed deserves and, we trust, will receive a generous reward in the prompt recognition of the merit of the work and its hearty reception by all persons interested in exploring and elucidating the fascinating history of Kentucky during the period of its infancy. We commend without reserve the entire volume here presented.

SAMUEL M. WILSON.

Lexington, Kentucky, January 1, 1931.

WILLIAM LITTELL

William Littell, the compiler of "Littell's Laws of Kentucky," is believed to have been born in New Jersey, about the year 1780, and to have been a second-cousin of the founder of the Living Age. This relationship, however, has not been positively established. What seems to rest on a firmer foundation is the fact that he was a brother of Absalom Littell, of New Albany, Indiana, and it is probable that he came to Kentucky from Indiana about 1804. He was first educated for the ministry, but abandoned that calling, studied medicine and practiced for a short time in Mt. Sterling, Ky. He next turned his attention to the law, and, in consequence of his legal attainments, exhibited mainly in his painstaking work as a compiler and editor, the degree of LL.D. was conferred upon him by Transylvania University in 1810. Collins, the historian, states that "he was a lawyer of no special reputation except as a land lawyer, a laborious workman, [and] a constant student." His erudition and industry, however, were undeniable. His contributions to the early political history of Kentucky were valuable, but his fame rests chiefly on his law compilations.

Littell married, January 22, 1816, Martha (Irwin) McCracken, a sister of John M. C. Irwin, of Fayette County, and widow of Elijah McCracken. He was twice married but the name of his wife, by his first marriage, has not been ascertained. He died in Frankfort, Ky., September 26, 1824, survived by his widow and two sons, William, born of the first marriage, and Philander, born of the second. Both were minors and Littell's will named as their guardians two ministers, one of whom was the celebrated George T. Chapman of Lexington. He died in straitened circumstances, leaving practically all of his property to his son, William, with the result that the General Assembly, in January, 1825, passed a special act for the relief of the younger son, Philander. This act recited that the testator's "property was not enough to pay his debts, unless sold by a person who has the interest of his estate at heart, who may thus pay his debts, and save something for his infant son."

Littell was renowned for his eccentricities, and Collins states that he was for a "part of his life a man of bad morals." No sufficient evidence of this, however, has been discovered, and it is, perhaps, an overstatement.

In 1805, he entered into a contract with the Commonwealth to collect and publish the Statute Laws of Kentucky, in three volumes, afterwards extended to five. These appeared successively in 1809, '10, '11, '14, and '19. A list of his works, exclusive of writings contributed to the newspapers, is as follows:

Epistles of William, Surnamed Littell, 12mo., Frankfort, Ky., 1806; (satirical pieces in Biblical language and dialogue style).

Narrative (of the Settlement of Kentucky), 12mo., Frankfort, 1806.

Political Transactions in and Concerning Kentucky, 8vo., Frankfort, 1806. (This was republished, with an Introduction by Temple Bodley, in 1926, under the auspices of the Filson Club.)

Principles of Law and Equity, Frankfort, 1808.

The Statute Law of Kentucky, in 5 vols., Frankfort, 1809–1819.

Festoons of Fancy, Consisting of Compositions Amatory, Sentimental and Humorous, in verse and prose, 12mo., Louisville, 1814. (The *Epistles* is sometimes found combined with the *Festoons of Fancy*.)

A Digest of the Statute Law of Kentucky, 2 vols. (in association with Jacob Swigert), Frankfort, 1822. (Annotated with citations of decisions by the Court of Appeals.)

Reports of Cases at Common Law and in Chancery, Decided by the Court of Appeals of the Commonwealth of Kentucky, in 5 vols., Frankfort, Ky., Vol. I, 1823, Vol. II, 1823, Vol. III, 1823, Vol. IV, 1824, Vol. V, 1824.

Cases Selected from the Decisions of the Court of Appeals of Kentucky, Not heretofore Reported, Frankfort, 1824. (Commonly called ''Littell's Selected Cases.'')

KEY TO DATES OF ACTS

	VOL.	PAGE
Acts of Virginia	3	537-588
Kentucky Acts:		
1792 June Session	1	59-114
1792 November Session	1	115-172
1793 November Session	1	173-221
1794 November Session	1	222-274
1795 November Session	1	275-360
1796 November Session	1	361-604
1797 February Session	1	605-696
1797 November Session	1	697-698
1798 January Session	2	1-183
1798 November Session	2	184-263
1799 November Session	2	264-368
1800 November Session	2	369-427
1801 November Session	2	428-492
1802 November Session	3	1-100
1803 November Session	3	101-165
1804 November Session	3	166-246
1805 November Session	3	247-324
1806 November Session	3	325-436
1807 December Session	3	437-536
1808 December Session	4	1- 83
1809 December Session	4	84-192
1810 December Session	4	193-283
1811 December Session	4	284-422
1812 December Session	5	1- 67
1813 December Session	5	68-136
1814 December Session	5	137-298
1815 December Session	5	299-424
1816 December Session	5	425-586

INDEX TO LITTELL'S LAWS OF KENTUCKY

	VOL.	PAGE
Abell, Robert (see Able)		
(a) Delegate from Washington County to second Constitutional Convention (1799).........	1	58
(b) Re-imbursed for supplies furnished frontier guards	1	355
Able, Robert (see Abell)		
Trustee of Washington Academy.............	2	242
Able, William		
Inspection site in Washington County.........	3	324

Academies and Seminaries
See Index of each under proper letter.

Allen	Greenup	Montgomery
Barren	Greenville	New Athens
Bethel	Hardin	Newport
Boone	Harrison	Newton
Bourbon	Harrodsburgh	Nicholas
Bracken	Hartford	Pendleton
Breckenridge	Henderson	Rittenhouse
Bullitt	Henry	Robertson
Caledonia	Jefferson	Rockcastle
Christian	Kentucky	Salem
Danville	Knox	Shelby
Daviess	Lancaster	Stanford
Estill	Lebanon	Summerset
Fleming	Lewis	Transylvania
Franklin	Lexington	Union
Franklinian	Liberty	Washington
Gallatin	Logan	Winchester
Glasgow	Madison	Woodford
Grayson	Manchester	

Adair, County of
(a) Formed from Green County December 11, 1801	2	429
(b) Part of added to Wayne County (1803)......	3	112
(c) Part of Cumberland County added to (1804)..	3	172
(d) Part of Cumberland County added to, reduced (1805)	3	251

ADAIR

	VOL.	PAGE
Adair, John		
(a) Delegate from Mercer County to second Constitutional Convention (1799)	1	58
(b) Trustee of Harrodsburgh Academy	2	240
Adams, Aaron		
Trustee of Mt. Sterling	1	125
Adams, Elizabeth		
Authorized to sue William Adams for divorce	2	362
Adams, George		
Trustee Town of Milford (Madison Co.)	3	567
Adams, James		
(a) Trustee of Beallsborough (Nelson Co.)	3	564
(b) Trustee of Bairdstown	3	566
Adams, John		
(a) Named in boundary of election precinct in Christian County	4	225
(b) Voting place at house in Warren County	5	473
Adams, Simon		
Trustee Town of Port William	1	340
Adams, Spencer		
(a) Trustee of Shelby Academy	2	241
(b) Allowed credit on settlement as Sheriff of Floyd County	5	437
Adams, Thomas		
Penalty for performing marriage ceremony as Justice of the Peace without authority remitted	4	13
Adams, William		
(a) Elizabeth Adams authorized to sue him for divorce	2	362
(b) Trustee Shelby Library Company	4	90
(c) Granted change of venue from Shelby to Mercer County on trial for larceny	5	74
Alderson, Isaac		
Trustee Lancaster Library Company	3	208
Alexander, Ebenezer		
Acts as Presiding Justice of Logan County confirmed	2	361
Alexander, James		
Trustee of Bullitt Academy	3	478
Alexander, James R.		
Trustee of Allen Seminary	5	433
Alexander, Robert		
(a) Trustee of Woodford Academy	2	243
(b) Promoter for Woodford County of Kentucky River Navigation Company	2	448
Alexander, Thomas		
Tried in Henry County for murder	2	484

ALLCORN

	VOL.	PAGE
Allcorn, William		
Named in boundary of election precinct in Clay County	5	472
Allen, Benjamin		
(a) Inspection site in Campbell County	2	457
(b) Trustee Town of Salisberry in Campbell County	3	369
(c) Voting place at house in Campbell County	3	413
Allen, Cary		
Trustee of Kentucky Academy	1	228
Allen, Chilton		
Trustee Winchester Library Company	4	195
Allen, County of		
(a) Formed from Warren and Barren Counties, April 1, 1815	5	157
(b) Part of added to Warren County (1816)	5	348
Allen, James (see Allin)		
(a) Trustee Town of Greensburg	1	273
(b) Trustee New Athens Seminary	3	302
(c) Trustee Salem Academy	3	580
Allen, John (see Allin)		
(a) Delegate from Bourbon County to Second Constitutional Convention (1799)	1	57
(b) Claim of title to town-site of Paris settled	1	112
(c) Trustee Town of Paris	1	188
(d) One of Commission to open Stoners Fork to navigation	1	193
(e) Act settling claim to town-site of Paris repealed	1	356
(f) Trustee of Bourbon Academy	2	237
(g) Trustee of Bourbon Academy	2	242
(h) Trustee Town of Greensburg	1	273
(i) Trustee of Shelby Academy	2	241
(j) Administrator of Elizabeth Snelling, deceased	3	242
Allen, John		
(k) Judge Circuit Court, Second District	3	507
Allen, Joseph		
(a) Trustee Town of Washington in Mason County	1	199
(b) Trustee to hold Breckenridge Seminary lands	5	401
Allen, Robert		
(a) Trustee Town of Greensburg	1	273
(b) One of Commission to open a road from Greensburg to the Tennessee line	3	22
(c) Trustee New Athens Seminary	3	302
Allen Seminary		
Incorporated at Scottville, January 31, 1817, with James R. Alexander, Thomas Gatton, John Godley, Alfred Payne, Daniel M. Jones, David A. Porter, Jacob W. Walker, John		

ALLEN 4

	VOL.	PAGE
Walker, John Wills and Samuel Garrison, Trustees	5	433

Allen, Thomas
(a) Delegate from Mercer County to Second Constitutional Convention (1799) 1   58
(b) Deeds as Attorney in Fact for Trustees of Harrodsburgh confirmed 2   169
(c) Trustee Town of Warwick in Mercer County.... 3   564

Allin, James (see Allen)
One of Commission to raise funds to open road from Greensburg to the Tennessee line 3   22

Allin, John (see Allen)
His military survey named in boundary of Jessamine County 2   214

Allington, Clarinda
She was taken captive by Cherokee Indians and compelled to become the wife of a chief by whom she had three children. She escaped and an allowance was made her for support of herself and children........................... 3   193

Alsop, John Senior
Allowed compensation for building a turnpike on the Madison Road 4   55

Anderson, George
Title of State to escheated land bought by him was released 4   325

Anderson, James
One of Commission to build bridge over Rockcastle River on road to Cumberland Gap..... 3   511

Anderson, John
Witness fees on his trial before the Legislature allowed 4   220

Anderson, Richard C.
(a) Trustee of Jefferson Academy 3   207
(b) Lands of Jefferson Seminary vested in him and others as 'Trustees 3   490

Anderson, Colonel Richard Clough
(a) Lands vested in him and others as Trustees of Jefferson Seminary 2   108
(b) One of Commission to sell lots in Louisville and adjust claims 3   545
(c) Named as boundary of election precinct in Jefferson County 5   308
(d) Same as (c) 5   334

ANDERSON

	VOL.	PAGE
Anderson, Stoke		
Inspection site in Mason County	3	323
Anderson, Thomas		
Justices of Pendleton County to meet at his house	2	198
Andrews, Robert		
Inspection site at his mill in Fleming County	3	451
Applegate, John		
Certificate for Spy Service ordered paid to Philip Bush, Jr., as assignee	3	408
Armstrong, James		
Certificate for Spy Service ordered paid to Philip Bush, Jr., as assignee	3	408
Armstrong, James, deceased		
Certificate for land ordered recorded	4	87
Armstrong, Johnson		
Promoter for Maysville of the Maysville and Lexington Turnpike Road Company	5	536
Armstrong, Joshua		
Trustee Town of Kennedysville in Green County	1	342
Armstrong, Richard		
Title of State to his lands, for which no grant had been issued, was released	5	329
Arnold, Stephen		
Trustee Town of Warwick in Mercer County	3	564
Arnold, Thomas		
(a) One of Commission to settle accounts of Clerk of the Fayette Quarterly Court	3	157
(b) Promoter for Paris of the Bank of Kentucky	3	390
Arthur, Colonel		
Road from his house to Somerset to be improved	5	392
Ashby, Bladen		
Trustee Hardin Academy	2	242
Ashby, Daniel		
Allowed a credit in settlement as Sheriff of Henderson County	3	272
Ashcraft, Daniel		
Named in boundary of election precinct in Grayson County	5	35
Ashridge Meeting House		
Trustees of Kentucky Academy to meet at	1	228
Atkins, Joel		
Trustee Town of Stanford	1	240
Atwood, James		
A marriage solemnized by him as Justice of the Peace without authority legalized	2	364

AUGUSTA 6

	VOL.	PAGE
Augusta, Town of
  (a) Powers given Trustees...................... 2 281
  (b) Made county seat of Bracken County 3 95
  (c) Road to Georgetown to be opened 3 201
Auxer, Michael
  Voting place at his house in Floyd County...... 5 155
Bailey, Elijah
  Inspection site in Logan County 1 370
Bailey, James
  Allowed pay as marker of road from Danville
    to Tellico 3 259
Bailey, John
  (a) Delegate from Logan County to second Constitutional Convention (1799) 1 58
  (b) Inspection site in Logan County 1 370
  (c) Same as (b) 2 140
  (d) Authorized to locate timber lands in Logan County for his bloomery 2 174
  (e) Given further time to locate lands in (d)....... 2 487
  (f) Trustee Newton Academy 2 241
  (g) Successor as Trustee Newton Academy named.. 3 277
Baird, David
  (a) Inspection site in Nelson County 2 139
  (b) Same as (a) 3 583
  (c) Bairdstown established on his lands 3 566
Baird, James
  (a) Trustee of Bairdstown 3 566
  (b) Trustee of Salem Academy 3 580
Baird, James, Junior
  One of Commission to build bridge over Rough Creek at Hartford 4 88
Bairdstown (see Bardstown)
Baker, Abner
  (a) Promoter for Garrard County of Kentucky River Navigation Company 2 448
  (b) Trustee Lancaster Library Company 3 208
  (c) Trustee Manchester Academy 4 18
Baker, John
  (a) Winchester established on his lands 1 187
  (b) Mention made of (a) 1 367
Baker, Joshua
  (a) Delegate from Mason County to second Constitutional Convention (1799) 1 58
  (b) Trustee Town of Newtown in Mason County.. 1 285
Baker, Martin, Jr.
  Justices of Nicholas County to meet at his house 2 366

	VOL.	PAGE
Baker, Robert		
Justices of Clay County to meet at his house....	3	338
Baker, William		
Trustee Town of Newtown in Mason County..	1	285
Balch (see Balsh)		
Baldwin, Samuel		
Trustee Town of Washington	2	393
Ballard, Bland W.		
(a) Trustee Shelby Academy	2	241
(b) Allowed pay for services as Quarter Master Sergeant of Militia	3	491
Ballengall, David		
One of Commission to locate county seat of Lewis County	3	340
Ballenger, Achilles		
Trustee Lancaster Library Company	3	208
Ballenger, John		
One of Commission to open road from Knox Court House to Pulaski	3	464
Ballenger, Joseph		
Trustee Town of Stanford	1	240
Balsh, Amos		
Trustee Newton Academy	2	241
Successor appointed	3	277
Bank of Kentucky		
(a) Incorporated December 27, 1806, with a capital stock of $1,000,000.00; with William Trigg, Daniel Weisiger and George Greer, of Frankfort; Alexander Parker, Thomas Hart, Junior, and Henry Purviance, of Lexington; William Scott, Thomas Arnold and Samuel Williams, of Paris; John Machir, Bazil Duke and Daniel Vertner, of Washington; Robert Caldwell, Thomas Howard and William Irvine, of Richmond; James Birney, Robert Craddock and Joshua Barbee, of Danville; William R. Hynes, Walter Brashears and John Caldwell, of Bairdstown; Thomas Prather, James Berthoud and Peter B. Ormsby, of Louisville; Adam Steele, Wingfield Bullock and James Bradshaw, at Shelbyville; Daniel Barry, Samuel Rose and Joshua Crow, of Hartford; and Joseph Ficklin, Armstead Morehead and James Wilson, of Russellville, as solicitors of subscriptions to its capital stock	3	390
(b) Private banking prohibited (1812)	4	399
(c) Capital stock increased to $3,000,000.00 (1814)	5	281

	VOL.	PAGE
(d) A part of its stock, reserved by the State, authorized sold by the Bank (1816)	5	517
Barbee, Elias		
(a) Trustee Town of Greensburg	1	273
(b) Trustee New Athens Academy	2	242
Barbee, Joshua		
(a) Trustee Danville Library Company	2	376
(b) Promoter, for Danville, of Bank of Kentucky	3	390
(c) Trustee Town of Danville	4	39
(d) Trustee of Danville Academy	5	480
Barbour, Ambrose		
Trustee Henderson Library Company	5	460
Barbour, Philip		
Inspection site, Town of Henderson	3	514
Barbour, Thomas		
Trustee Jefferson Academy	3	207
Barclay, James		
Trustee Lewis Academy	4	17
Bardstown		
Established by Virginia in 1788 on lands of David Baird and John C. Owing, with Isaac Morrison, Walter Beall, James Baird, John Ried, Andrew Hynes, Philip Philips, John Caldwell, Gabriel Cox, James Adams, James Morrison, and Michael Campbell, as Trustees	3	566
Barger, Adam		
Charged with murder of John Coffman	4	148
Barlow, Ambrose		
Allowed pay for guarding families moving through Cumberland Gap in 1786	3	407
Barner, John		
Trustee Gallatin Academy	5	13
Barnes (see also Barns)		
Barnes, Joshua		
Inspection site in Washington County	3	451
Barnes, William (see Barns)		
Voting place at house in Pendleton County	3	489
Barnet, Alexander		
Trustee Hartford Academy	2	242
Barnett, Alexander		
(a) Trustee Bourbon Academy	2	237
(b) Trustee Bourbon Academy	2	242
Barnett, Andrew		
Price paid for land had been credited in name of Anthony Barnett: error corrected	5	428

	VOL.	PAGE

Barnett, Elizabeth
    Authorized, with Polly Mason, to survey and patent 400 acres of land on an entry made by their ancestor, Abraham Holt............. 5   22

Barnett, James
    (a) One of Commission to open road in Madison County 1   231
    (b) Trustee Madison Academy.................. 2   241
    (c) Trustee Madison Academy.................... 3   278
    (d) Promoter for Madison County of Kentucky River Navigation Company................ 2   448
    (e) Trustee Town of Milford in Madison County... 3   567
    (f) Given time to file certificate of survey......... 5   208

Barnett, Joseph, deceased
    (a) Sale of his lands authorized.................. 1   603
    (b) Directs manner of applying proceeds of sale of lands 2   177
    (c) Directs settlement of estate with County Court of Hardin County........................ 2   186

Barnet, Joseph
    Trustee Salem Academy..................... 3   580

Barnett, Joseph, et als.
    (a) Authorized to locate land on Horse Lick Fork of Rockcastle adjoining their salt spring on line between Clay and Madison Counties........ 4   137
    (b) Given further time to locate lands............ 5   138
    (c) Given further time to locate lands............ 5   428

Barnet, William
    Given time to settle accounts as Sheriff of Green County 2   186

Barns, John
    Price of land in Pulaski County remitted, he being insane 5   18

Barns, William (see Barnes)
    Voting place at house in Pendleton County.... 3   319

Barr, Robert
    (a) One of Commission to open road in Madison County 1   231
    (b) Trustee Lexington Library Association........ 2   375

Barr, Thomas
    Trustee Lexington Library Association........ 2   375

Barr, Thomas T.
    Promoter of Kentucky Assurance Society...... 4   254

BARREN COUNTY 10

	VOL.	PAGE
Barren County		
(a) Formed May 10, 1799, from Green and Warren	2	222
(b) Part of Cumberland County added to (1799)..	2	265
(c) Allen County, in part, carved from (1815)....	5	157

Barrett, William
Trustee New Athens Seminary............... 3   302

Barrow, David
Incorporator of Mt. Sterling Library Company 5   177

Barrow, Nathan, deceased
Lands of authorized sold.................... 5   437

Barry, Daniel
(a) Granted change of venue from Bardstown to Danville on trial for murder............... 2   486
(b) Promoter for Hartford of Bank of Kentucky... 3   391
(c) Trustee Town of Hartford................... 3   443

Bartholemy, Francis
Nancy Bartholemy authorized to sue him in Campbell County for divorce............... 3   163

Bartholemy, Nancy
Authorized to sue Francis Bartholemy in Campbell County for divorce................... 3   163

Bartlett, Anthony
Promoter for Gallatin County of the Ohio Steam Boat Company 5   344

Bartlett, Edmund
(a) One of the Commissioners for Henry County to survey the Henry-Shelby line............... 5   103
(b) Member of second Commission to survey Henry-Shelby line 5   330
(c) One of Commission to open road from Newcastle to mouth of Licking...................... 5   131

Bartlett, James
(a) One of Commissioners for Henry County to open road from Newcastle to mouth of Licking.... 3   365
(b) Trustee Henry Academy..................... 5   134

Bartlett, William
Named in Nicholas-Fleming boundary......... 5   366

Barty, David
Trustee Lebanon Academy................... 4   193

Bast, George
Trustee Danville Academy................... 5   480

Bates, John
(a) Trustee Jefferson Academy................. 3   207
(b) Lands of Jefferson Academy vested in him and others, as Trustees........................ 3   490

	VOL.	PAGE
(c) One of Commission to open South Fork of Kentucky River to navigation..................	4	94
(d) One of Commissioners from Clay County to open a road in Clay and Estill Counties..........	5	566

Bath County
Formed February 1, 1811, from Montgomery County 4 215

Batterton, Moses
Named in boundary of Rockcastle County...... 4 92

Bayles, Benjamin
(a) Trustee Town of Washington................ 2 393
(b) Trustee Franklin Academy.................. 3 255
(c) Promoter for Washington of Kentucky Assurance Society 4 254

Baylor, Walker
(a) Director Vineyard Society of Lexington....... 2 268
(b) Acts as one of Commission to replace Fayette Burnt Records confirmed.................. 3 154
(c) Trustee Town of Stanford................... 3 559

Beal, Samuel T.
One of a Commission to conduct a lottery...... 5 570

Beall, Benjamin
Purchaser of lands of William Kennedy, deceased 3 163

Beall, Benjamin, deceased
Division and sale of his lands in Campbell County authorized....................... 5 566

Beall, Jannett H., deceased
Division and sale of her lands in Campbell County authorized 5 566

Beall, Richard
Given time to settle as Sheriff of Washington County 2 364

Beall, Walter
(a) Greensburg established on his lands.......... 1 272
(b) Inspection site in Hardin County............. 1 330
(c) Inspection site in Hardin County............. 2 279
(d) Inspection site in Mercer County............. 2 139
(e) Inspection site in Mercer County............. 3 582
(f) Inspection site in Nelson County............. 2 139
(g) Inspection site in Nelson County............. 3 582
(h) Trustee Salem Academy in Nelson County.... 3 580
(i) Town of Warwick in Mercer County established on his lands 3 563
(j) Trustee of Bardstown...................... 3 566

BEALLSBOROUGH 12

	VOL.	PAGE

Beallsborough, Town of
    Established in 1787 on Salt River at mouth of Beech Fork in Nelson County on lands of Walter Beall, with James Morrison, Francis Parepoint, Samuel Pottinger, Isaac Morrison, James Adams, Isaac Cox, Cuthbert Harrison, George Harrison, Andrew Hinds, John Kennedy, William Kendell and Adkin Hill, Trustees 3   564

Bean, Thomas
    Named in boundary of election precinct in Hardin County 5   473

Beatty, Adam
    (a) Promoter for Town of Washington of Kentucky Assurance Society....................... 4   254
    (b) One of the incorporators of the Washington Library Company 4   273
    (c) One of Commission to raise by lottery a fund to improve road from Maysville to Town of Washington 4   279

Beatty, Cornelius
    Trustee Transylvania University.............. 2   234

Beatty, Otho
    (a) Trustee Kentucky Seminary................. 2   389
    (b) Inspection site at Frankfort................ 2   456

Beaty, Henry
    Mill on Drowning Creek named in Madison-Estill boundary 3   473

Beaty, James
    One of Commission to build bridge over North Elkhorn in Scott County................ 4   88

Beckwith, John W.
    (a) Trustee Bullitt Academy..................... 3   478
    (b) One of Commission to raise by lottery a fund to open Salt River to navigation.............. 4   249

Bedford, Benjamin
    (a) One of Commission to open Stoners Fork of Licking to navigation.................... 1   193
    (b) Trustee Town of Boonesborough (1787)...... 3   540
    (c) One of Commission to erect a turnpike on road from Fleming County to the Big Sandy.... 4   154

Bedford, Town of
    Established in Henry County February 6, 1816, on lands of Henry Young. Jack Pryor, Charles Eastin, Charles Dorsey, Jr., and Daniel Farley, with Henry Davidge, Archelaus Hoskins, Daniel

BEDINGER

	VOL.	PAGE
Farley, Jack Pryor and William Gatewood as Trustees	5	350

Bedinger, George M.
(a) Given time to complete locks at mill-dam on Licking River ... 2 ... 313
(b) Given further time ... 2 ... 455
(c) Mill on Main Licking referred to ... 3 ... 257
(d) Mill on Main Licking referred to ... 3 ... 366

Beelor, Eleanor
Authorized to sue Nathaniel Beelor for divorce in Jefferson County ... 3 ... 516

Beelor, Nathaniel
Eleanor Beelor authorized to sue him for divorce in Jefferson County ... 3 ... 516

Bell, Benjamin
Trustee Town of Warwick in Mercer County ... 3 ... 564

Bell, David
(a) Promoter for Danville of Kentucky Assurance Society ... 4 ... 254
(b) Trustee Danville Academy ... 5 ... 480

Bell, John
Delegate from Fayette County to Second Constitutional Convention (1799) ... 1 ... 58

Bellis, Peter
Tolls to be charged on bridge over Dix River fixed ... 5 ... 70

Bembridge, Peter
Trustee Lancaster Library Company ... 3 ... 208

Benham, Daniel
Trustee Lebanon Academy ... 4 ... 193

Bennett, Caty
See Thomas Bennett ... 5 ... 478

Bennett, Rosa
See Thomas Bennett ... 5 ... 478

Bennett, Thomas, deceased
Title of State by escheat released to his heirs, Caty and Rosa Bennett ... 5 ... 478

Berry, Benjamin
Inspection site in Henderson County ... 2 ... 278

Berry, James
Trustee Lebanon Academy ... 5 ... 323

Berry, Richard
One of Commission to open a road from Springfield toward Frankfort ... 3 ... 203

Berry, Samuel, Jr.
One of Commissioners for Woodford County to open road from Buckley's Ferry to Bardstown ... 3 ... 463

	VOL.	PAGE
Berry, Washington		
(a) Trustee Town of Newport	1	281
(b) Trustee Newport Academy	2	240
Berthoud, James		
(a) Incorporator of Ohio Canal Company	3	260
(b) Promoter for Louisville of Bank of Kentucky	3	391
Berthoud, Nicholas		
Inspection site at Shippingsport in Jefferson County	3	514
Best, Josiah		
One of Commission to open Nolinn Creek in Hardin County to navigation	4	221
Bethel Academy		
(a) Incorporated February 10, 1798 with Francis Paythress, John Knobler, Nathaniel Harris, John Metcalf, Barnabas McHenry, James Crutcher, James Hord and Richard Masterson, Trustees	2	174
(b) Granted 6000 Acres of land on Green River	2	107
(c) Authorized to sell lands for benefit of public schools of Jessamine County	4	151
Bibb, George M.		
Copies of his Reports of the Court of Appeals to be furnished Judges and Clerks of Circuit Courts	5	413
Big Barren River		
(a) Declared navigable to mouth of Bays Fork and Jacob Skiles, Alexander Graham, George G. Minor, Thomas Starrat and Benjamin Lawless appointed Commissioners to render it navigable	4	116
(b) Declared navigable to mouth of Long Creek in Barren County, and Alexander Davidson Jr., Samuel Parker and John Godly appointed Commissioners to render it navigable	4	198
Biggerstaff, Samuel		
Inspection site in Madison County	2	139
Biggs, Andrew		
Granted change of venue from Montgomery to Harrison County on trial for murder	4	250
Bilbo, Archibald		
Trustee Town of Perryville	5	454
Bilbo, John		
Given time to file delinquent tax list as Deputy Sheriff of Henderson County	3	345
Bilderbacks, William		
Voting place at house in Lewis County	5	184

	VOL.	PAGE
Birdsong, William		
Trustee Caledonia Academy	5	3
Birney, James		
(a) Trustee Town of Danville	4	39
(b) Trustee Danville Library	2	376
(c) Promoter for Mercer County of Kentucky River Navigation Company	2	448
(d) Promoter for Danville of the Bank of Kentucky	3	390
(e) Promoter for Danville of the Ohio Canal Company	3	221
Black, Mary		
Authorized to sue Robert Black for divorce	2	195
Black, Robert		
Mary Black authorized to sue him for divorce	2	195
Blackburn, William B.		
Incorporator of Versailles Library Company	4	356
Blain, John		
One of Commissioners for Lincoln County to survey Lincoln-Casey County line	5	105
Blair, James		
(a) Trustee Kentucky Seminary	2	389
(b) Trustee Kentucky Seminary	4	319
Blakely, Charles		
Price of head-right land remitted	4	323
Blanchard, John		
Trustee Bracken Academy	2	242
Bland, John		
Granted 160 Acres of land in Cumberland County for his support	3	96
Blane, Alexander		
Trustee Town of Stanford	3	559
Bledsoe, Moses		
Trustee Montgomery Academy	3	438
Bledsoe, William		
Trustee Lancaster Academy	2	242
Bledsoe, William M.		
(a) Delegate from Garrard County to second Constitutional Convention (1799)	1	58
(b) Trustee Lancaster Library Company	3	208
Blince, Benjamin		
Voting place at house in Breckenridge County	4	328
Blue, James		
Relieved of effect of irregularities with respect to some head-right lands	4	340
Blue Licks—Upper and Lower		
Salt works at to be fenced	2	188

BLUE 16

	VOL.	PAGE
Blue, Uriah		
Trustee Town of Carthage in Union County..	5	83
Blythe, James		
(a) Trustee Kentucky Academy................	1	228
(b) Trustee Transylvania University.............	2	234
Bodine, Catherine		
Authorized sale of land...................	5	437
Bodley, Thomas		
(a) Director of the Vineyard Society of Lexington	2	268
(b) His acts as Commissioner to replace Fayette County Burnt Records confirmed..........	3	154
(c) One of Commission to settle accounts of the Clerk of the Fayette Quarterly Court......	3	157
(d) One of a Commission to raise by lottery a fund to erect a Grand Masonic Hall in Lexington..	5	181
(e) Promoter for Lexington of the Maysville and Lexington Turnpike Road Company......	5	536
Bohannon, George		
Trustee Harrodsburg Academy..............	2	240
Boler, Sally W.		
State price of land remitted................	5	481
Bond, John		
Trustee Bracken Academy..................	2	242
Bondurant, Joseph		
Trustee Shelby Library Company............	4	90
Bonta, Abraham, deceased		
(a) Sale of his lands authorized...............	3	165
(b) Credit terms of sale extended.............	3	166
Bonta, Peter		
Trustee Harrodsburg Academy..............	2	240
Booker, Paul J.		
Trustee Washington Academy...............	5	15
Books—farm		
Named in Montgomery-Bath County line......	4	215
Boone Academy		
Incorporated January 8, 1814 with Absolem Graves, Moses Scott, John Flournoy, Jacob Rouse, Jeremiah Kirtley, John Brown and Mr. —— Bosson, Trustees...............	5	76
Boone County		
Formed from Campbell County, June 1, 1799..	4	535
Boone, Daniel		
(a) Trustee of Boonesborough.................	3	538
(b) Trustee Town of Washington (1786)........	3	555
(c) Trustee of Maysville.....................	3	565
Boone, Jacob		
Trustee of Maysville......................	3	565

	VOL.	PAGE
Boone, Jesse		
Trustee Greenup Academy	4	128
Boone, Joseph		
Inspection site in Warren County	3	323
Boonesborough		
(a) Established October —, 1779 with Richard Callaway, Charles Minn Thruston, Levin Powell, Edmund Taylor, James Estre, Edward Bradley, John Kennedy, David Gist, Pemberton Rollings and Daniel Boone as Trustees	3	538
(b) The Trustees declined to act and Thomas Kennedy, Aaron Lewis, Robert Rhodes, Green Clay, Archibald Woods, Benjamin Bedford, John Sappington, William Irvine, David Crews and Higgerson Grubbs were appointed (1787)	3	539
(c) Ferry established at (1779) and Richard Callaway was granted the right to operate it	3	585
(d) Time given lot owners to build	1	341
(e) Trustees authorized to set apart and sell one acre of the Commons for the purpose of having a salt works erected thereon	1	221
(f) Inspection site at (1798)	2	139
Bosson, Mr.——		
Trustee Boone Academy	5	76
Boswell, Captain		
Given power to appoint surveyors (1783)	1	442
Boswell, Bushrod		
Promoter, at Lexington, of Maysville and Lexington Turnpike Road Company	5	536
Boswell, Hartwell		
Incorporator of Cynthiana Manufacturing Company	5	378
Boswell, William E.		
(a) Delegate from Harrison County to second Constitutional Convention (1799)	1	58
(b) Trustee Harrison Academy	2	241
(c) Allowed pay as Commissioner of Harrison County	2	485
Bourbon Academy		
(a) Incorporated December 22, 1798 with William Garrard, David Purviance, Augustine Eastin, John Edwards, Andrew Todd, John Allen, William Kelly, Thomas Jones Sr., Hugh Brent, John Metcalfe, Alexander Barnett, James Brown Sr., Barton W. Stone, James Matson, and James Kinney, as Trustees	2	237

BOURBON COUNTY 18

	VOL.	PAGE
(b) Trustees granted 6000 acres of land on Green River	2	242

Bourbon County
- (a) Formed from Fayette County, May 1, 1786.. 1 627
- (b) Mason County carved from (1788) 1 628
- (c) Clarke County, in part, carved from (1792).... 1 630
- (d) Harrison County, in part, carved from (1794).. 1 631
- (e) Further portions of added to Harrison County 4 63
- (f) Nicholas County, in part, carved from (1800) 2 366
- (g) Further portion of added to Nicholas County 5 452

Bourbon Furnace
- (a) Licking River and Slate Creek declared navigable to................................ 1 277
- (b) Act (a) repealed........................... 4 366

Bowen, William R.
Trustee Henderson Academy................ 5 72

Bowles, James
Trustee Town of Carthage (Union County).. 5 83

Bowling, George
Certificate for military services ordered paid to Philip Bush, Jr., as assignee thereof........ 3 408

Bowling Green, Town of
- (a) Commissioners to locate County Seat of Warren County to meet there.................... 3 447
- (b) Made County Seat of Warren County........ 4 9

Bowman, John
Trustee Transylvania Seminary.............. 3 572

Bowmar, Harman
Trustee Woodford Academy................ 3 181

Boyd, Robert
One of Commission to open a road from Knox Court-House to Pulaski.................. 3 464

Boyle, John, Jr.
- (a) Trustee Lancaster Academy................ 2 242
- (b) Trustee Lancaster Library Company.......... 3 208

Bozerth, John
- (a) Named in boundary of Grayson County...... 4 130
- (b) Voting place at house in Grayson County...... 4 130

Bracken Academy
Incorporated December 22, 1798 with Philip Buckner, Nathaniel Patterson, Samuel Brooks, William Brook, John Blanchard, Francis Wells, Robert Davis, John Bond, John Fee, John Pattie, and Joseph Logan as Trustees.. 2 242

	VOL.	PAGE
Bracken County
  (a) Formed June 1, 1797 from Mason and Campbell Counties 1   366
  (b) Pendleton County, in part, carved from (1799) 2   197
Bradford, Daniel
  One of Commission to raise by lottery a fund to erect a Grand Masonic Hall in Lexington 5   181
Bradford, John
  (a) Trustee Transylvania University............. 2   234
  (b) Director Vineyard Society, of Lexington...... 2   268
  (c) Trustee Lexington Library Association........ 2   375
  (d) Acts as one of Commission to replace Fayette County Burnt Records confirmed.......... 3   154
  (e) Promoter for Lexington of the Ohio Canal Company 3   221
  (f) Incorporator of Ohio Canal Company........ 3   260
  (g) Promoter, for Lexington, of Madison Hemp Company 3   533
Bradford, William
  One of Commission to locate County Seat of Union County........................... 4   213
Bradfort's Mill
  Rolling Fork in Washington County to be opened to navigation to.................. 3   346
Bradley, Edward
  Trustee of Boonesborough (1779)............ 3   538
Bradley, Samuel
  Justices of Henderson County to meet at his Tavern 2   227
Bradshaw, Benjamin
  Promoter for Jessamine County of Kentucky River Navigation Company................ 2   448
Bradshaw, Edward
  (a) Allowed pay for preparing exhibits for use in the William Rodgers impeachment.......... 4   127
  (b) Trustee Christian Academy.................. 5   450
Bradshaw, James
  Promoter for Shelbyville of Bank of Kentucky 3   391
Bradshaw, John
  Over-payment of taxes refunded............. 4   206
Brand, James W., deceased
  Conveyance of lands authorized.............. 5   478
Brandenburgh, Solomon
  Inspection site in Hardin County............ 3   322
Brands, Johannes
  Heir of Robertus Samuel Brands, deceased.. 2   362

	VOL.	PAGE

Brands, Robertus Samuel, deceased
  (a) Purchase of land in Shelby County when an alien, confirmed........................... 1   603
  (b) His title and that of Johannes Brands, as his heir to lands in Shelby County, vested in Isaac and Nicholas Governeur.................. 2   362

Branham, John
  Rachel Branham authorized to sue him in Montgomery County for divorce................ 3   171

Branham, Rachel
  Authorized to sue John Branham in Montgomery County for divorce................ 3   171

Brashear, Dennis
  Trustee Town of Danville.................... 4   39

Brashear, Thomas C.
  Tax Commissioner of Bullitt County.......... 2   186

Brashear, Walter
  (a) Authorized to survey 400 acres of land in Jefferson County as assignee of Samuel Gill and John Strother........................ 3   100
  (b) Promoter for Bardstown of Bank of Kentucky 3   390
  (c) Trustee Salem Academy...................... 5   7

Brashears, Nacy
  Trustee Town of Shepherdsville.............. 1   183

Brasher, Henry
  Trustee Town of Newport................... 1   281

Brashiers, Marsham
  Trustee of Louisville........................ 3   540

Breckenridge, Alexander
  Trustee Town of Campbell-Town (1785).... 3   554

Breckenridge County
  Formed January 1, 1800 from Hardin County 2   271

Breckenridge, John
  Delegate from Fayette County to second Constitutional Convention (1799).............. 1   58

Breckenridge, John, deceased
  (a) His heirs being mostly infants, the Fayette Circuit Court was authorized to appoint a trustee to manage their property............ 4   395
  (b) Act (a) amended............................ 5   47

Breckenridge, Robert
  (a) Trustee of Campbell-Town (1785)............ 3   554
  (b) One of Commissioners to sell, and adjust claims respecting lots in Louisville (1786)........ 3   545
  (c) Trustee Jefferson Seminary.................. 2   378
  (d) Re-appointed Trustee Jefferson Seminary.... 3   207

21   BRECKENRIDGE SEMINARY

	VOL.	PAGE
(e) Lands of Jefferson Seminary vested in him and others as Trustees	3	490
(f) Incorporator of Louisville Hospital	5	574

Breckenridge Seminary
Joseph Allen and John P. Oldham named Trustees to hold its lands 5   401

Breckenridge, William
Lands descended to him authorized sold 5   511

Breeding, John
His settlement on Green River named in boundary of election precinct in Adair County   3   173

Brehmer, Jacob, deceased
(a) Lands in Nelson County authorized sold by Henry Floyd, Sr., Henry Floyd, Jr., John Floyd, Nathaniel Floyd and Austin Hubbard   3   217
(b) Act (a) amended and Austin Hubbard, Henry Floyd, Jr. and Clement Hamilton named commissioners to sell lands 3   470

Brent, Colonel
Empowered to appoint surveyors (1783) 1   442

Brent, Hugh
(a) Trustee Bourbon Academy 2   237
(b) Trustee Bourbon Academy 2   242
(c) Promoter for Paris of Ohio Canal Company 3   221
(d) Promoter for Paris of Maysville and Lexington Turnpike Road Company 5   536

Brent, Innes B.
Deputy Sheriff of Fayette County 1   113

Brents, Samuel
Trustee New Athens Seminary (Greensburg).. 3   302

Bridges, John L.
Trustee Danville Seminary 3   381

Brinckman, Martin
Lot owners of Middletown to meet at his house to elect trustees 2   275

Brinker, Joseph
(a) One of Commissioners to open road from Newcastle to mouth of Licking 5   131
(b) Trustee Henry Academy 5   134

Briscoe, George H.
Trustee Town of Perryville 5   454

Briscoe, Hezekiah
(a) Grants 100 acres of land for town-site of Versailles 1   63
(b) Adverse claims to lands at (a) adjusted 1   226

Briscoe, John
Guardian of Hezekiah Briscoe 1   63

	VOL.	PAGE
Briscoe, Parmenas		
Trustee of Versailles.........................	1	63
Bristoe, Benjamin, deceased		
Heirs given time to pay for land..............	4	6
Bristoe, James, deceased		
(a) Heirs given time to pay for land...........	3	465
(b) Recited that Benjamin Bristoe's heirs were intended at (a)............................	4	6
Broadis, Beverly (see Broadus, Broaddus, Broddas)		
Trustee Manchester Academy................	4	18
Broaddus, Beverly (see Broadis, Broadus, Broddas)		
One of Commission to raise by lottery a fund to open Kentucky River to navigation........	4	210
Broadus, Beverly (see Broadis, Broaddus, Broddas)		
Re-appointed on Commission to raise by lottery a fund to open Kentucky River to navigation	4	318
Broadnax, Henry P.		
Judge Circuit Court, Sixth District............	3	507
Broadrick, David (see Broderick, Brodrick)		
Trustee of Newtown in Mason County........	1	285
Brock, Henry		
Certificate to John Holder for services in the Wabash Expedition, and assigned to him, was ordered renewed......................	3	100
Broddas, Beverly (see Broadis, Broaddus, Broadus)		
One of Commission to open South Fork of Kentucky River to navigation..............	4	94
Broderick, David (see Broadrick, Brodrick)		
Trustee Franklin Academy..................	1	296
Brodrick, David		
Trustee Town of Washington in Mason County	1	199
Brook, William		
Trustee Bracken Academy..................	2	242
Brooke, George		
(a) Trustee Woodford Academy................	2	243
(b) Trustee Woodford Academy................	3	181
Brooks, Abijah		
Trustee Montgomery Academy................	2	241
Brooks, Joseph		
(a) Trustee Town of Shepherdsville..............	1	183
(b) Named as boundary of New-Town..........	1	233
(c) Title of State to lands claimed by him released	4	133
Brooks, Samuel		
Trustee Bracken Academy..................	2	242
Brooks, Thomas		
Trustee of Maysville (1787)................	3	565

	VOL.	PAGE
Brown, Daniel		
(a) Trustee Newton Academy	2	241
(b) Trustee New Athens Seminary (Greensburg)	3	302
Brown, David		
Trustee Bullitt Academy	3	478
Brown, George		
Trustee of Georgetown	1	220
Brown, James, Sr.		
(a) Trustee Bourbon Academy	2	237
(b) Trustee Bourbon Academy	2	242
Brown, James		
Justices of Floyd County to meet at his house	2	283
Brown, James		
Promoter at Frankfort of Lexington and Louisville Turnpike Road Company	5	519
Brown, John		
(a) Authorized to build bridge over Kentucky River at Frankfort	3	311
(b) Same as (a)	4	350
(c) One of Commission to erect a State House	5	123
(d) Trustee of Harrodsburg (1785)	3	552
(e) Trustee Kentucky Seminary (Franklin County)	4	319
(f) One of Commission to settle accounts at penitentiary	5	276
(g) One of Commission to raise by lottery a fund to improve the road from Maysville to the Town of Washington	4	279
(h) Trustee Boone Academy	5	76
Brown, Patrick		
Trustee Hardin Academy	2	242
Brown, Samuel		
Director Vineyard Society of Lexington	2	268
Brown, William		
(a) Granted change of venue from Caldwell to Christian County on trial for perjury	4	358
(b) Incorporator of Cynthiana Manufacturing Company	5	378
Brownfield, Richard		
Named in boundary of election precinct in Christian County	4	225
Browning, John		
One of Commission to open Mud River in Logan County to navigation	4	115
Brunner, Peter		
Delegate from Mercer County to second Constitutional Convention (1799)	1	58

BRUNTS 24

	VOL.	PAGE

Brunts, Solomon
   Authorized to locate land for use in Manufac-
      turing iron............................. 2   488
Bryan, Daniel
   Incorporator of Fayette Paper Manufactur-
      ing Company........................... 5   409
Bryan, John
   (a) Trustee Hopkinsville Library Company........ 5   361
   (b) Trustee Christian Academy.................. 5   450
Bryant, John
   (a) Trustee Lancaster Academy.................. 2   242
   (b) Trustee Lancaster Library Company.......... 3   208
Buchanan, James
   Voting place at house in Nicholas County.... 2   385
Buck, Charles
   One of Commission to raise by lottery a fund
      to open Kentucky River to navigation...... 4   210
Buckannan, John
   Trustee of Scottville in Allen County.......... 5   483
Buckhannon, Nathaniel
   Inspection site in Adair County.............. 3   23
Buckley, Jeremiah
   (a) Inspection site in Woodford County.......... 3   332
   (b) Commissioner for Franklin County to open road
      from Buckley's Ferry to Bairdstown...... 3   463
   (c) Authorized to build a floating bridge over
      Kentucky River at Buckley's Ferry........ 5   332
Buckner, John C.
   Trustee of Covington....................... 5   283
Buckner, Philip
   (a) Delegate from Bracken County to second Con-
      stitutional Convention (1799).............. 1   57
   (b) Trustee Franklin Academy.................. 1   296
   (c) Trustee Bracken Academy.................. 2   242
   (d) Reimbursed for a boat impressed by General
      Clarke in 1786........................... 2   426
   (e) Commissioner for Bracken County to open road
      from Georgetown to Augusta.............. 3   201
Buckner, Robert
   Given time to settle as surety for William
      Morrow insolvent Sheriff of Bourbon County 3   163
Buckner, William
   (a) Trustee of Greensburg..................... 1   273
   (b) Trustee New Athens Academy at Greensburg.. 2   241
   (c) Granted patent for head-right land surveyed
      in irregular shape........................ 5   32

	VOL.	PAGE

Buford, Abraham
  (a) Trustee Rittenhouse Academy 2   240
  (b) Assignor to Joseph Hart of claim for 3000 acres of land 4   70

Buford, Henry P.
  Trustee Rockcastle Academy 4   114

Buford, William
  (a) Lancaster established on his lands 2   172
  (b) Trustee Lancaster Library Company 3   208

Bullitt Academy
  (a) Incorporated December 22, 1798 with Henry Crist, Benjamin Summers, Benjamin Pope, Daniel Donaldson, Samuel Crow, Richard Summers, Joseph Saunders, John Lewis, Thomas Speed, Armstead Morehead and Thomas Greenfield as Trustees 2   243
  (b) New Board of Trustees appointed February 19, 1808, viz., Henry Crist, Frederick W. S. Grayson, John W. Beckwith, James Alexander, David Brown, William Summers, Samuel Crow, Benjamin Summers and Thomas Sanders 3   478

Bullitt, Alexander S. (Scott)
  (a) One of Commission to sell, and adjust claims respecting lots in Louisville (1786) 3   545
  (b) George Wilson allowed pay for forage furnished him as County Lieutenant of Jefferson County, Virginia in 1787 3   391
  (c) Trustee of Louisville (1789) 3   547
  (d) Speaker of Kentucky Senate (1798) 4   536
  (e) Delegate from Jefferson County to, and President of, Second Constitutional Convention (1799) 1   57
  (f) One of Commission to locate penitentiary (1798) 2   15
  (g) Trustee Jefferson Seminary (1798) 2   108
  (h) Trustee Jefferson Academy (1804) 3   207
  (i) Lands of Jefferson Academy vested in him and others as Trustees (1807) 3   490

Bullitt County
  (a) Formed January 1, 1797 from Jefferson and Nelson Counties 1   364
  (b) Part of Jefferson County added to 4   219

Bullitt, Cuthbert
  (a) Trustee Washington Library 4   354
  (b) Promoter at Louisville of Lexington & Louisville Turnpike Road Company 5   519

	VOL.	PAGE
Bullitt's Lick		
Shepherdsville established on road to	1	183
Bullitt, Thomas		
Incorporator of Louisville Hospital	5	574
Bullock's & Hill's Mill		
Made head of navigation on Chaplin's Fork in Nelson County	3	316
Bullock, David		
(a) Trustee of Winchester	1	187
(b) Trustee Winchester Academy	2	217
(c) Promoter for Clarke County of Kentucky River Navigation Company	2	448
Bullock, Edmund		
(a) One of Commission to assess damages to property owners of Milford caused by removal of Madison County Seat therefrom	2	165
(b) Speaker Kentucky House of Representatives (1798)	4	534
Bullock, Edward		
(a) Voting place at house in Perryville	5	438
(b) Co-founder of Town of Perryville	5	454
Bullock, Garland		
(a) Trustee Town of Port-William in Gallatin County	2	337
(b) Trustee Gallatin Academy	5	13
Bullock, Josiah		
Trustee of Winchester	1	187
Bullock, Patterson		
Trustee Winchester Academy	2	217
Bullock, Thomas		
Promoter for Woodford County of Kentucky River Navigation Company	2	448
Bullock, Wingfield		
(a) Promoter for Shelbyville of Ohio Canal Company	3	221
(b) Incorporator of Ohio Canal Company	3	260
(c) Promoter for Shelbyville of Bank of Kentucky	3	391
(d) Trustee Washingtonian Library	4	354
Bundy, George		
Mary Bundy authorized to sue him in Montgomery County for divorce	3	170
Bundy, Mary		
Authorized to sue George Bundy in Montgomery County for divorce	3	17
Burch, John		
Marriage to Polly McKinley by unauthorized Justice of the Peace was made legal	2	36

	VOL.	PAGE

Burdett, John
  (a) Trustee Rockcastle Academy............... 4   114
  (b) Made manager for Rockcastle County of Turnpike and Wilderness Road................. 4   264
Burk, James
  One of Commission to build bridge over Floyds Fork of Salt River in Bullitt County......... 5   22
Burke, Andrew, et als.
  Relief granted as to head-right lands........ 4   415
Burke, Mary
  Granted patent to 100 acres in Nelson County.. 4   332
Burks, Isham
  Trustee of Greensburg..................... 1   341
Burks, Nicholas
  One of Commission to survey road from Greensburg to Tennessee line................... 3   21
Burks, Samuel
  (a) Trustee of Greensburg..................... 1   273
  (b) Justices of Cumberland County to meet at his house 2   202
Burnet, Robert
  Voting place at his house in Washington County 4   330
Burnside, Robert
  One of Commission to raise by lottery a fund to open Kentucky River to navigation...... 4   318
Burriss, Sarah
  Granted 100 acres of land in consideration of her husband's service at New Orleans...... 5   428
Burwell, Captain Nathaniel
  (a) Empowered to appoint surveyors (1783)...... 1   442
  (b) Inspection site in Christian County.......... 2   279
Bush, Matthias
  Trustee Harrodsburg Academy.............. 2   240
Bush, Philip
  Trustee Harrodsburg Academy.............. 2   240
Bush, Philip, Jr.
  Auditor directed to pay certificates for military services assigned to him by the holders...... 3   407
Bush, William
  (a) Trustee of Winchester..................... 1   187
  (b) Authorized to locate 1000 acres of mountain land on which he and Samuel Newell had discovered iron ore......................... 3   163
  (c) Authorized to locate iron ore lands............ 3   413
Butler County
  (a) Formed May 1, 1810 from Logan and Ohio Counties 4   110

BUTLER 28

	VOL.	PAGE
(b) Part of Logan County added to	5	70

Butler, Isaac
Title to land on Green River confirmed 1   604

Butler, Mann
(a) Incorporator Washington Library Company.... 4   273
(b) Trustee Louisville Library Company 5   359

Butler, William
(a) Named in Cumberland-Green County boundary 2   202
(b) Commissioner for Henry County to open a road from Newcastle to mouth of Licking 3   365
(c) Allowed pay for military services in 1787 and 1793 3   516
(d) Trustee Newcastle Library Company 4   35

Caits, Joshua (see Cates)
Purchase of 7350 acres of land in Christian County from Greenup and Greenville Academies confirmed ..'....................... 5   138

Calahan, Edward
Voting place at his house in Clay County 4   106

Caldwell, Charles
(a) Trustee Hopkinsville Library Company 5   361
(b) Trustee Christian Academy 5   450

Caldwell County
Formed May 1, 1810 from Livingston County... 4   22

Caldwell, David
(a) Trustee of Springfield..................... 1   176
(b) Trustee Newton Academy................... 2   241
(c) Adjustment made in price to be paid for Green River lands.............................. 2   423
(d) Named in Lincoln-Mercer County boundary.. 4   86

Caldwell, James
Commissioner for Harrison County to open road from Georgetown to Augusta.............. 3   201

Caldwell, John
(a) Trustee Salem Academy, Nelson County (1788) 3   586
(b) Authorized to erect mill-dam on Beech Fork in Nelson County.......................... 2   48
(c) Promoter at Bairdstown of Bank of Kentucky 3   39
(d) Trustee of Bairdstown (1788) 3   56
(e) One of Commission to raise by lottery a fund to open Salt River to navigation 4   24
(f) One of Commission to raise by lottery a fund to pave the streets of Bairdstown 5   57
(g) Trustee Kentucky Academy 1   22
(h) Trustee Newton Academy in Logan, Warren or Christian County 2   24

	VOL.	PAGE
(i) Deceased and successor as Trustee of Newton Academy appointed	3	277
Caldwell, Philips and Samuel		
(a) Authorized to locate lands around a salt lick	2	489
(b) Ambiguity in Act (a) corrected	3	97
(c) Price to be paid for land at (a) reduced	4	381
Caldwell, Philips, deceased		
Fee allowed Sheriff of Ohio County in suit by Commonwealth against his estate	3	305
Caldwell, Robert		
(a) Trustee Town of Milford in Madison County	1	226
(b) One of Commission to assess damages to property owners in Milford upon removal of county seat of Madison County therefrom	2	166
(c) Trustee Madison Academy	2	241
(d) Promoter for Richmond of Bank of Kentucky	3	390
(e) Manager for Madison County of the Turnpike and Wilderness Road	4	264
(f) Director of Turnpike and Wilderness Road	4	265
Caldwell, Samuel		
(a) Trustee Logan Vineyard Society	3	139
(b) Trustee Logan Academy	3	206
(c) Trustee Newton Academy	3	409
Caldwell, Samuel and Philips		
See Philips Caldwell		
Caldwell, William		
(a) Surveyor of road from Springfield toward Frankfort	3	22
(b) Trustee Robertson Academy	5	125
(c) Named as vendor of lot in Paris	5	397
Caledonia Academy (Caldwell County)		
Incorporated December 22, 1812, with John M. Walker, William Mitchuson, Fidelio Sharp, Josiah Whitnell, William Birdsong, Richard Hays and Samuel Smith as Trustees	5	2
Calhoon, George		
Authorized to give bond as Sheriff of Henry County as Collector of the Revenue	4	151
Calhoon, John		
Trustee Washington Academy	5	15
Callaham, Isaac		
Granted change of venue from Clay to Knox County on trial for murder	5	425
Callaway, Richard		
(a) Trustee of Boonesborough (1779)	3	538
(b) Granted ferry franchise at Boonesborough (1779)	3	585

CALLOWAY 30

	VOL.	PAGE
Calloway, John		
(a) One of Commissioners for Henry County to survey Henry-Shelby County line	5	103
(b) Also member of second Commission for same purpose as (a)	5	330
Calmes, Marquis		
(a) Trustee of Versailles	1	63
(b) Trustee Woodford Academy	2	243
(c) Trustee Woodford Academy	3	181
(d) Lands of James Trimble, deceased, ordered sold to pay a debt due him	3	243
Cameron, Angus		
Commissioners named to sell his lands	2	53
Cameron, Archibald		
Commissioner to sell lands of Angus Cameron	2	53
Cameron, John		
Commissioner to sell lands of Angus Cameron	2	53
Campbell, Andrew		
(a) Voting place at his house in Green County	5	317
(b) Founder of Campbellsville in Green County	5	430
Campbell, Archibald		
Trustee of Georgetown	3	570
Campbell County		
(a) Formed May 10, 1795, from Harrison, Scott, and Mason Counties	1	632
(b) Bracken County carved from	1	366
(c) Pendleton County, in part, carved from	2	197
(d) Boone County carved from	4	535
Campbell, David		
(a) Trustee Greenville Academy	4	113
(b) Trustee of Campbellsville	5	430
(c) Promoter, at Versailles, of Lexington and Louisville Turnpike Road Company	5	519
Campbell, Duncan		
One of Commission to open road from Lindsey's Station in Scott County to the Ohio	5	272
Campbell, George		
His addition included in Frankfort	1	641
Campbell, John		
(a) Lands named as boundary of Louisville (1780)	3	540
(b) Asserted title to town-site of Louisville (1783)	3	542
(c) Town-site of Louisville ordered surveyed so as to exclude his lands (1783)	3	542
(d) Claim to town-site of Louisville adjusted (1784)	3	543
(e) To share in proceeds of sales of lots in Louisville (1786)	3	540

	VOL.	PAGE
(f) Title of State to 1000 acres of land adjoining town-site of Louisville vested in him (1791)	3	548
(g) Campbell-Town, at Falls of the Ohio, established on his lands (1785)	3	554
(h) Inspection site on lands of at Falls of the Ohio	3	580
(i) Ferry authorized from his lands across the Ohio (1785)	3	586
(j) Speaker Pro Tem of Kentucky Senate (1798)	4	534
(k) Allowed pay for services on Wabash Expedition	3	97
(l) Trustee Transylvania Seminary (1783)	3	572
(m) Suit against him by Breckenridge County Court authorized on account of covenant broken to survey Seminary lands	5	496
(n) Trustee Liberty Academy (Casey County)	4	114

Campbell, John, deceased
Acts as Surveyor of Christian County confirmed ... 3 ... 337

Campbell, Lawrence
Trustee of Campbellsville ... 5 ... 430

Campbell, Michael
(a) Authorized to erect mill-dam on Beech Fork in Nelson County ... 2 ... 489
(b) Trustee of Bairdstown (1788) ... 3 ... 566

Campbell, Robert
Granted 200 acres Green River land by way of pension ... 2 ... 187

Campbell, William
(a) Trustee Newton Academy ... 2 ... 241
(b) Trustee Greenville Academy ... 4 ... 113
(c) Inspection site on Cumberland River ... 2 ... 456
(d) Trustee Lancaster Academy ... 2 ... 242

Campbell, William F.
Surety for John Campbell on bond to survey Seminary lands for Breckenridge County ... 5 ... 496

Campbell-Town
Established at Falls of the Ohio in 1785 on lands of John Campbell with Richard Taylor, Edmund Taylor, James Sullivan, Alexander Breckenridge and Robert Breckenridge as Trustees ... 3 ... 554

Campbellsville (Green County)
Established January 3, 1817, on lands of Andrew Campbell, with Pleasant Kirtley, William Rutter, Joseph Robertson, David Campbell and Lawrence Campbell as Trustees ... 5 ... 430

Camper, James (Kemper)
Trustee Kentucky Academy ... 1 ... 228

	VOL.	PAGE
Canihaw, John, Sr.		
Trustee Hardin Academy	2	242
Canine, Peter		
Allowed to withdraw survey of lands on Green River	3	158
Cannon, James		
Named in boundary of election precinct in Christian County	5	80
Canterberry, Nimrod		
Voting place at house in Greenup County	4	330
Canton, Simon (see Kenton)		
(a) Maysville established on his lands (1787)	3	565
(b) Inspection site in Bourbon (Mason) County (1787)	3	582
Cantral, William		
Special term of Bath Circuit Court authorized to try Samuel Danley for murder of	5	25
Carland, Thomas		
Inspection site in Shelby County	1	370
Carmack, John, Sr.		
Named in boundary of election precinct in Livingston County	3	488
Carneal, Thomas		
Inspection site in Boone County	2	383
Carneal, Thomas D.		
Co-founder of Covington	5	283
Carneel, Thomas		
Trustee Newport Academy	2	240
Carothers, John, et als.		
Authorized to patent small tracts of land in Montgomery and Nelson Counties	4	134
Carpenter, George		
(a) Named in Lincoln-Casey County boundary	3	326
(b) Named in Lincoln-Casey County boundary	5	105
Carr, Walter		
Delegate from Fayette County to second Constitutional Convention (1799)	1	58
Carrell, Sandford, deceased		
Administrator authorized to sell lands	5	382
Carrington, Capt. Mayo		
Empowered to appoint surveyors (1783)	1	442
Carson, William		
Trustee Rockcastle Academy	4	114
Carter, John		
Charged with murder of James Miller	4	148
Carter, John, deceased		
Commissioners authorized to sell lands	5	357

	VOL.	PAGE
Carter, William		
Patent allowed for land in Wayne County....	5	74
Carthage, Town of (Union County)		
Sales of lots by Benjamin Fry, James Houston, James Bowles, Uriah Blue, and William Quigley as Trustees confirmed	5	83
Cartwright, Justinian		
Montgomery Academy authorized to sell enough of the lands donated it by the State to pay Cartwright for services in perpetuating testimony and establishing the donations to Montgomery Academy	4	243
Casey County		
(a) Formed May, 1807, from Lincoln County	3	325
(b) Part of returned to Lincoln County	3	474
(c) Commissioners appointed to survey Casey-Lincoln County line	5	105
Casey, Peter		
(a) Trustee Harrodsburg Academy	2	240
(b) Trustee of Harrodsburg (1785)	3	552
Casey, William		
(a) Delegate from Green County to second Constitutional Convention (1799)	1	58
(b) Trustee of Greensburg	1	273
(c) Named in boundary of Cumberland County....	2	202
(d) Trustee New Athens Academy	2	242
(e) Trustee Robertson Academy	5	125
Cassidy, Michael		
Trustee Fleming Academy	2	241
Cates, Joshua (see Caits)		
(a) Authorized to re-locate donation land purchased from Harrison Seminary	5	310
(b) Given time to locate lands at (a)	5	317
Cave, William		
(a) Trustee of Georgetown (1790)	3	570
(b) Justices of Boone County to meet at house....	4	535
Cavenaugh, William		
Trustee Winchester Academy	2	217
Cavens, Abraham		
Trustee Town of Preston in Shelby County....	1	347
Centreville, Town of		
Established December 17, 1806, and made county seat of Livingston County	3	354
Chaffin, Joseph, et als.		
Given time to make surveys under Virginia land claims	4	381

CHAMBERS 34

	VOL.	PAGE

Chambers, James
    One of Commission to raise by lottery a fund to improve road from Maysville to Town of Washington 4   279
Chambers, John
    (a) One of Commission to raise by lottery a fund to improve road from Maysville to Town of Washington 4   279
    (b) Promoter, for Maysville, of the Maysville and Lexington Turnpike Road Company......... 5   536
Champion, Thomas
    Voting place at house in Livingston County... 5   462
Chapeze, Henry
    Authorized to sue Sarah Chapeze in Nelson County for divorce 3   160
Chapeze, Sarah
    See Henry Chapeze
Chaplaine, Abraham
    Trustee of Harrodsburg (1785) 3   552
Chapline, William, deceased
    Fees due him as Clerk of Warren County ordered collected by present Clerk for benefit of his estate 4   330
Chapman, Mr. ——
    Named in Bullitt County boundary........... 1   364
Chapman, Thomas
    Inspection site in Warren County 2   279
Charlestown (in Bourbon—later Mason—County)
    Established in 1787 on lands of Ignatius Mitchell at mouth of Lawrence Creek on the Ohio with John Grant, Charles Smith, Jr., Thomas Warren, Miles Withers Conway, Henry Lee, John Machir and Robert Rankin as Trustees   3   562
Chasten, Joseph, deceased
    Commissioners authorized to sell a mill descended to his heirs 4   410
Chiles, David
    Trustee of Germantown 1   329
Chism, B.
    Named in boundary of election precinct in Green County 5   317
Chism, John (see Chisom)
    Adjustment made in settlement as Sheriff of Green County 2   423
Chisom, John (see John Chism)
    Trustee of Greensburg 1   341

	VOL.	PAGE

Christ, Henry (see Crist)
   Trustee Bullitt Academy 3   478
Christian Academy
   Incorporated January 17, 1817, with Rezin Davidge, Peter Ferguson, Edward Bradshaw, John Clark, Ferdinand Wadlington, Benjamin H. Reeves, John Bryan, John D. Patton, and Charles Caldwell as Trustees 5   450
Christian County
   (a) Formed March 1, 1797, from Logan County... 1   365
   (b) Livingston County carved from 2   198
   (c) Henderson County carved from 2   227
   (d) Muhlenberg County, in part, carved from..... 2   205
   (e) Muhlenberg line further defined.............. 2   378
Christian, William
   (a) Trustee of Harrodsburg (1785) 3   552
   (b) Trustee Transylvania Seminary (1783) 3   571
Christian, William, deceased
   Lands to be conveyed to Matthews Flournoy.. 3   99
Churchill, Armistead
   Granted change of venue from Jefferson to Bullitt County 5   515
Churchill, Henry
   (a) Trustee Jefferson Seminary 2   108
   (b) Trustee Jefferson Academy 3   207
Churchill, Samuel
   Promoter, for Louisville, of the Lexington and Louisville Turnpike Road Company 5   519
Cincinnati
   Road to from Frankfort to be opened......... 1   185
Cissill, William
   Allowed pay for services on the Wabash Expedition in 1786 3   188
Clack, Moses
   (a) Voting place at house in Fleming County..... 5   426
   (b) Voting place removed 5   447
Clark, Bennett
   (a) Trustee Montgomery Academy 2   241
   (b) Trustee Town of Irvine 4   339
Clarke, Bennett
   One of Commissioners from Estill County to open road in Estill and Clay Counties....... 5   566
Clarke, Cary L.
   Judge Circuit Court Fourth District 3   507
Clarke County
   (a) Formed February 1, 1793, from Fayette and Bourbon Counties 1   630

CLARK 36

	VOL.	PAGE
(b) Montgomery County carved from	1	366
(c) Estill County, in part, carved from	3	441

Clark, David
(a) Trustee Town of Lebanon 5 191
(b) Named in boundary of election precinct in Clay County 5 472

Clarke, Gen. George Rogers
(a) He and his officers and men granted 150,000 acres in Northwestern Territory (1783) 1 444
(b) Trustee Transylvania Seminary (1783) 3 572

Clarke, Col. Henry
Named in boundary of election precinct in Christian County 4 224

Clark, Henry
One of Commission to open Red Bird Fork of Kentucky River to navigation 5 149

Clark, James
Trustee Winchester Library Company 4 195

Clarke, John
(a) Trustee of Newtown in Mason County 1 285
(b) One of Commission to sell, and adjust claims respecting lots in Louisville 3 545

Clark, John
Trustee Christian Academy 5 450

Clarke, Nicholas
Promoter, for Frankfort of Ohio Canal Company 3 221

Clarke, Robert (see Senior and Junior)
(a) Delegate from Clarke County to second Constitutional Convention (1799) 1 58
(b) Inspection site in Harrison County 3 123
(c) Inspection site in Washington County 3 239

Clark, Robert, Sr.
(a) Trustee Winchester Academy 2 217
(b) Inspection site in Madison County 2 383

Clark, Robert, Jr.
(a) One of Commission to assess damages to property owners in Milford upon removal of Madison County seat therefrom 2 165
(b) Trustee Winchester Academy 2 217
(c) Promoter for Clarke County, of the Kentucky River Navigation Company 2 448
(d) Promoter for Winchester, of Ohio Canal Company 3 222

Clarke, Brigadier General
Empowered to appoint surveyors (1783) 1 443

	VOL.	PAGE
Clarke, Lieutenant Colonel		
Empowered to appoint surveyors (1783)......	1	442
Clarke and Smith		
Inspection site at their iron works on Red River in Clarke County	3	324
Clarksburg (in Harrison County)		
Lot owners given time to improve (1789)......	3	552
Clay Academy (see Manchester)		
Clay County		
(a) Formed April 1, 1807 from Madison, Knox and Floyd Counties	3	338
(b) Part of added to Madison County.............	4	406
(c) Part of added to Estill County...............	5	162
Clay, Green		
(a) Delegate from Madison County to second Constitutional Convention (1799)	1	58
(b) Inspection site in Madison County............	2	196
(c) Inspection site in Madison County............	3	332
(d) Trustee Madison Academy	2	241
(e) Inspection sites in Madison County (2)........	2	279
(f) Trustee Town of Milford....................	3	567
(g) Trustee of Boonesborough...................	3	540
(h) One of commissioners to raise by lottery a fund to open Kentucky River to navigation.......	4	210
(i) Same as (h)...............................	4	318
(j) Irvine established on his lands...............	4	339
(k) Repaid purchase price of land bought by him at Sheriff's sale, the sale having been quashed..	5	129
Clay, Henry		
Promoter of Madison Hemp Company.........	3	532
Clay, Henry, Jr.		
Commissioner for Bourbon County to open the South and Stoners Forks of Licking to navigation	3	193
Clay, Samuel		
One of Commission to open Stoner's Fork of Licking to navigation	1	193
Clay, Thomas		
Delegate from Madison County to second Constitutional Convention (1799)	1	58
Clemons, Jeremiah		
(a) Voting place at his house in Danville.........	3	377
(b) Trustee Danville Seminary	2	381
(c) Trustee of Danville	4	39

		VOL.	PAGE

Cleney, Vincent
    One of Commission to raise by lottery a fund to improve the road from Maysville to the Town of Washington 4   279

Cleveland, Eli
    Given time to settle accounts as Sheriff of Fayette County 1   156

Cleveland's Landing
    Inspection site at (1792) 1   135

Clever, Stephen
    (a) Trustee Hartford Academy 2   242
    (b) Trustee Hartford Academy 3   278

Cobb, Jesse
    Trustee Town of Irvine 4   339

Cobbs, John
    Trustee Transylvania Seminary lands (1780).. 3   571

Coburn, John
    (a) Trustee Franklin Academy 1   296
    (b) One of Commission to locate penitentiary...... 2   15
    (c) One of Commission to survey the Virginia-Kentucky boundary line 2   276

Cocke, Stephen
    Trustee Washington Academy 5   15

Cofield, Major
    Named in boundary of election precinct in Livingston County 4   327

Coffman, John
    A citizen of Indiana, was murdered, and Adam Barger, John Fisher and William Walker were charged with the offense................... 4   148

Cole, John
    (a) Inspection site in Warren County............ 2   456
    (b) Named in boundary of election precinct in Warren County 5   16

Coleman, Edward S.
    Voting place at house in Frankfort............ 5   474

Coleman, Francis
    Inspection site in Livingston County......... 2   457

Coleman, Henry
    (a) Delegate from Harrison County to second Constitutional Convention (1799) 1   58
    (b) Trustee of Cynthiana 1   179
    (c) Trustee Harrison Academy................. 2   241

Coleman, James
    (a) Commissioner for Harrison County to open a road from Georgetown to Augusta........... 3   201
    (b) Inspection site in Harrison County.......... 3   324

COLEMAN

	VOL.	PAGE
Coleman, Robert		
Trustee Lebanon Academy	4	193
Colley, Jacob		
(a) Voting place at house in Christian County....	5	80
(b) Act (a) repealed	5	141
Collier, John		
Inspection site in Madison County (1787)	3	582
Collins, Bartlett		
(a) Trustee of Georgetown	1	220
(b) Trustee Transylvania University	2	234
(c) Trustee Rittenhouse Academy	2	240
(d) Promoter for Scott County of Kentucky River Navigation Company	2	448
Collins, Dillard		
(a) One of Commission to assess damages to property owners in Milford upon removal of Madison County seat therefrom	2	165
(b) Trustee Winchester Academy	2	217
(c) Promoter for Clarke County of Kentucky River Navigation Company	2	448
Collins, Edmund		
Trustee of Newtown in Mason County	1	285
Collins, Henry (a British subject)		
His lands were declared escheated and donated to Kentucky County for Seminary purposes (1780)	3	571
Collins, Lewis		
Patent for 200 acres of land granted to Benjamin Sawyer, his assignee	5	70
Combs, Benjamin		
Trustee of Winchester	1	187
Comfort, Daniel		
Trustee Henderson Library Company	5	460
Conard, Jonathan		
Trustee New Athens Academy	2	242
Conn, Notley		
(a) Trustee of Hopewell (Paris) (1789)	3	568
(b) Trustee of Falmouth	1	181
(c) Trustee Kentucky Academy	1	228
Connolly, John		
(a) Louisville established on his lands (1780)	3	540
(b) Title to townsite of Louisville disputed by John Campbell (1783)	3	542
(c) Louisville townsite ordered surveyed so as to exclude John Campbell's land (1783)	3	542
(d) Claim to Louisville townsite adjusted (1784)..	3	543

CONNOR 40

	VOL.	PAGE
(e) Mortgage by him to John Campbell and Joseph Simon covering Louisville townsite ordered paid out of proceeds of sales of lots in the Town of Louisville (1786)	3	546

Connor, Daniel
Francis Triplett granted change of venue from Montgomery to Bourbon County on trial for shooting Connor with intent to kill.......... 4   163

Conway, Miles W.
(a) Trustee Town of Washington (1786).......... 3   555
(b) Re-appointed Trustee of Washington (1790)... 3   556

Conway, Miles Withers
Trustee of Charlestown (1787)............... 3   562

Cook, John
(a) Falmouth established on his lands............ 1   181
(b) Trustee of Falmouth 1   181
(c) Further reference made to (a)............... 5   583

Cooke, John
Trustee of Versailles 1   63

Cook, Samuel
(a) Trustee of Falmouth....................... 1   181
(b) Trustee Harrison Academy 2   241

Cooke, Thomas
Named in Allen-Warren County line.......... 5   348

Coombs, Adam
(a) Mill made limit of navigation on Nolinn Creek in Hardin County 4   221
(b) One of Commission to open Nolinn Creek to navigation 4   221
(c) Confirmation of Act (a) 5   34

Coombs, Adin
See (c) under Adam Coombs................ 5   34

Cooper, Frederick
Named in boundary of election precinct in Wayne County 5   3(

Cooper, Robert
Voting place at house in Butler County........ 4   11!

Cornetts, William
Voting place at house in Clay County......... 5   7!

Corporations (Business) (see under name of each corporation)
Bank of Kentucky
Cynthiana Manufacturing Company
Fayette Paper Manufacturing Company
Frankfort Bridge Company No. 1
Frankfort Bridge Company No. 2
Gallatin-Ohio Steamboat Company
Green River Iron Manufacturing Company

CORWINE

Hope Distillery Company
Kentucky Insurance Company
Kentucky Mutual Assurance Society
Kentucky River (Navigation) Company
Lexington and Louisville Turnpike Road Company
Lexington Manufacturing Company
Lexington White Lead Manufacturing Company
Licking Iron Company
Logan Vineyard Society
Madison Hemp Company
Maysville and Lexington Turnpike Road Company
Ohio Canal Company
Paris Hydraulic Company
Petersburg Steam Mill Company
Vineyard Society, of Lexington
Winchester Steam Mill Company

Corwine, Matthias
    Trustee Town of Wilmington 1   175
Corwine, Richard
    Trustee Town of Washington (1790) 3   556
Cosby, Fortunatus
    Trustee Jefferson Seminary 2   378
Cotton
    Inspection of provided for in order to encourage its cultivation 3   20
Couchman, Melchi
    Allowed pay for services on Wabash expedition   3   162
Couchman, Michael, deceased
    Commissioners named to sell lands descended to his heirs 5   42
Covington, Town of
    Established February 8, 1815, Founded by Richard M. Gano, Thomas D. Carneal and John S. Gano on lands bought of Thomas Kennedy. Trustees, Uriel Sebree, Alfred Sandford, Joseph Kennedy, William Hubble, and John C. Buckner............................... 5   283
Covington, Elijah M.
    Authorized to locate 1000 acres of land in Warren County for use in his iron-works........ 2   427
Covington, Thomas A.
    One of Commission to open Drake Creek in Warren County, to navigation.................. 4   361
Cowan, John
    (a) Trustee to hold Seminary lands (1780) 3   571
    (b) Trustee Transylvania Seminary (1783) 3   572

COWEN 42

	VOL.	PAGE
(c) Trustee of Harrodsburg (1785)	3	552

Cowen, Thomas
    Inspection site in Pulaski County ... 2   384
Cox, Finis
    Trustee Newton Academy ... 2   241
Cox, Gabriel
    Trustee of Bairdstown (1788) ... 3   566
Cox, Isaac
    (a) Trustee of Beallsborough (1787) ... 3   564
    (b) Trustee Transylvania Seminary (1783) ... 3   572
Cox, Samuel
    Voting place at house in Knox County ... 4   205
Crab Orchard
    (a) Road from to Cumberland Gap to be opened (1795) ... 1   275
    (b) Road from to Powells Valley mentioned (1794) ... 1   231
    (c) Town incorporated February 6, 1816 on lands of John Daviss, with Daniel Owsley, Rane McKinney, John Daviss, Thomas Owsley, Archibald Shanks and Archibald S. Letcher as Trustees ... 5   351
Craddock, Robert
    (a) Named as owner of lot in Danville ... 2   179
    (b) Trustee Danville Library ... 2   376
    (c) Promoter for Danville of Bank of Kentucky .. 3   390
Craig, Andrew
    (a) Road from his house on Wilderness Road to Lower Goose Creek Salt Works to be cleared and repaired ... 4   242
    (b) Part of turnpike fees on Wilderness Road to be used in repairing road at (a) ... 5   201
    (c) Made manager for Knox County of Wilderness Road ... 4   264
Craig, Benjamin
    Co-founder of Town of Port William ... 1   232
Craig, Elijah
    (a) Authorized to operate a ferry at East Frankfort ... 2   231
    (b) Trustee Rittenhouse Academy ... 2   240
    (c) Founder of Georgetown (1790) ... 3   570
    (d) Promoter for Georgetown of Lexington and Louisville Turnpike Road Company ... 5   520
    (e) Trustees of Georgetown authorized to sue his heirs to quiet title to Townsite ... 5   397
    (f) Suit to remove him as Justice of Gallatin County prosecuted by Martin Hawkins ... 3   99

	VOL.	PAGE
(g) Craig's costs in suit at (f) ordered paid by him	3	99
(h) Witness fees in suit at (f) allowed John Gardner	3	161
(i) John Hardin allowed his costs in an impeachment proceeding against Craig to remove him as Justice of Gallatin County	3	162

Craig, James
Given time to complete tax collections as Sheriff of Muhlenburg County ... 2 ... 486

Craig, Jeremiah
Trustee of Port William ... 1 ... 232

Craig, Joel
Trustee Georgetown Library ... 2 ... 376

Craig, John
(a) Trustee Transylvania Seminary (1783) ... 3 ... 572
(b) Lands terminus of Ferry over Kentucky River at Stone Lick (1785) ... 3 ... 586
(c) Trustee of Frankfort (1786) ... 3 ... 557
(d) Lands of named in boundary of Town of Washington (1790) ... 3 ... 556

Craig, John H.
(a) Named as grantee of land—no location ... 1 ... 603
(b) A lost certificate for services as Lieutenant in the Wabash Campaign in 1786 was renewed ... 2 ... 485
(c) Commissioner for Boone County to open road from Newcastle to mouth of Licking ... 3 ... 365
(d) Administrator of Elizabeth Snelling, deceased ... 3 ... 242

Craig, Lewis
Division of lands with heirs of John May authorized ... 1 ... 113

Craig, Robert
Given further time to repair Wilderness Road ... 2 ... 211

Craig, Toliver
(a) Trustee Rittenhouse Academy ... 2 ... 240
(b) Trustee of Georgetown (1790) ... 3 ... 570

Craig, Whitfield
Trustee of Germantown ... 1 ... 329

Cravens, Jesse
(a) Trustee of Stanford ... 1 ... 240
(b) Trustee Hartford Academy ... 2 ... 242
(c) Trustee Hartford Academy ... 3 ... 278
(d) One of Commission to erect bridge over Rough Creek at Hartford ... 4 ... 88
(e) Fees of witnesses on his trial before the Legislature ordered paid ... 4 ... 220
(f) Granted change of venue from Ohio to Hardin County on his trial for perjury ... 4 ... 228

	VOL.	PAGE
(g) Granted change of venue from Ohio to Hardin County on his trial for forgery	4	358

Cravens, Nehemiah
Re-survey of land authorized	5	459

Crawford, James
(a) Trustee Kentucky Academy	1	228
(b) Trustee Transylvania University	2	234
(c) Promoter for Mt. Sterling of Ohio Canal Company	3	221
(d) Trustee Montgomery Academy	3	438
(e) He and Solomon Tabor and William Stewart authorized to locate 1000 acres of land in Barren County to include a salt spring	5	202

Crawford, Thomas
Authorized to locate land in Mercer County	5	135

Crawford, Thomas, Sr.
Trustee of Perryville	5	454

Crawford, Thomas J.
Trustee of Perryville	5	454

Crews, David
(a) Trustee of Boonesborough (1779)	3	540
(b) Lands at mouth of Jacks Creek in Lincoln County named as terminus of a ferry over Kentucky River to Fayette County (1785)	3	586

Crist, Henry (see Henry Christ)
(a) Trustee Bullitt Academy	2	243
(b) Re-appointed Trustee of Bullitt Academy	3	478
(c) Inspection site in Bullitt County	2	287
(d) Authorized to convey lands of Solomon Spears, deceased	2	487

Crist, Nicholas
Appointment as tax collector of Bullitt County confirmed	2	361

Crittenden, John
(a) Trustee of Versailles	1	355
(b) Trustee Newport Academy	2	240
(c) Trustee Transylvania Seminary (1783)	3	572

Crockett, Anthony
Trustee Kentucky Academy	2	389

Crockett, Joseph
(a) Commissioner to repair Wilderness Road and erect a turnpike thereon	1	688
(b) Trustee Transylvania University	2	234
(c) Trustee of Frankfort (1786)	3	557
(d) Trustee of New Market (1786)	3	560

Croghan, John
Incorporator of Louisville Hospital........... 5   574
Croghan, William
(a) Commissioner to locate Military lands at head of Green River........................... 1   349
(b) Trustee Jefferson Seminary................. 2   108
(c) Allowed compensation for running line from Green River to Cumberland Mountain...... 2   182
Crow, Joel
Allowed pay for guarding families moving through Cumberland Gap in 1786.......... 3   407
Crow, John
First session of Trustees of Transylvania Seminary to be held at his Station in Lincoln County.................................3   574
Crow, Joshua
(a) Trustee Hartford Academy.................. 2   242
(b) Trustee Hartford Academy.................. 3   277
(c) Promoter for Hartford of Bank of Kentucky.. 3   391
(d) Trustee of Hartford........................ 3   443
(e) One of Commission to build bridge over Rough Creek at Hartford....................... 4   88
Crow, Samuel
(a) Trustee of Shepherdsville................... 1   183
(b) Trustee Bullitt Academy.................... 2   243
(c) Re-appointed Trustee Bullitt Academy......... 3   478
Crutcher, Henry
Trustee Glasgow Academy................... 4   85
Crutcher, James
(a) Trustee Bethel Academy.................... 2   174
(b) One of Commission to raise by lottery a fund to open Salt River to navigation............. 4   249
Cumberland County
(a) Formed July 1, 1799 from Green County..... 2   202
(b) Part of added to Barren County.............. 2   265
(c) Wayne County, in part, carved from......... 2   392
(d) Part of added to Adair County.............. 3   172
(e) Part added to Adair County decreased........ 3   251
Cumberland Gap
Road opened from Crab Orchard to.......... 1   275
Cummins, Moses
Named in Ohio-Daviess County line.......... 5   299
Cummins, Peter
Allowed compensation for apprehending fugitives from justice........................ 4   148
Cumpton, Levi
Inspection site in Warren County............ 2   279

CUNNINGHAM 46

	VOL.	PAGE
Cunningham, Francis		
Authorized to locate land in Mercer County..	4	332
Cunningham, John		
Trustee Grayson Seminary	5	325
Cunningham, William		
Trustee Grayson Seminary	5	325
Curd and Edwards		
Inspection site at mill in Logan County	3	323
Curd, John		
(a) Inspection site in Mercer County	2	139
(b) Trustee Newton Academy	2	241
(c) Trustee Newton Academy	3	409
(d) Inspection site in Mercer County	3	559
(e) Town of New Market at mouth of Dick's River in Mercer County established (1786) on his lands and ferry established	3	560
Curd, Newton		
Inspection site in Jessamine County	3	337
Currens, James		
Inspection site in Livingston County	2	389
Cynthiana		
Established December 10, 1793 on lands of Robert Harrison, with Benjamin Harrison, Morgan Vanmetre, Jeremiah Robinson, John Wall, Sr., and Henry Coleman as Trustees..	1	178
Cynthiana Manufacturing Company		
Incorporated February 10, 1816 by William Moore, William Brown, Samuel Hall, Hartwell Boswell and Isaac Miller	5	377
Dabney, Colonel		
Empowered to appoint surveyors (1783)	1	442
Dallam, Richard		
Promoter, for Russellville of the Kentucky Assurance Society	4	254
Dallam, William S.		
Incorporator of Fayette Paper Manufacturing Company	5	409
Dallard, John, deceased		
Heirs given warrant for 100 acres of land....	5	347
Dallum, William S.		
(a) Trustee Logan Vineyard Society	3	139
(b) Trustee Logan Academy	3	206
(c) Removed from County and his successor appointed at (b)	3	277
Damril, Lazarus		
Named in boundary of election precinct in Floyd County	3	255

DANIEL

	VOL.	PAGE
Daniel, Robert		
Co-founder of Danville	3	561
Daniel, Walker		
(a) Co-founder of Danville	3	561
(b) Claims of his heirs to townsite of Danville quieted	2	178
(c) Trustee Transylvania Seminary	3	572
(d) Correction made of errors in filing plats, and certificates of survey of 23,692 acres of land in Fayette County assigned to him by Bernard Todd in 1782	4	133
Danley, Samuel		
Special term of Bath Circuit Court authorized to try him for murder of William Cantral	5	25
Danville		
(a) Established in 1787 on lands of Walker and Robert Daniel, with John Jouit, William McDowell, Harry Innes, Christopher Greenup, Samuel McDowell. Sr., Abraham Irvin, Sr., George Muter, and William Kennedy, Trustees	3	561
(b) Title to townsite quieted	2	178
(c) Plat of the town, as made by John Thomas, confirmed	2	178
(d) John Rochester, James Birney, Joshua Barbee, Richard Davenport, Jeremiah Clemons, Jeremiah Fisher, Ephraim McDowell, Daniel McIlvoy and Dennis Brashear, named Trustees 1808	4	39
(e) Road from to Tellico, Tennessee, to be opened and William Whitley, Jonathan Forbes and Joseph Evans named commissioners to survey the route therefor	3	204
(f) Robert Modrel, Tunstall Quarles and Jonathan Smith named commissioners to make contracts for building road at (e)	3	275
Danville Academy		
(a) Incorporated January 30, 1817 with Joshua Barbee, Jeremiah Fisher, George Bast, Richard Davenport, Ephraim McDowell, David Bell, and Michael Hope, as Trustees	5	480
(b) Part of public square in Danville vested in Willis Green, John Rochester, Jeremiah Clemons and John L. Bridges as Trustees for its benefit	3	381

DANVILLE LIBRARY 48

	VOL.	PAGE
Danville Library		
Incorporated November 29, 1800 with Willis Green, William McDowell, Robert Craddock, James Speed, Sr., James Birney, Woodson Wren, Ephraim McDowell, Joshua Barbee, Barnabas Hughes, James Speed, Jr., and John Rochester, Trustees	2	376
Davenport, Richard		
(a) Trustees of Danville Library to meet at his house	2	376
(b) Trustee of Danville	4	39
(c) Promoter for Danville of Kentucky Assurance Society	4	254
(d) Trustee Danville Academy	5	480
Davidge, Henry		
(a) Incorporator of Gallatin-Ohio Steamboat Company	5	343
(b) Trustee Town of Bedford	5	350
Davidge, Reazin		
(a) Trustee Logan Academy	3	206
(b) Removed from County and successor as Trustee Logan Academy named	3	277
Davidge, Rezen		
Trustee Hopkinsville Library Company	5	361
Davidge, Rezin		
Trustee Christian Academy	5	450
Davidson, Alexander, Jr.		
One of Commission to open Big Barren River to navigation in Warren and Barren Counties	4	198
Davidson, Elias		
(a) One of Commission to raise by lottery a fund to open Salt River to navigation	4	249
(b) Trustee Washington Academy	5	15
Davidson, George		
(a) Trustee of Standford	1	240
(b) Trustee Stanford Academy	2	240
Davidson, James		
Trustee of Stanford	5	166
Davidson, John		
Adjustment made in settlement for Green River lands	2	423
Davidson, Michael		
(a) Trustee of Stanford	5	166
(b) Trustee Stanford Library Company	5	455
Davidson, Samuel		
Reward allowed for apprehending Hugh Ross, who was charged with felony	1	358

	VOL.	PAGE

Davies, John
    Trustee Town of Port William 2   337
Daviess County
  (a) Formed June 1, 1815 from Ohio County and Benjamin Fields, John Daviess, David Glenn, Sr., John McFarlan, Edward Hayden and John Leaman named commissioners to locate County Seat 5   159
  (b) County seat located at Rossborough, later Owensboro 5   501
  (c) Daviess-Ohio County line defined 5   299
Daviess, John
    One of Commission to locate Daviess County Seat   5   160
Daviess, Joseph H.
  (a) Trustee Kentucky Seminary 2   389
  (b) One of Commission to open a road from Paris or Mt. Sterling to the Big Sandy 3   4
Davis, Azariah, deceased
    Executors authorized to sell lands 5   565
Davis, Baxter
  (a) Inspection site in Pulaski County 3   243
  (b) Named in boundary of election precinct in Ohio County 4   416
  (c) Named in Ohio-Daviess County line 5   160
Davis, Benjamin
    Elizabeth Davis authorized to sue him for divorce   2   173
Davis, Charles
  (a) Trustee Newton Academy 2   241
  (b) Given time to settle as Sheriff of Henderson County 2   423
  (c) One of Commission to locate County Seat of Union County 4   213
Davis, David (see David Daviss)
  (a) Trustee Town of Washington 1   199
  (b) Trustee Town of Washington 2   393
Davis, Elizabeth
    See Benjamin Davis 2   173
Davis, Hardin
    Trustee Glasgow Academy 4   85
Davis, John (see John Daviss)
  (a) Allowed pay for services on the Wabash Expedition 3   162
  (b) Assignor of land to Deacon Payne 3   191
  (c) Trustee Lebanon Academy 5   323
Davis, Joseph
    Named in boundary of election precinct in Hopkins County 4   328

DAVIS 50

	VOL.	PAGE
Davis, Richard		
Given time to settle as Sheriff of Hopkins County	4	200
Davis, Robert		
Trustee Bracken Academy..................	2	242
Davis, Solomon		
Allowed pay for slave executed..............	3	94
Davis, Thomas		
Trustee of Germantown.....................	1	329
Davis, William		
(a) Inspection site in Garrard County.............	1	606
(b) Inspection site in Garrard County.............	2	196
(c) Trustee Stanford Academy..................	3	334
Davison, Alexander		
Delegate from Warren County to second Constitutional Convention (1799)................	1	58
Daviss, David		
Trustee Franklin Academy...................	3	255
Daviss, John		
Founder and Trustee of Crab Orchard.........	5	351
Dedman, Nathan		
Trustee Woodford Academy.................	3	181
Demaree, David		
Trustee Shelby Library Company............	4	90
Dennis, John		
Justices of Muhlenberg County to meet at his house	2	205
Denny, James		
Trustee Town of Jefferson..................	2	380
Denton, Robert		
Voting place at house in Casey County........	4	226
Depan, John		
Trustee Liberty Academy...................	4	114
Depeaw, Charles		
Named in Lincoln-Casey County boundary.....	3	326
Derrett, William		
Trustee Town of Lewisbourgh in Mason County	1	295
Dewees, Evan		
Price of land credited in name *Dowers* was given proper entry	5	428
Dewees, William		
Price of land credited in name *Dowers* was given proper entry	5	428
Dibrill, Charles		
Inspection site in Wayne County..............	3	325
Dicken, Ephraim (see Dickins)		
Relieved of consequences of mistakes as proprietor of head-right claims	4	30

	VOL.	PAGE
Dickens, Thomas		
Named in boundary of election precinct in Knox County	4	205
Dickins, Ephraim (see Dicken)		
Inspection site in Cumberland County	3	23
Dickison, Nancy		
Authorized to sue Thomas Dickison in Shelby County for divorce	3	464
Dickison, Thomas		
See Nancy Dickison		
Dilliard, James, deceased		
Balance of purchase price of 200 acres of land in Livingston County remitted	4	332
Dinwiddy, James		
One of Commission to assess damages to property owners in Milford upon removal of Madison County seat therefrom	2	166
Disher, Christopher		
Named in boundary of election precinct in Bracken County	3	487
Dismukes, Joseph		
(a) Lands on Indian Creek named in boundary of election precinct in Lincoln County	2	400
(b) Named in Lincoln-Casey County boundary	3	325
Dixon, John		
Named in boundary of election precinct in Warren County	5	16
Dobyns, Thomas		
(a) Acts as tax collector of Mason County confirmed	2	424
(b) Act (a) amended	2	488
Dodd, John C.		
Voting place at house in Caldwell County	4	203
Donald, Samuel		
Named in Bourbon-Nicholas County boundary	5	452
Donaldson, Daniel		
Trustee Bullitt Academy	2	243
Donaldson, William		
Trustee to sell lands of John Elliott, deceased	4	9
Donophan, Joseph		
One of Commission to locate County seat of Greenup County	3	117
Dooley, Jacob		
Pay allowed for services as Lieutenant on frontier of Clarke County in 1795	3	516
Dooley, Moses		
Named in Cumberland-Barren County boundary	3	103

DOOM   52

	VOL.	PAGE
Doom, Jacob		
(a) Inspection at warehouse in Washington County	1	330
(b) Inspection at warehouse in Washington County	2	213
(c) Inspection at warehouse in Washington County	3	384
Doran, Thomas		
(a) Rolling Fork to be made navigable to his mill..	3	199
(b) Rolling Fork declared navigable to his mill....	3	316
(c) Rolling Fork declared navigable above his mill	3	346
(d) Inspection site at mill in Washington County..	3	323
Dorsey, Charles, Jr.		
Co-founder of Town of Bedford..............	5	350
Dougherty, Elizabeth		
Repaid money expended by her deceased husband (William Dougherty, former jailer of Jefferson County) for the apprehension of John Lee, a felon who had escaped jail....	5	385
Dougherty, Henry		
(a) Named in Shelby-Henry County boundary....	2	200
(b) Named in Shelby-Gallatin County boundary....	2	203
Dougherty, Robert		
(a) Tax Commissioner of Clarke County..........	1	188
(b) An omitted credit due him was given on the Treasurer's books	5	46
Dougherty, Thomas		
One of Commission to locate County Seat of Bath County	4	215
Dougherty, William		
See Elizabeth Dougherty		
Dowdal, John		
Inspection site in Washington County.........	2	383
Dowdy, William		
A certificate for military services by him was paid to Philip Bush, Jr., assignee...........	3	408
Dowery, Samuel		
Trustee of Mt. Sterling.....................	1	125
Downing, Job		
Named in Christian-Muhlenberg County boundary	2	378
Downing, Joel		
(a) Named in Christian-Muhlenberg County boundary	2	205
(b) Reference to him at (a) recited to be error.....	2	371
Downing, John		
Stockholders of Madison Hemp Company to meet at his tavern in Lexington..................	3	53

DOWNING

	VOL.	PAGE

Downing, Rachael
   Authorized, as Administratrix, to sell lands of
     William Downing, deceased 1   359
Downing, William, deceased
   See Rachael Downing
Dozier, Henrietta
   She had been surreptitiously divorced. The act
     authorized her to marry again 5   6
Drake, Abraham
   One of Commission to locate County Seat of
     Greenup County 3   117
Drake Creek in Warren County
   Declared navigable and George Harris, George
   Hudspeth, Thomas A. Covington, William
   Skiles and Jesse Kirby named commissioners to
     clear it to navigation 4   361
Dudley, Jepthah
   (a) One of Commission to raise by lottery a fund
     to open Kentucky River to navigation 4   210
   (b) Same as (a)—re-appointed 4   318
   (c) One of Commission to erect a State-House 5   123
   (d) One of Commission to clear Kentucky River at
     Frankfort to navigation 5   390
Dueling
   (a) Act to suppress (1799) 2   285
   (b) Officers to take oath regarding (1811) 4   383
Duffey, John
   Commissioner for Wayne County to mark Pu-
     laski-Wayne line 5   563
Dufour, John James
   Promoter of the Vineyard Society of Lexington 2   269
Dugan, Col. James (see James Duggan)
   Named in Logan-Warren boundary 1   369
Duggan, Daniel
   Trustee of Newport 1   281
Duggan, Col. James
   Named in Logan-Warren boundary 2   177
Duke, Alexander
   Named in boundary of election precinct in
     Lewis County 5   426
Duke, Basil
   (a) Trustee Franklin Academy 1   296
   (b) Trustee Franklin Academy 3   255
   (c) Promoter for Town of Washington of the Bank
     of Kentucky 3   390
   (d) Incorporator of Washington Library Company 4   273

DUNCAN 54

	VOL.	PAGE

Duncan, James
  (a) Trustee of Hopewell (Paris) (1789).......... 3   568
  (b) Delegate from Bourbon County to second Constitutional Convention (1799)................ 1   57
  (c) One of Commission to open Mud River, in Logan County, to navigation..................... 4   115
Duncan, Samuel
  (a) Trustee Town of Kennedysville............... 1   342
  (b) Voting place at house in Caldwell County...... 4   327
Duncan, Seth
  Compromise settlement with him as surety of James Little, Sheriff of Bourbon County authorized 5   45
Dunlap, Alexander
  Trustee Woodford Academy................. 2   243
Dunn, James
  Allowed pay for military services in 1787 and 1793 3   516
Dunn, James, deceased
  Commissioners named to sell lots in Lexington.. 5   324
Dupey, William (see William Dupuy)
  Trustee Greenup Academy................... 4   128
Dupuy, Joseph
  (a) Inspection site in Henry County.............. 2   279
  (b) Extra pay allowed as sheriff of Henry County 2   484
Dupuy, Joseph, deceased
  (a) Commissioners named to compromise conflicting claims as to his lands..................... 5   389
  (b) Lands of, authorized sold.................... 5   511
Dupuy, Samuel
  Promoter for Shelbyville of Lexington and Louisville Turnpike Road Company......... 5   519
Dupuy, William (see Dupey)
  Patents allowed on Virginia rights though barred by limitations 5   272
Durbin, Christopher
  Turnpike keeper on Wilderness Road......... 4   264
Durrett, Richard
  Trustee Franklin Academy................. 1   296
Duval, Samuel P. (see Duvall)
  Trustee Harrodsburg Academy............... 2   240
Duval, William P. (see Duvall)
  Promoter for Bardstown of Kentucky Assurance Society 4   254
Duvall, Samuel (see Duval)
  Named in boundary of election precinct in Logan County 5   14C

                                                              VOL.   PAGE
Duvall, William P. (see Duval)
  Trustee Salem Academy..................... 5   7
Dye, John
  Named in boundary of election precinct in Hardin County 5   473
Dysert, James
  Trustee Rockcastle Academy................ 4   114
Dysert, John
  Trustee Rockcastle Academy................ 4   114
Eagler's Mill
  South Fork of Licking declared navigable to.. 4   222
Earley, Mathias
  Voting place at house in Christian County.... 5   141
Eastin, Achilles, deceased
  Commissioners named to sell lands............ 4   412
Eastin, Augustine
  (a) Trustee Bourbon Academy.................. 2   237
  (b) Trustee Bourbon Academy.................. 2   242
Eastin, Charles
  Co-founder Town of Bedford................ 5   350
Eastland, Thomas
  Trustee Woodford Academy................. 3   181
Edgman, Thomas K.
  Relieved of consequences of irregular proceedings relative to head-right lands............... 4   98
Edlin, George, deceased
  Witnesses in his trial before the Legislature ordered paid 4   217
Edwards, Amos
  (a) Trustee Logan Vineyard Society.............. 3   139
  (b) Trustee Logan Academy..................... 3   277
  (c) Promoter for Russellville of Kentucky Assurance Society 4   254
Edwards, Curds and
  Inspection site at mill in Logan County........ 3   323
Edwards, James
  Inspection site on lot in Maysville............. 2   384
Edwards, John
  (a) Trustee Bourbon Academy.................. 2   237
  (b) Trustee Bourbon Academy.................. 2   242
  (c) Trustee of Hopewell (Paris) (1789)........... 3   568
  (d) Trustee Transylvania Seminary (1783)........ 3   572
  (e) Promoter for Louisville of Lexington and Louisville Turnpike Road Company............. 5   519

EDWARDS   56

	VOL.	PAGE
Edwards, Ninian		
(a) Trustee Logan Academy	3	206
(b) Promoter for Russellville of Ohio Canal Company	3	221
(c) Trustee Newton Academy	3	277
Eggleston, Edmund, Jr., deceased		
Lands authorized sold	5	584
Elder, Edward M.		
Trustee Town of Lebanon	5	191
Elizabeth (Christian County)		
Named changed to Hopkinsville	3	183
Elizabethtown		
Road from Mann's Lick to Big Barren to run through	2	492
Elkins, Joel		
Convicted of murder in Clay County	3	464
Elkins, Robert		
Trustee Winchester Academy	2	217
Elliott, James, deceased		
Executors to qualify in Jefferson County	1	272
Elliott, James		
Trustee to sell lands of John Elliott, deceased	4	9
Elliott, John		
Trustee of Winchester	1	187
Elliott, John, deceased		
(a) Sale of land authorized	3	96
(b) Further sales of land authorized	3	515
(c) Daniel McGary and James Elliott, two of the commissioners to sell lands at (a) failed to act and James McElhany and William Donaldson were appointed in their stead	4	9
Elliott, Robert, deceased		
Sale of lands in Woodford County authorized	3	208
Ellis, Israel		
Inspection site in Pendleton County	2	456
Ellis, James		
(a) County seat of Nicholas County (Ellisville) located on his lands on Paris-Limestone Road about two miles from Lower Blue Licks	3	18!
(b) Part of land at (a) to be re-conveyed to him	5	8!
Ellis, Jezareel		
Inspection site in Pendleton County	3	45:
Ellis, John		
Named in Lincoln-Madison County boundary	1	62'
Ellis, John, deceased		
Sale of lands authorized	1	69:

Ellisville

	VOL.	PAGE
Ellisville		
(a) Made County Seat of Nicholas County	3	183
(b) Public lands at, to be sold	5	563
Ellison, Samuel		
Named in boundary of election precinct in Christian County	4	329
Emberson, Walter		
Named in Pulaski-Wayne County boundary	5	562
Embree, Joshua		
Inspection site in Cumberland County	3	24
Emerson, Francis, deceased		
Lands authorized sold	5	7
Emmerson, John		
(a) Trustee of Greensburg	1	273
(b) One of Commission to raise funds to open road from Greensburg to the Tennessee line	3	22
English's Station		
Named in Rockcastle County boundary	4	92
Erickson, Benjamin		
Trustee of Louisville (1789)	3	547
Essery, John		
Trustee of Shepherdsville	1	183
Estill County		
(a) Formed April 1, 1809 from Madison and Clarke Counties	3	441
(b) Part of returned to Madison County	3	473
(c) Part of Clay County added to	5	162
(d) Part of Montgomery County added to	5	327
Estill Courthouse		
Road from to Goose Creek Salt Works and to State Road near Cumberland River authorized and Bennett Clarke and James Whitt, of Estill County, and John Bates and Hugh White of Clay County named commissioners to open it	5	566
Estill, John, deceased		
Town of Milford in Madison County established on his lands (1789)	3	567
Estill, Samuel		
(a) Town of Milford in Madison County established on his lands (1789)	3	567
(b) Trustee of Milford	1	226
Estill Seminary		
Name of Jefferson Seminary changed to	5	509
Estre, James		
Trustee of Boonesborough	3	538

EVANS 58

	VOL.	PAGE
Evans, Joseph		
One of Commission to open road from Danville to Tellico, Tennessee	3	204
Evans, Richard		
Allowed a credit on settlement as Sheriff of Floyd County	4	212
Evinger, George		
His mill named in boundary of election precinct in Jefferson County	5	308
Ewing, Baker		
(a) One of Commission to erect a jail at Frankfort	1	263
(b) His addition included in Frankfort	1	641
(c) Trustee Kentucky Seminary	2	389
Ewing, Charles		
(a) Trustee Washington Academy	2	242
(b) Henrietta Ewing authorized to sue him in Nelson County for divorce	3	446
Ewing, Fines		
Trustee Lebanon Academy	4	193
Ewing, George, deceased		
Patents allowed despite some irregularities	4	170
Ewing, Henrietta		
See (b) under Charles Ewing		
Ewing, Reuben		
(a) Delegate from Logan County to second Constitutional Convention (1799)	1	58
(b) Trustee Logan Academy	3	206
(c) One of Commission to locate County Seat of Warren County	3	447
Ewing, Robert		
(a) Trustee Newton Academy	2	241
(b) Trustee Logan Academy	3	206
Ewing, Samuel, deceased		
Estate given credit in settlement as Sheriff of Mercer County	5	556
Ewing, Urbin		
(a) Trustee Newton Academy	3	409
(b) One of Commission to open Mud River in Logan County to navigation	4	115
Ewing, Young		
(a) Delegate from Christian County to second Constitutional Convention (1799)	1	58
(b) Tax Commissioner of Logan County	1	168
(c) Trustee Newton Academy	2	241
(d) Trustee Lebanon Academy	4	193
(e) One of Commission to sell part of public square in Hopkinsville	5	511

                                             VOL.   PAGE
Falmouth
  (a) Established December 10, 1793 on lands of John
      Cook, John Waller and William McDowell with
      Notley Conn, John Hughes, John Cook, John
      Vance, Samuel Cook, Joseph Hume, William
      Monroe, James Little and George Standiford
      as Trustees 1   181
  (b) Trustees authorized to have a survey and plat of
      the town made 4   364
Faris, Edward
  Over-payment for land refunded............. 2   423
Faris, John
  (a) Justices of Fleming County to meet at his house 2   176
  (b) Justices of Fleming County to meet at his house 2   189
  (c) Trustee Fleming Academy 2   241
  (d) Promoter for Flemingsburg of Ohio Canal
      Company 3   222
Farley, Daniel
  Co-founder and Trustee of Town of Bedford.. 5   350
Farris, Elijah
  Conveyance of lands to him by the Administrator
    of Joseph Hale was authorized............. 1   354
Farris, Isham
  Owned a bridge over Big Laurel River on the
    Wilderness Road 4   266
Fayette County
  (a) Formed November 1, 1780 from Kentucky
      County 1   626
  (b) Bourbon County carved from................ 1   627
  (c) Woodford County carved from............... 1   628
  (d) Clarke County, in part, carved from.......... 1   630
  (e) Jessamine County carved from............... 2   213
  (f) Fayette-Jessamine line surveyed 2   297
Fayette Hospital
  Incorporated February 10, 1816, "for the accom-
    modation of lunatics and other distempered and
    sick poor" of Fayette County............. 5   415
Fayette Paper Manufacturing Company
  Incorporated February 10, 1815 by William S.
    Dallam, Luther Stephens, Hallet M. Winslow,
    Daniel Bryan, Thomas January and William
    Roman 5   409
Fee, John
  Trustee Bracken Academy................... 2   242
Felty, John
  Trustee of Louisville....................... 3   547

	VOL.	PAGE

Ferguson, James
    Lands of Jefferson Seminary vested in him and others as Trustees........................ 3   490

Ferguson, James, deceased
    Suit against his unknown heirs by Thomas Rankin, Sr., to obtain a sale of a lot in Cynthiana was authorized..................... 5   498

Ferguson, Joshua
    (a) One of Commission to open Beech Fork to navigation 2   312
    (b) Inspection site at mill on Beech Fork in Washington County 2   383
    (c) His mill and dam excepted from an act concerning navigation on Beech Fork............. 3   82
    (d) Beech Fork to be kept open to navigation to his mill 3   316

Ferguson, Peter
    (a) Trustee Hopkinsville Library Company........ 5   361
    (b) Trustee Christian Academy 5   450

Ferguson, Richard
    Incorporator of Louisville Hospital............ 5   574

Ferries
    (a) At Boonesborough, franchise granted Richard Callaway in 1779......................... 3   585
    (b) Across Kentucky River at mouth of Hickman connecting lands of James Hogan (1785).... 3   586
    (c) Across Kentucky River at mouth of Jacks Creek at David Crews' (1785).................... 3   586
    (d) Across Kentucky River at Stone Lick connecting lands of William Steele in Fayette County with lands of John Craig in Lincoln County (1785) 3   586
    (e) Across the Ohio River from lands of John Campbell in Jefferson County (1785)............ 3   586
    (f) Across Cumberland River in Lincoln County connecting lands of Joseph Martin and William Hord (1791) 3   586
    (g) Across Kentucky River from lands of John Curd in Mercer County at mouth of Dick's River 3   561
    (h) From Port William across the Ohio (1812).... 5   19
    (i) Across Rockcastle River on Wilderness Road.. 5   313
    (j) Across Kentucky River at Frankfort (1786).... 3   558
    (k) Across Kentucky River one mile above Frankfort at Elijah Craig's........................ 2   231

Fetter, David
    Incorporator of Louisville Hospital........... 5   574

	VOL.	PAGE
Ficklin, Joseph		
Promoter for Russellville of Bank of Kentucky..	3	391
Field, Abner		
(a) Trustee of New-Town	1	233
(b) Trustee Jefferson Seminary	2	378
(c) Trustee Jefferson Seminary	3	207
(d) Lands of Jefferson Seminary vested in him and others as Trustees	3	490
Fields, Aquilla		
(a) Trustee Hartford Academy	2	242
(b) Trustee of Hartford	3	443
Fields, Benjamin		
(a) Trustee Hartford Academy	2	242
(b) Trustee Hartford Academy	3	278
(c) One of Commission to locate County Seat of Daviess County	5	160
Fields, Curtis		
Trustee Madison Academy	5	133
Field, John		
(a) Certificate for military services directed to be paid to Philip Bush, Jr., assignee	3	408
(b) Devisee of Benjamin Roberts of land on which Flemingsburg was located	5	187
Fields, Lewis		
(a) Trustee of Williamsville	1	118
(b) Trustee of New-Town	1	233
Fincastle County		
Kentucky County formed from (1776)	1	626
Finley, Robert		
Trustee Kentucky Academy	1	228
Finly, Samuel		
Trustee Stanford Academy	2	240
Finn, John		
Authorized to locate 200 acres of land south of Green River	2	358
Fishback, Jacob		
Trustee Winchester Academy	2	217
Fisher, Benjamin		
Given time as assignee of Joseph Love, to locate land for iron works	5	463
Fisher, Jeremiah		
(a) Trustee of Danville	4	39
(b) Trustee Danville Academy	5	480
Fisher, John		
Charged with murder of John Coffman	4	148
Fitzhugh, Dennis		
Incorporator of Louisville Hospital	5	574

FLEMING

	VOL.	PAGE

Fleming Academy
    Established December 22, 1798 with Michael Cassidy, Robert Morrison, John Hart, Hugh Fulton, George Stockden, Andrew Kincaid, John Home, John Faris and Richard Tilton, Trustees 2   241

Fleming County
    (a) Formed March 1, 1800 from Mason County.... 2   175
    (b) Floyd County, in part, carved from........... 2   282
    (c) Part of Nicholas County added to............ 5   365

Fleming, William
    Trustee Transylvania Seminary lands (1783)... 3   571

Fleming, William P.
    One of Commission to locate County Seat of Lewis County 3   340

Flemingsburg
    (a) Made County Seat of Fleming County......... 2   176
    (b) Made County Seat of Fleming County......... 2   188
    (c) Plat of, ordered made....................... 4   358

Fletcher, Spencer, deceased
    Balance due on head-right land remitted....... 5   384

Fletcher, Thomas
    One of Commission to open road from Fleming County to Big Sandy..................... 3   350

Flint, Mary
    Co-respondent in suit of Henrietta Ewing against Charles Ewing for divorce................ 3   446

Flipping, Thomas
    Voting place at house in Barren County....... 3   103

Flournoy, David
    (a) Tax Commissioner of Scott County........... 1   168
    (b) Promoter for Scott County of Kentucky River Navigation Company 2   448
    (c) One of Commission to build a bridge over North Elkhorn in Scott County................. 4   88

Flournoy, Francis
    Inspection site in Campbell County............ 2   457

Flournoy, John
    Trustee Boone Academy.................... 5   76

Flournoy, Matthews, deceased
    (a) Lands of William Christian, deceased, to be conveyed to heirs of Flournoy.............. 3   99
    (b) Additional commissioners appointed to make the conveyance at (a)....................... 3   301

Floyd County
    (a) Formed June 1, 1800 from Fleming, Mason and Montgomery Counties.................... 2   282

	VOL.	PAGE
(b) Clay County, in part, carved from	3	338
(c) Part of Madison County added to	3	339

Floyd, Henry, Sr.
One of Commission to locate and convey lands
of Jacob Brehmer, deceased................ 3   217

Floyd, Henry, Jr.
(a) One of Commission to locate and convey lands
of Jacob Brehmer, deceased............... 3   217
(b) Re-appointed for same purpose as at (a)...... 3   470

Floyd, John
(a) One of Commission to locate and convey lands
Jacob Brehmer, deceased................... 3   217
(b) Trustee of Louisville (1780)................. 3   540
(c) Lexington located partly on his lands (1782).. 3   549
(d) Trustee Transylvania Seminary (1783)........ 3   571

Floyd, Joseph
Trustee of Wilmington...................... 1   175

Floyd, Nathaniel
One of Commission to locate and convey lands of
Jacob Brehmer, deceased.................. 3   217

Fogle, Robert H.
Co-founder and Trustee of Lebanon........... 5   191

Forbes, Jonathan
(a) Surveyor of Lincoln County.................. 2   192
(b) Trustee Stanford Academy................... 2   240
(c) One of Commission to open road from Danville
to Tellico, Tennessee........................ 3   204
(d) Trustee of Stanford......................... 1   240

Forbis, Hugh
Mt. Sterling, in part, established on his land... 1   125

Forbis, William
Trustee Stanford Library Company........... 5   455

Ford, James
Trustee Shelby Library Company............. 4   90

Ford, William
Released from payment of interest on settlement
as Sheriff of Fayette County............... 2   422

Foreman, Thomas
Trustee Town of Washington................. 1   199

Foreste, Richard
Co-founder of Lebanon 5   191

Forsythe, William
Inspection site in Logan County.............. 3   243

Fort, Micajah
Named in boundary of election precinct in Christian County 4   225

Forwood, William
Named in boundary of election precinct in Jefferson County 5 308
Fowler, John
(a) Provided for a town on his lands in Mason County. Town never established 1 154
(b) Allowed compensation for bringing land title papers from Virginia 1 272
(c) Inspection site in Montgomery County 2 279
(d) One of Commission to erect a turnpike on road from Fleming County to the Big Sandy.... 4 154
(e) Patents issued despite some irregularities..... 4 170
(f) Title of State by escheat to lands in Campbell County bought by Fowler from Jacob Robsammon, was released..................... 4 253
Fowler, John, Jr.
Trustee of Frankfort (1786)................. 3 557
Fox, Arthur
(a) Deeds to lots in Town of Washington confirmed 1 200
(b) Deeds to lots in Town of Washington confirmed 2 395
(c) Trustee Town of Washington (1786).......... 3 555
(d) Lands part of boundary of Town of Washington (1790) 3 556
(e) Re-appointed Trustee Town of Washington (1790) 3 556
(f) Trustee of Maysville (1787).................. 3 565
Fox, Richard
(a) Trustee of Versailles........................ 1 63
(b) One of Commissioners for Woodford County to survey Woodford-Franklin County line...... 5 447
Fox, Samuel
One of Commission to assess damages to property owners in Town of Milford upon removal of Madison County Seat therefrom............. 2 166
Fox, William
Trustee Somerset Academy................... 3 37
Francis, John
(a) Authorized to locate 1000 acres of land in Wayne County to include a salt spring...... 4 257
(b) Given further time to locate lands............ 5 138
(c) Given still further time to locate lands......... 5 428
Frankfort
(a) Established in 1786 on lands of James Wilkinson, with Caleb Wallace, Thomas Marshall, Joseph Crocket, John Fowler, Jr., John Craig, Robert Johnston and Benjamin Roberts as Trustees .... 3 55'

	VOL.	PAGE
(b) Ferry established at (1786)	3	558
(c) A subdivision by John Logan, William Murray, George Campbell and Baker Ewing on south side of Kentucky River included in the town (1797)	1	640
(d) John Logan, Thomas Todd, Daniel Weisiger, James Roberts, and Issac E. Gano appointed Trustees (1793)	1	247
(e) Road from to Cincinnati opened	1	185

Frankfort Bridge Company, No. 1
Incorporated December 21, 1799 by Christopher Greenup, Daniel Weisiger and William Trigg   2   303

Frankfort Bridge Company, No. 2
(a) Incorporated January 25, 1810 by Thomas V. Loofbourrow and William Trigg   4   137
(b) Capital Stock increased and given time to complete bridge (1815)   5   335

Frankfort Library Company
Incorporated January 31, 1812   4   359

Franklin Academy
(a) Incorporated December 15, 1795 at Washington, in Mason County, with Thomas Waring, Thomas Sloo, John Coburn, Nathaniel Wilson, David Broderick, Edward Harris, George Lewis, William Ward, Robert Rankin, John Johnson, John Machir, William Wood, Basil Duke, William Goforth, William Roe, George Stockton, Alexander Marshall, Philip Buckner, Lewis Moore, Richard Durrett, Winslow Parker, Alexander D. Orr, Thomas Marshall and Philemon Thomas, Trustees   1   296
(b) By Act of December 19, 1805 Bazil Duke, John Machir, Benjamin Bayless, John Johnson, Thomas Marshall, Baldwin B. Stith, David Daviss, Francis Taylor and William Heddleston were named Trustees   3   255
(c) Granted 6000 acres Green River Lands   2   107

Franklin County
(a) Formed May 1, 1795 from Mercer, Shelby and Woodford Counties   1   632
(b) Gallatin County, in part, carved from   2   203
(c) Survey of Franklin-Woodford line ordered   5   447

Franklinian School, in Mercer County
Lands of High Dutch Lutheran Congregation to be sold for its benefit   3   458

Frazier, Joseph
Lands assigned by him to Simon Kenton named

FRAZIER 66

	VOL.	PAGE
as boundary of Town of Washington	3	556

Frazier, Martin
Trustee of Kennedysville 1   342
Frazier, Robert
Incorporator Madison Hemp Company 3   532
Frazer, William
Patent granted for 3000 acres, Knox County.... 5   70
Frederick, Samuel
Voting place at house in Jefferson County...... 5   308
French, James
(a) One of Commission to assess damages to property owners in Milford upon removal of Madison County Seat therefrom 2   166
(b) Trustee Town of Milford 3   567
(c) One of Commission to open a road from Fleming County to the Big Sandy 3   167
(d) Trustee Montgomery Academy 3   438
French, William
Incorporator of Gallatin-Ohio Steamboat Company 5   343
Frizzle, Jacob
Voting place at house in Lewis County........ 5   427
Froman, Jacob
(a) Trustee Kentucky Academy.................. 1   228
(b) Inspection site in Woodford County.......... 2   278
Fruit, James
Named in boundary of election precinct in Christian County 4   329
Fry, Benjamin
Trustee of Carthage in Union County......... 5   83
Fugued, William
Trustee Greenup Academy................... 4   128
Fulton, Hugh
Trustee Fleming Academy................... 2   241
Funk, John
Authorized to sue Susanna Funk for divorce... 2   54
Funk, Susanna
See John Funk
Funkhouser, Christopher
Inspection site in Logan County............... 2   456
Fuquay, Joseph
Trustee Henderson Academy................. 5   72
Gains, Richard
(a) Trustee Stanford Academy.................. 2   240
(b) Trustee Stanford Academy.................. 3   334
Gaither, Nathan
Trustee Robertson Academy................... 5   125

GALLATIN ACADEMY

	VOL.	PAGE

Gallatin Academy (at Port Royal)
    Incorporated January 13, 1813 with Carter Tarent, William Winslow, John Barner, Garland Bullock and Robert Plummer, Trustees.. 5   13

Gallatin County
    Formed May, 1799 from Franklin and Shelby Counties 2   203

Gallatin-Ohio Steamboat Company
    Incorporated February 1, 1816 by Robert King, John Pugh, John McIntire, Henry Davidge and William French...................... 5   343

Galt, William C.
    Trustee Louisville Library Company.......... 5   360

Gano, Isaac E.
    (a) Trustee of Frankfort 1   247
    (b) Trustee Kentucky Seminary 2   389

Gano, Rev. John, deceased
    Error in will corrected to permit sale of lands.. 3   305

Gano, John S.
    Co-founder of Covington 5   283

Gano, Richard M.
    (a) One of Commissioners for Scott County to open road from Georgetown to Augusta.......... 3   201
    (b) Co-founder of Covington 5   283
    (c) He having died the remaining proprietors and Trustees of Town of Covington were authorized to act 5   408
    (d) Commissioners authorized to sell lands......... 5   501

Gardner, John
    Allowed witness fees against Elijah Craig..... 3   161

Garner, Henry
    Justices of Pulaski County to meet at his house.. 2   392

Garnett, Richard
    (a) One of Commission to locate County Seat of Warren County 3   447
    (b) Trustee Glasgow Academy 4   85

Garrard County
    (a) Formed June 1, 1797 from Lincoln, Madison and Mercer Counties 1   384
    (b) Part of Madison County added to............ 2   270
    (c) Part of Lincoln County added to............ 2   461

Garrard, Daniel
    (a) Trustee Manchester Academy................ 4   18
    (b) One of Commission to open South Fork of Kentucky River to navigation................. 4   94

	VOL.	PAGE
Garrard, James		
(a) Trustee of Hopewell (Paris) (1789)	3	568
(b) Trustee Transylvania University	2	234
(c) Governor (1798)	4	534
Garrard, James, and Sons		
Goose Creek to be opened to navigation to their salt works, from South Fork of Kentucky River	4	94
Garrard, William		
(a) Trustee Bourbon Academy	2	237
(b) Trustee Bourbon Academy	2	242
(c) Allowed pay for services as quartermaster of militia	3	491
Garrard, William, Jr.		
Trustee Paris Library Company	3	455
Garris, Benjamin		
Inspection site in Muhlenberg County	2	456
Garrison, Samuel		
(a) Trustee Allen Seminary	5	433
(b) Trustee of Scottville	5	483
Garth, Elijah		
Trustee Lebanon Academy	5	323
Gatewood, John		
Authorized to re-locate his settlement so as to include his house	4	211
Gatewood, William		
Trustee Town of Bedford	5	350
Gatton, Thomas		
(a) Trustee Allen Seminary	5	433
(b) Trustee of Scottville	5	483
George, Dolly		
Price of head-right land remitted	4	220
Georgetown		
(a) Established in 1790 on lands of Elijah Craig with Robert Johnson, William Cave, Rodes Thompson, Toliver Craig, John Grant, Archibald Campbell and William Henry, Trustees	3	570
(b) John Hawkins, George Brown and Bartlett Collins added to Board of Trustees (1793)	1	220
(c) Authority given to raise by subscription a fund to erect a Linen Manufactory	1	232
(d) William Henry and Richard M. Gano, of Scott County, Samuel McMillion, James Caldwell and James Coleman, of Harrison County, and William Woodward and Philip Buckner, of Bracken County, appointed commissioners to open a road to Augusta	3	201

	VOL.	PAGE
Georgetown Library		
Incorporated November 29, 1800 by John Hawkins, John Thompson, John Hay, John Payne, Robert Sanders, Samuel Shepherd, Richard Johnston, William Garrett Johnston, William Storey, Josiah Pitts and Joel Craig	2	376
Georgia Settlements		
(a) Named in Logan-Warren County boundary	1	369
(b) Named in Logan-Warren County boundary	2	177
Georgia, State of		
This State to connect with road from	2	422
Germantown		
(a) Established December 19, 1795 on lands of Philemon Thomas with David Chiles, Whitfield Craig, Spencer Record, Thomas Davis and Thomas Hubbard, Trustees	1	329
(b) Purchasers of lots to be secured by bond of Philemon Thomas against adverse claims	1	653
Getridge, John (see Gutridge)		
Trustee of Newtown in Mason County	1	285
Gherry, Nicholas		
Trustee of Salisberry in Campbell County	3	369
Gibbs, Hugh		
Allowed pay for guarding families moving through Cumberland Gap in 1786	3	407
Gibson, James, Jr.		
Named in Allen-Warren County boundary	5	348
Gilbert, John		
(a) One of Commission to open Red Bird Fork of Kentucky River to navigation. His lands also made head of navigation on Red Bird Fork	5	149
(b) Road from his salt works in Clay County to the Wilderness Road ordered improved	5	392
Gilchrist, Robert		
Trustee Union Academy	5	80
Gill, Samuel		
(a) Trustee Lancaster Academy	2	242
(b) Authorized, with John Strother, to survey 102,912 acres in Jefferson County	3	100
Gillock, Lawrence		
Patent for 200 acres Green River land allowed despite some irregularities	2	364
Gilmore, John		
Trustee of Harrodsburg (1785)	3	552
Gist, David		
Trustee of Boonesborough (1779)	3	538

GIVEN 70

	VOL.	PAGE
Given, Thomas		
Trustee Shelby Academy	2	241
Glasgow Academy		
Incorporated December 23, 1809, with Hardin Davis, John Gorin, Henry Crutcher, Richard Garnett, John McFerren, John Monroe, William Logan, Samuel Murrell and Joel Yancey, Trustees	2	242
Glenn, David		
Trustee Hartford Academy	2	242
Glenn, David, Sr.		
One of Commission to locate County seat of Daviess County	5	160
Godley, John		
Trustee Allen Seminary	5	433
Godly, John		
One of Commission to open to navigation Big Barren River in Warren and Barren Counties	4	198
Goforth, William		
Trustee Franklin Academy	1	296
Goggin, John		
Inspection site in Madison County	2	173
Goggins Warehouse		
Inspection site in Madison County	3	323
Gooding, John		
One of Commission to lease the road from Fleming County to the Big Sandy	4	236
Goodlett, John		
Special proceeding to collect a debt due him was authorized	5	459
Goodloe, William		
One of Commission to build bridge over Rockcastle River on Wilderness Road	3	511
Goose Creek		
Declared navigable	4	94
Goose Creek Salt Works		
(a) Road to from Richmond and Pulaski to be opened	3	95
(b) Named in Clay County boundary	3	338
(c) Road to from Estill Courthouse authorized	5	566
Gordon, Ambrose, deceased		
Sale of lands authorized	2	363
Gorham, Hannah		
Allowed pay for boarding a jury in Bourbon County	5	586

	VOL.	PAGE

Gorin, John
  (a) One of Commission to raise funds to open a road
      from Greensburg to the Tennessee line 3   21
  (b) Trustee Glasgow Academy 4   85

Governeur, Isaac

Governeur, Nicholas
    Title to lands of Robertus Samuel Brands declared vested in them 2   363

Graham, Alexander
  (a) One of Commission to open Big Barren River to navigation 4   116
  (b) Permitted to buy part of Main Street in Bowling Green on which his building encroached 5   320

Graham, David
    Co-founder and Trustee of Lebanon 5   191

Graham, Edward
    Over-payment for land refunded 4   317

Graham, James
    Tried for felony in Nelson County 2   207

Graham, James M.
    One of Commission to lease road from Fleming County to the Big Sandy 4   236

Graham, Walter
    Given time to file plats and Certificate on a military warrant 5   12

Grant, John
  (a) Town of Wilmington established on his land.... 1   175
  (b) Trustee Newport Academy 2   240
  (c) Trustee of Charlestown 3   562
  (d) Trustee of Georgetown 3   570

Grant, Squire
    Trustee of Wilmington 1   175

Graves, Absolem
    Trustee Boone Academy 5   76

Graves, Bartlett
  (a) Inspection site in Campbell County 3   323
  (b) Trustee Town of Salisberry 3   369

Graves, Major Benjamin
    Was wounded at the Raisin but was not known to be dead. A tract of his land was ordered sold   5   316

Gray, James
    Trustee Union Academy 5   80

Gray, John
  (a) Authorized to change location of his survey.... 3   191
  (b) Named in boundary of election precinct in Christian County 4   225

GRAY 72

	VOL.	PAGE
Gray, Presley		
Trustee of Port William	2	337
Gray, William F.		
One of Commission to open Kentucky River at Frankfort to navigation	5	390
Grayson County		
Formed April 1, 1800 from Hardin and Ohio Counties	4	129
Grayson, Frederick W. S.		
Trustee Bullitt Academy	3	478
Grayson, Robert H.		
Voting place at house in Greenup County	4	226
Grayson Seminary		
Incorporated January 29, 1816 with Jack Thomas, Robert E. Yates, William Cunningham, John Yates, John Cunningham, Isaac Thomas and William Love, Trustees	5	325
Greathouse, Isaac		
Patent to issue on copy of plat and certificate	5	490
Green County		
(a) Formed January 1, 1793 from Lincoln and Nelson Counties	1	631
(b) Pulaski County, in part, carved from	2	189
(c) Cumberland County carved from	2	202
(d) Barren County, in part, carved from	2	222
(e) Adair County carved from	2	429
(f) Part of Hardin County added to	3	198
Green, Henry, Jr.		
Title to lands of Alexander Holland, deceased, vested in	1	171
Green, John		
Rebecca Green authorized to sue him for divorce	2	173
Green, Rebecca		
See John Green		
Green River, Lands on South Side of		
(a) Lands on opened to settlement	1	350
(b) Lands on opened to settlement	1	682
(c) Penalty for illegal surveys on	2	110
(d) 6000 acres on vested in Samuel Hopkins, Harry Toulmin, and David Walker. Trustees to promote establishment of manufactories	2	290
(e) Purchase price of lands on allowed to be paid in installments	2	380
(f) Actual settlement on lands dispensed with	2	459
(g) Provides for sale of salt springs	3	49
(h) Settlers given further time to make survey	3	151
(i) Reservation of salt springs released	3	175

	VOL.	PAGE

Green River Iron Manufacturing Company
    Incorporated February 4, 1817 5   552

Green, Thomas
  (a) Farm on Licking River in Fleming County made terminus of road from the Big Sandy ... 3   166
  (b) One of Commission to open road from Licking to the Big Sandy 3   350

Green, Willis
  (a) Deputy Register—Land Office 1   159
  (b) Trustee Danville Library 2   376
  (c) Trustee Danville Seminary 3   381
  (d) Trustee Transylvania Seminary (1783) 3   572

Greenfield, Thomas
  Trustee Bullitt Academy.................... 2   243

Greensburg, Town of
  (a) Established December 4, 1794 on lands of Walter Beall with William Casey, William Buckner, Elias Barbee, John Hall, Samuel Burks, Robert Allen, John Allen, John Emmerson, Richard Thurman and James Allen, Trustees 1   272
  (b) Road from to the Tennessee line opened, and Robert Allen, Nicholas Burks, and Haydon Trigg named to survey a route, and John Emmerson, James Allin and John Gorin to raise a fund to pay for the survey 3   21

Greenup Academy
  Incorporated January 23, 1810 with Francis Waring, Sr., Jesse Boone, William Dupey, John Poage and William Fugued, Trustees 4   127

Greenup, Christopher
  (a) Trustee Transylvania Seminary (1783) 3   572
  (b) Trustee of Danville 2   179
  (c) Trustee of Danville 3   562
  (d) Trustee Town of Warwick in Mercer County... 3   564
  (e) Incorporator of Frankfort Bridge Company.... 2   304
  (f) Promoter for Franklin County of the Kentucky River Navigation Company 2   448
  (g) One of Commission to cut new channel for Kentucky River at Fish Trap Island below Frankfort 3   121
  (h) Inspection site on lands on Benson Creek...... 3   332
  (i) Seven hundred dollars appropriated in 1806 to buy a fire engine to protect the public buildings at Frankfort, had been paid to him as the then Governor, but no engine had been purchased. Demand was to be made of him for the money

GREENUP COUNTY 74

	VOL.	PAGE
and upon his failure to refund, suit to recover it was authorized	4	147
(j) Trustee Kentucky Seminary	4	319
(k) Ordered to alter mill dam on Main Licking so as not to obstruct navigation	5	374

Greenup County
    Formed February 1, 1804 from Mason County.. 3   117

Greenville Academy
    Incorporated January 18, 1810 with Charles F. Wing, Claiborne Rice, David Campbell, William Campbell, Jeremiah Langby, Jesse Reno, Alney McClean, John C. Russell, and James Weare, Trustees 4   113

Greenwood, Nimrod
    Trustee of Perryville 5   454

Greer, George
    Promoter at Frankfort of the Bank of Kentucky 3   390

Griffin's Mill, (Scott County)
    Road from to Lexington opened............... 4   88

Griffin, Thomas
    Error in land certificate corrected............. 5   331

Griffith, Joshua
    Trustee of Hartford 3   443

Griffith, William
    Delegate from Bourbon County to second Constitutional Convention (1799) 1   57

Grisal, Andrew
    Donated head-right land 4   159

Grubbs, Hickerson
    Trustee Madison Academy 2   241

Grubbs, Higgerson
    Trustee of Boonesborough (1787).............. 3   540

Grundy, Felix
    (a) Delegate from Washington County to second Constitutional Convention (1799).......... 1   58
    (b) Trustee Washington Academy 2   242

Gullion, Jeremiah
    Inspection site in Gallatin County............ 3   23

Gunsaulis, Henry
    Johannah Gunsaulis authorized to sue him in Mason County for divorce 3   439

Gunsaulis, Johannah
    See Henry Gunsaulis

Gutridge, John (see Getridge)
    (a) Trustee Town of Washington (1786).......... 3   555
    (b) Trustee Town of Washington (1790).......... 3   556
    (c) Trustee Town of Washington 1   199

	VOL.	PAGE
Gwathmey, John		
Promoter for Louisville of Kentucky Assurance Society	4	254
Gwinn, Thomas J.		
Trustee of Shelbyville	1	151
Hadden, William		
(a) Allowed pay for services in Logan's Expedition in 1786	3	344
(b) State price of 113 acres of land remitted	5	556
Haden, William		
Trustee of Port William	1	340
Hahn, Christian		
Inspection site in Nelson County	3	452
Hale, John		
Authorized as administrator to convey lands of Joseph Hale in Mercer County	1	354
Hale, Joseph, deceased		
See John Hale		
Hall, Aaron		
Trustee of Mt. Sterling	1	125
Hall, Caleb		
Error in certificate for headright land corrected	4	330
Hall, Cornelius		
One of Commission to locate County Seat of Lewis County	3	340
Hall, Horatio		
Trustee of Paris	1	188
Hall, James		
Named in Logan-Warren County boundary	1	369
Hall, John		
Trustee of Greensburg	1	273
Hall, M. W.		
Error in charge against him as collector of Barren County corrected	3	174
Hall, Samuel		
Incorporator of Cynthiana Manufacturing Company	5	378
Hall, Sylvester		
Road to his ferry named in Allen County boundary	5	157
Hall, Thomas		
Trustee of Kennedysville	1	342
Hall, William		
(a) Patent to him ordered recorded	5	116
(b) Co-founder of Perryville	5	454

| | VOL. | PAGE |

Hamford, Thomas
    Justices of Pulaski County to meet at his house.. 2   190
Hamilton, Clement
    One of Commission to locate and convey lands
      of Jacob Brehmer, deceased................ 3   470
Hamilton, Joseph
    Trustee Newton Academy 3   409
Hamilton, Walter
    Given time to file delinquent tax list as former
      Deputy Sheriff of Washington County........ 5   414
Hamm, Joel, deceased
    Sale of lands authorized 5   257
Hammond, Peter
    Named in Clay County boundary 3   338
Hammons, John
    Voting place at house in Floyd County........ 5   156
Hann, John (see Hanna)
    (a) One of Commission to raise by lottery a fund to
      open Kentucky River to navigation........ 4   210
    (b) Same as at (a)   4   318
Hanna, John
    Same as (b)—John Hann
Hanna, Stephen, deceased
    Sale of lands authorized 5   408
Hansberry, Peter
    One of Commission to open Mud River in Logan
      County to navigation 4   115
Hanson, Samuel
    (a) Trustee Paris Library...................... 3   455
    (b) Trustee Winchester Library Company......... 4   195
Harbert, John
    Donated 200 acres of land for support......... 3   162
Harbison, Samuel
    Named in boundary of an addition to Shelbyville 5   256
Harbourg, Joseph
    Named in boundary of election precinct in Christian County 4   225
Hardgrove, James
    Trustee Somerset Academy 3   37
Hardin Academy
    Incorporated December 22, 1798, with John Paul, Thomas Helm, John Vantreese, Benjamin Helm, John Canihaw, Sr., Bladen Ashby, Robert Hodgins, Patrick Brown, Stephen Roling and Jacob Larne, Trustees 2   242

HARDIN

	VOL.	PAGE
Hardin, Benjamin (see Benjamin Harding)		
(a) Named in Logan-Christian County boundary...	1	366
(b) Named in Logan-Christian County boundary...	2	378
(c) Named in Muhlenberg County boundary	2	205
(d) Trustee Washington Academy	2	242
Hardin County		
(a) Formed February 20, 1793 from Nelson County	1	631
(b) Ohio County carved from	2	208
(c) Breckenridge County carved from	2	271
(d) Part of added to Green County	3	198
(e) Grayson County, in part, carved from	4	129
Hardin, John		
Allowed costs in suit against Elijah Craig	3	162
Hardin, Martin		
(a) Inspection site in Washington County	2	457
(b) Granted change of venue from Hardin to Nelson County on trial for shooting with intent to kill	5	74
Hardin, Martin D.		
Promoter for Richmond of Ohio Canal Company	3	221
Hardin, Samuel		
Trustee Newton Academy	2	241
Hardin, William		
Justices of Breckenridge County to meet at his house	2	271
Harding, Benjamin (see Hardin)		
Trustee of Springfield	1	176
Hardwick, John		
Given credit in settlement as Sheriff of Montgomery County	3	413
Harel, Isaac		
A parole sale of land to him was confirmed	5	500
Harges, William, Jr.		
Name in boundary of election precinct in Christian County	4	225
Harmon's Lick		
Named in Garrard-Madison County boundary	1	384
Harp, Micajah		
Was killed resisting arrest for murder	2	365
Harper, Hans		
Error in credit for land corrected	4	195
Harpool, John		
Named in boundary of election precinct in Warren County	5	473
Harrell, William, deceased		
Balance of price of land remitted	5	490

HARRIS   78

	VOL.	PAGE
Harris, Edward		
(a) Trustee Town of Washington	1	199
(b) Trustee Franklin Academy	1	296
Harris, Edward, Sr.		
Trustee Town of Washington	2	393
Harris, George		
One of Commission to open Drake Creek in Warren County to navigation	4	361
Harris, John		
His merchant mills made head of navigation of Drake Creek in Warren County	4	361
Harris, Nathaniel		
Trustee Bethel Academy	2	174
Harris, Samuel		
Trustee of Paris	1	188
Harris, William, deceased		
Balance of State price of land remitted	5	490
Harrison Academy		
Incorporated December 22, 1798 with Benjamin Harrison, William E. Boswell, Henry Coleman, Hugh Miller, Sr., John Wall, Samuel Lamb, Samuel McMullin, Samuel Cook and Robert Hingson, Trustees	2	241
Harrison, Benjamin		
(a) Trustee of Cynthiana	1	179
(b) One of Commission to open the South Fork of Licking to navigation	1	193
(c) Trustee Harrison Academy	2	241
Harrison, Burr		
Trustee Salem Academy	5	7
Harrison County		
(a) Established February 1, 1794 from Bourbon and Scott Counties	1	631
(b) Part of Bourbon added to	4	63
(c) Part of Nicholas County added to	5	365
(d) Part of Nicholas County added to	5	452
(e) Campbell County, in part, carved from	1	632
Harrison, Cuthbert		
(a) Trustee of Beallsborough	3	564
(b) Trustee Salem Academy	3	580
Harrison, Elisha		
Named in boundary of election precinct in Clay County	5	472
Harrison, George		
(a) Trustee of Beallsborough	3	564
(b) Trustee Salem Academy	3	580

HARRISON

	VOL.	PAGE

Harrison, H.
   Delegate from Fayette County to second Constitutional Convention (1799) 1   58

Harrison, Jesse
   Error in credit of a payment for head-right land was corrected 5   130

Harrison, John
   (a) Trustee Lancaster Academy 2   242
   (b) Promoter for Garrard County of Kentucky River Navigation Company 2   448

Harrison, Micajah
   (a) Promoter for Mt. Sterling of Ohio Canal Company 3   221
   (b) Incorporator of Mt. Sterling Library Company 5   177

Harrison, Robert
   Founder of Cynthiana 1   178

Harrod, James
   (a) See Ann Tadlock 3   196
   (b) Trustee of Harrodsburg (1785) 3   552

Harrodsburg
   (a) Established in 1785 with William Christian, John Brown, Robert Mosby, Samuel Lapsley, Peter Casey, John Smith, Samuel Taylor, John Cowan, John Gilmore, James Harrod, Abraham Chaplaine, William Kennedy and Benjamin Logan, Trustees 3   552
   (b) Deeds to lots in, made by Thomas Allen, on behalf of the Trustees, confirmed 2   169

Harrodsburg Academy
   Incorporated December 22, 1798 with Samuel Taylor, John Adair, Philip Bush, Gabriel Slaughter, George Thompson, Matthias Bush, George Bohannon, Peter Casey, Samuel P. Duval, Peter Bonta, John Thomas and Augustine Passmore, Trustees 2   240

Harrow, James
   Title to lands perfected 2   426

Harrow, John, deceased
   Commissioners named to convey mills descended to his heirs 4   405

Hart, Aaron
   One of Commission to open Nolinn Creek in Hardin County to navigation 4   221

Hart, Israel
   Inspection site in Pulaski County 3   324

Hart, John
   Trustee Fleming Academy 2   241

HART

	VOL.	PAGE
Hart, Joseph		
Plats and certificates for 3000 acres of land, due him as assignee of Abraham Buford, ordered filed	4	70
Hart, Josiah		
(a) Trustee of Winchester	1	187
(b) Winchester, in part, located on his lands	1	367
Hart, Nathaniel, deceased		
Inspection site in Clarke County on his lands	2	278
Hart, Nathaniel		
Incorporator of Versailles Library Company	4	356
Hart, Thomas, Sr.		
Trustee Lexington Library Association	2	375
Hart, Thomas, Jr. (see Harte)		
Promoter for Lexington of Bank of Kentucky	3	390
Hart's Old Ferry		
On Cumberland River—named in Wayne-Pulaski boundary	5	562
Harte, Thomas, Jr.		
One of Commission to cut new channel for Kentucky River at Fish Trap Island below Frankfort	3	121
Hartford (in Ohio County)		
Established February 3, 1808 on lands of the late Gabriel Madison, with Thomas Moseley, Joshua Crow, James Love, Daniel Barry, Aquilla Field, Joshua Griffith, and Robert Moseley, Trustees	3	443
Hartford Academy		
(a) Incorporated December 22, 1798 with Alexander Barnet, Ignatius Pigman, Joshua Crow, William Bailey Smith, Benjamin Fields, Jesse Cravens, Harrison Taylor, Stephen Clever, Aquilla Fields, and David Glenn, Trustees	2	242
(b) Joshua Crow, Harrison Taylor, Samuel Work, Jesse Cravens, Benjamin Fields, Christopher Jackson and Stephen Clever appointed Trustees (1805)	3	278
Hartgrove, James		
Commissioner for Pulaski to mark the Pulaski-Wayne County line	5	563
Hartgrove, Capt. Willis		
Voting place at house in Berrysville in Logan County	3	345
Harwood, William McWilliam		
Granted change of venue from Breckenridge to Hardin County on trial for larceny	5	328

	VOL.	PAGE
Haskins, Robert		
Trustee New Athens Academy	2	242
Hatton, Elizabeth		
Widow of Robert Hatton		
Hatton, Robert, deceased		
Sale of lots in Frankfort authorized	1	696
Hauskins, Jesse		
Polly Hauskins authorized to sue him for divorce	3	290
Hauskins, Polly		
See Jesse Hauskins		
Hawkins, Henry		
Escheated lands in Henry County released to him	2	486
Hawkins, James		
Co-founder of Port William	1	232
Hawkins, James, deceased		
Lands authorized sold	5	42
Hawkins, James W.		
Promoter for Frankfort of Lexington and Louisville Turnpike Road Company	5	519
Hawkins, John		
(a) Trustee of Georgetown	1	220
(b) Trustee Rittenhouse Academy	2	240
(c) Trustee Georgetown Library	2	376
Hawkins, Joseph H.		
Incorporator of Lexington White Lead Manufacturing Company	5	204
Hawkins, Littleberry		
Incorporator of Lexington White Lead Manufacturing Company	5	204
Hawkins, Martin		
(a) Refunded his costs in suit against Elijah Craig to remove him as Justice of Gallatin County	3	99
(b) Authorized to build a mill dam at Fish Trap Island below Frankfort	3	120
(c) Ordered to remove mill dam at (b)	3	121
(d) Promoter for Georgetown of Ohio Canal Company	3	221
Hawkins, Thomas W.		
(a) One of Commission to settle accounts at the penitentiary	5	276
(b) One of Commission to open Kentucky River at Frankfort to navigation	5	390
Hawley, Hezekiah		
Trustee Louisville Library Company	5	360
Hawthorn, James		
Claimant of site of Centreville in Livingston County	3	354

HAY 82

	VOL.	PAGE
Hay, Fanny		
Madison Circuit Court directed to appoint a Trustee of her estate, she being of unsound mind	4	225
Hay, John		
(a) Trustee of Wilmington	1	175
(b) Trustee Georgetown Library	2	376
Haycraft, Samuel		
One of Commission to locate County seat of Warren County	3	447
Hayden, Edward		
One of Commission to locate County seat of Daviess County	5	160
Hayden, William C.		
Incorporator Mt. Sterling Library Company	5	177
Haydon, Richard		
Inspection site in Madison County	3	451
Hays, James		
Inspection site in Harrison County	2	456
Hays, Richard		
Trustee Caledonia Academy	5	3
Head, Benjamin		
Promoter, for Middletown, of Lexington and Louisville Turnpike Road Company	5	519
Head, Jesse		
(a) Promoter, for Springfield, of Ohio Canal Company	3	221
(b) His witnesses on his trial before the Legislature ordered paid out of the treasury	4	217
Heath, Col. William		
Empowered to appoint surveyors (1783)	1	442
Hebberd, John		
Trustee Manchester Academy	4	18
Heddleston, William		
(a) Trustee Town of Washington	2	393
(b) Trustee Franklin Academy	3	255
Hedrick, Michael		
Inspection site at mill in Fleming County	3	451
Heighsmith, Thomas		
Register authorized to correct some irregularities respecting settlement rights	5	71
Helm, Benjamin		
Trustee Hardin Academy	2	242
Helm, John		
Trustee Washington Academy	2	242

	VOL.	PAGE
Helm, Thomas		
(a) Trustee Hardin Academy	2	242
(b) Trustee of Stanford	5	166
(c) Trustee Stanford Library Company	5	455
Henderson Academy		
Incorporated December 31, 1813 with Adam Rankin, Joseph Fuquay, Daniel McBride, William R. Bowen, James Hillyer, Richard Henderson, and Wyatt H. Ingram, Trustees	5	72
Henderson County		
(a) Formed May 15, 1799 from Christian County	2	227
(b) Hopkins County carved from	3	346
(c) Part of Ohio County added to	4	10
(d) Union County carved from	4	213
Henderson, Hugh, et als.		
Patents ordered issued on certified copies of lost plats and certificates	5	455
Henderson, Isham		
(a) Trustee Newcastle Library Company	4	35
(b) Trustee Henry Academy	5	134
Henderson Library Company		
Incorporated January 27, 1817 by Daniel Comfort, Samuel Hopkins, Adam Rankin, Samuel Legate, Ambrose Barbour and Uel Wilson	5	460
Henderson, Okey		
Justices of Lewis County to meet at his house	3	340
Voting place at house in Lewis County	4	225
Henderson, Richard		
Trustee Henderson Academy	5	72
Henderson, Richard and Company		
(a) Granted 200,000 acres at mouth of Green River in consideration of services in procuring settlers (1778)	3	587
(b) No entry to be made on lands of	1	411
Henderson, William		
Trustee of Lexington (1782)	3	549
Henry Academy		
Incorporated February 1, 1814, with Rowland Thomas, Isham Henderson, Robert Thurston, James Bartlett, and Joseph Bunker, Trustees	5	134
Henry County		
(a) Formed June 1, 1799 from Shelby County	2	200
(b) Andrew Holmes, William Taylor, David Standiford and Lowry Jones, of Shelby County, and William Neil, John Calloway, William M. Rice, and Edmund Bartlett of Henry County,		

HENRY 84

	VOL.	PAGE
appointed commissioners to survey Shelby-Henry County line	5	103
(c) Thomas Mitchell, David Standiford, and Andrew Holmes, of Shelby County, and James Bartlett, John Calloway and William Neil, of Henry County, appointed a new commission to survey Shelby-Henry County line	5	330

Henry, William
(a) Delegate from Scott County to second Constitutional Convention (1799)	1	58
(b) Trustee of Wilmington	1	175
(c) Trustee Kentucky Academy	1	228
(d) Authorized conveyance to him of lands of the Vestry of Russell Parish	1	603
(e) Trustee Rittenhouse Academy	2	242
(f) Promoter for Scott County of Kentucky River Navigation Company	2	448
(g) One of Commissioners for Scott County to open road from Georgetown to Augusta	3	201
(h) Trustee of Georgetown	3	570

Herndon, Richardson
(a) Inspection site in Knox County	3	323
(b) One of Commission to open road from Knox Court House to Pulaski	3	464
(c) Authorized to locate 2000 acres of land on Cumberland River adjoining his salt spring	4	220

Herod, John
Allowed pay for military services in 1787 and 1793	3	516

Hewett, Russell
A marriage solemnized by him as Justice of Henderson County, without authority was legalized	3	220

Hibbard, Lemuel
Required to make settlement as Turnpike keeper on Wilderness Road	5	199

Hickman, John
Promoter for Paris of Kentucky Assurance Society	4	254

Hickman, Pascal, deceased
Administratrix authorized to sell lands	5	356

Hickman, R.
Delegate from Clarke County to second Constitutional Convention (1799)	1	58

Hickman, Richard
(a) Trustee of Winchester	1	**187**
(b) Trustee of Winchester	1	**340**

	VOL.	PAGE
Hieronymous, Henry		
Inspection site in Clarke County	3	513
Higgins' Mill		
On Highland Creek—named in Henderson-Union County boundary	4	213
Higgins, Richard		
Incorporator of Lexington White Lead Manufacturing Company	5	204
Higgins, Robert		
(a) Trustee of Winchester	1	340
(b) Sheriff of Clarke County	2	195
Hill, Adkin		
Trustee of Beallsborough	3	564
Hill, Atkinson		
One of Commissioners to open Beech Fork of Salt River to navigation	2	312
Hill, Brooke		
Trustee Louisville Library Company	5	360
Hill, Henry		
Named in Warren-Allen County boundary	5	157
Hill's, Bullock's and		
Their mill made head of navigation on Chaplin Fork in Nelson County	3	316
Hilliard's and Moss' Mill		
Inspection site in Green County	3	322
Hillyer, James		
Trustee Henderson Academy	5	72
Hinch, Samuel		
Allowed credit on settlement as Deputy Sheriff of Jefferson County	4	60
Hinds, Andrew (see Hynes)		
Trustee of Beallsborough	3	564
Hinds, William R.		
Promoter for Bardstown of Ohio Canal Company	3	221
Hingson, Robert		
Trustee Harrison Academy	2	241
Hinkson, William		
Pay as spy allowed	2	358
Hite, Abraham		
Trustee of Jefferson Seminary	2	378
Trustee Jefferson Seminary	3	207
Lands of Jefferson Seminary vested in him and others as Trustees	3	490
One of Commission to sell, and adjust claims respecting lots in Louisville (1790)	3	547

HITE AND HOGG 86

	VOL.	PAGE
Hite and Hogg		
Inspection site in Henry County	2	384
Hix's, Richard, heirs, and		
Hix, Zilpha		
Donated 50 acres of land	5	448
Hoagland, Cornelius		
Inspection site in Gallatin County	3	322
Hoard, James (see Hord)		
Trustee of New-Market	3	560
Hoard, Jesse		
Trustee of Lewisbourgh	1	295
Hodge, Amos		
(a) Voting place at house in Lincoln County	2	400
(b) Act (a) repealed	3	327
Hodgens, Robert (see Hodgins)		
Given time to settle as Sheriff of Hardin County	2	423
Hodges, Samuel, Sr.		
Named in boundary of election precinct in Christian County	4	225
Hodgins, Robert (see Hodgens)		
Trustee Hardin Academy	2	242
Hogan, James		
(a) Named as terminus of ferry over Kentucky River at mouth of Hickman Creek (1785)	3	586
(b) Inspection site in Lincoln County (1787)	3	581
(c) Inspection site in Fayette County (1787)	3	582
(d) Inspection site in Fayette County	1	370
(e) Inspection site in Garrard County	1	606
(f) Inspection site in Garrard County	2	139
(g) Inspection site in Fayette County	2	139
(h) Required to file settlement as turnpike keeper on Wilderness Road	5	199
Hogan, William		
Turnpike keeper on the Madison Road	4	54
Hogg and Hite		
Inspection site in Henry County	2	384
Hogland, Amos, deceased		
Widow and heirs allowed reduction in price of land	2	364
Hogland, Sena		
Widow of Amos Hogland, deceased	2	364
Hogshead, William		
His plat of Town of Westport confirmed	2	408
Hoke, Adam		
Trustee Town of Jefferson	2	380

Holder, John
(a) Granted stay in proceedings against him as surety for Robert Higgins, Sheriff of Clarke County .... 2 — 195
(b) Certificate for services in Wabash Expedition renewed to Henry Brock, assignee........... 3 — 100
(c) He having died the penalty and interest on his obligation at (a) was remitted.............. 4 — 336

Holland, Alexander, deceased
Land held by him under a title bond was directed to be conveyed to Henry Green, his devisee .... 1 — 171

Holliday, Benjamin
Trustee of Milford in Madison County........ 1 — 226

Holmes, Andrew
(a) Contributor to cost of public buildings........ 1 — 220
(b) Operator of ferry on Kentucky River in Franklin County............................... 1 — 225
(c) Director of Vineyard Society, of Lexington.... 2 — 268
(d) Commissioner for Shelby County to survey Shelby-Henry County line................. 5 — 103
(e) Named on second commission to survey Shelby-Henry County line...................... 5 — 330

Holmes, Samuel
Granted change of venue.................... 5 — 202

Holt, Abraham
Elizabeth Barnett and Polly Mason granted 400 acres of land as his heirs................. 5 — 22

Holt, Thomas
Commissioner for Harrison County to open South and Stoners Forks of Licking to navigation .... 3 — 193

Home, John
Trustee Fleming Academy................... 2 — 241

Hood, Andrew
Justices of Greenup County to meet at his house 3 — 117

Hooker, Robert
Title of his assignee, Samuel Short, to land in Hopkins County confirmed................ 4 — 105

Hootten, Thomas
(a) Named in Rockcastle County boundary........ 4 — 92
(b) Named in Rockcastle-Madison County boundary 4 — 406

Hope Distillery Company
Incorporated January 27, 1817............... 5 — 458

Hope, Michael
Trustee Danville Academy................... 5 — 480

HOPE 88

	VOL.	PAGE
Hope, Richard		
Trustee of Perryville	5	454
Hopewell, Town of		
(See Paris)		
Hopkins, Lt. Col.		
Empowered to appoint surveyors (1783)	1	442
Hopkins County		
Formed May 1, 1807 from Henderson County	3	346
Hopkins, Samuel		
(a) Trustee Newton Academy	2	241
(b) Trustee to locate settlers south of Green River	2	290
(c) Promoter at Henderson of Ohio Canal Company	3	222
(d) Trustee Henderson Library Company	5	460
Hopkins, Major General Samuel		
Provides for payment of officers who attended the Court of Inquiry called to examine charges against him	5	105
Hopkinsville		
(a) Name changed from "Elizabeth"	3	183
(b) Trustees authorized to alter plan of the town	3	367
(c) Sale of part of public square are authorized	5	511
Hopkinsville Library Company		
Incorporated February 8, 1816 by Peter Ferguson, James H. McLaughlin, John Bryan, Rezen Davidge, Benjamin Shackleford, Samuel A. Miller, John D. Patton and Charles Caldwell	5	361
Hopper, Thomas		
Escaped from penitentiary—reward allowed for his capture	3	414
Hord, James (see Hoard)		
Trustee Bethel Academy	2	174
Hord, William		
Terminus of a ferry on Cumberland River in Lincoln County (1791)	3	586
Hornbeck, Isaac		
Trustee of New-Town	1	233
Hornsby, Joseph		
Trustee Shelby Academy	2	241
Hoskins, Archelaus		
Trustee Town of Bedford	5	350
Hospitals		
Fayette, Incorporated February 10, 1816	5	415
Louisville, Incorporated February 5, 1817	5	574
Hough, Joseph		
One of Commission to build bridge over Floyds Fork in Bullit County	5	22

	VOL.	PAGE
Houston, James		
Trustee of Carthage	5	83
How, Capt. James		
Named in boundary of election precinct in Greenup County	4	225
How, Joseph		
Trustee Montgomery Academy	3	438
Howard, Benjamin		
One of Commission to open road from Paris or Mt. Sterling to the Big Sandy	3	4
Howard, George		
Incorporator Mt. Sterling Library Company	5	177
Howard, John		
Inspection site in Clarke County	3	323
Howard, Thomas		
Promoter for Richmond of Bank of Kentucky	3	390
Howard, Thomas C.		
(a) Promoter for Madison County of the Madison Hemp Company	3	533
(b) One of Commission to raise by lottery a fund to open Kentucky River to navigation	4	210
(c) Promoter for Richmond of Kentucky Assurance Society	4	254
Hoy, Jones		
Trustee Town of Irvine	4	339
Hubbard, Austin		
(a) Tax Commissioner, Washington County	1	169
(b) One of Commission to locate and convey lands of Jacob Brehmer, deceased	3	217
(c) Re-appointed on second commission at (b)	3	470
Hubbard, Simon M.		
Allowed compensation, as Deputy Sheriff of Warren County for arresting an escaped felon	3	364
Hubbard, Thomas		
Trustee of Germantown	1	329
Hubble, William		
Trustee of Covington	5	283
Hudspeth, George		
One of Commission to open Drake Creek in Warren County to navigation	4	361
Hudspeth, Joel		
Voting place at house in Logan County	5	140
Hughes, Barnabas		
(a) Trustee Danville Library	2	376
(b) Promoter for Danville of Ohio Canal Company	3	221

	VOL.	PAGE

Hughes, James
  (a) Trustee of Lexington 1   577
  (b) Director of Vineyard Society, of Lexington 2   268
  (c) Promoter for Springfield of Ohio Canal Company   3   221
Hughes, John
  Trustee of Falmouth 1   181
Hughes, Thomas
  Promoter for Paris of Ohio Canal Company 3   221
Hume, Joseph
  (a) Trustee of Falmouth 1   181
  (b) Trustee Montgomery Academy 2   241
Humphreys, Charles
  Promoter for Lexington of Lexington and Louisville Turnpike Road Company 5   519
Hunsaker, Jacob
  Inspection site in Muhlenberg County 2   457
Hunt, Bazil, Sr.
  Voting place at house in Fleming County 5   447
Hunt, Isaiah
  Voting place at house in Ohio County 4   416
Hunt, John
  (a) One of Commission to erect a turnpike on road from Fleming County to the Big Sandy 4   154
  (b) Act (a) repealed and he was named on a commission to lease the road 4   235
Hunt, John W.
  (a) One of Commission to raise by lottery a fund to open Kentucky River to navigation 4   210
  (b) Re-appointed on second commission as at (a) .. 5   12
  (c) Promoter for Lexington of Lexington and Louisville Turnpike Road Company 5   519
Hunter, James
  (a) Promoter for Louisville of Ohio Canal Company   3   221
  (b) Incorporator of Ohio Canal Company 3   260
Hunter, John
  (a) Trustee Rittenhouse Academy 2   240
  (b) One of Commission to open new channel in Kentucky River at Fish Trap Island below Frankfort 3   121
Hunter, Robert
  Authorized to file delinquent list as Collector for Scott County 3   175
Hunter, William
  (a) Trustee Kentucky Seminary 2   389
  (b) Trustee Kentucky Seminary 4   319
  (c) One of Commission to erect a State House 5   123

	VOL.	PAGE

(d) One of Commission to settle accounts at the penitentiary 5 296

Hurst, John
One of Commission to build a bridge over North Elkhorn in Scott County................. 4 88

Huston, Joseph
Inspection site in Breckenridge County........ 2 383

Huston, Matthew
Trustee Madison Academy 2 241

Huston, N.
Delegate from Lincoln County to second Constitutional Convention (1799).............. 1 58

Huston, Nathan
Trustee Stanford Academy 2 240

Hutcherson, Charles
Allowed pay for making a press for the Adjutant General's office..................... 5 180

Hynes, Andrew (see Hinds)
(a) Trustee of Louisville (1780)................ 3 540
(b) Trustee of Bairdstown (1788).............. 3 566
(c) Trustee Salem Academy (1788)............. 3 580

Hynes, Isaac
Named in Grayson County boundary.......... 4 129

Hynes, William R.
(a) Promoter for Bairdstown of Bank of Kentucky 3 390
(b) One of Commission to raise by lottery a fund to open Salt River to navigation............ 4 249

Iles, Thomas
One of Commission to lease road from Fleming County to the Big Sandy.................. 4 236

Ingram, Samuel, deceased
Widow and heirs authorized to convey lands he had sold under contract 4 412

Ingram, Wyatt H.
Trustee Henderson Academy 5 72

Innes, Harry
(a) Delegate from Franklin County to second Constitutional Convention (1799) 1 58
(b) One of Commission to erect jail at Frankfort.. 1 263
(c) Authorized to convey lands belonging to Vestry of Russell Parish 1 603
(d) One of Commission to locate penitentiary...... 2 15
(e) Trustee of Danville 2 179
(f) Trustee of Danville (1787) 3 562
(g) Trustee Town of New-Market (1786)......... 3 560

Inspections
See Appendix

Instone, John
(a) One of Commission to open new channel for Kentucky River at Fish Trap Island below Frankfort 3   121
(b) Promoter for Frankfort of Kentucky Assurance Society 4   254

Ireland, John
Trustee of Winchester 1   340

Irish Station
Named in Bourbon-Nicholas County boundary 2   366

Irvan, William
Error in patent corrected 4   330

Irvine
Established January 28, 1812 on lands of Green Clay, with Stephen Trigg, Bennett Clark, John Oldham, Jones Hoy and Jesse Cobb, as Trustees, and made County Seat of Estill County...... 4   339

Irvin, Abraham, Sr.
Trustee of Danville (1787)................. 3   562

Irvine, Betsy
Commissioners named to sell lands for her benefit 5   357

Irvine, David C.
Given time to survey land................... 5   5

Irvine, William
(a) Trustee of Boonesborough (1787)............. 3   540
(b) Trustee of Milford (1789)................... 3   567
(c) Delegate from Madison County to second Constitutional Convention (1799)............... 1   58
(d) One of Commission to open road in Madison County 1   231
(e) One of Commission to assess damages to property owners in Milford upon removal of Madison County Seat therefrom................ 2   166
(f) Trustee Madison Academy 3   278
(g) Promoter for Richmond of Bank of Kentucky.. 3   390
(h) Promoter for Richmond of Kentucky Assurance Society 4   254

Irwin, Christopher
Trustee Madison Academy 2   241

Irwin, John
Trustee Winchester Academy 2   217

Jackman, William
Inspection site in Wayne County............. 3   243

JACKSON

	VOL.	PAGE

Jackson, Burwell
  (a) Trustee Newton Academy 2   241
  (b) Presiding Judge of Logan County............. 2   361
Jackson, Christopher
  (a) Trustee Hartford Academy 3   278
  (b) One of Commission to build bridge over Rough Creek at Hartford 4   88
Jackson, Hezekiah
  Voting place at house in Cumberland County.. 4   328
Jackson, Joel
  Trustee Newcastle Library Company.......... 4   35
Jackson, John
  (a) Relieved of consequences of some irregular proceedings respecting head-right lands........ 4   13
  (b) One of Commission to raise by lottery a fund to open Kentucky River to navigation....... 4   318
  (c) Voting place at house in Knox County........ 5   426
Jackson, John, deceased
  Commissioners named to convey lands......... 5   478
Jackson, William
  Inspection site in Wayne County............. 3   23
James, David
  Credit allowed on settlement as surety for an insolvent sheriff.......................... 5   578
James, Henry, et als.
  Authorized to locate iron-ore lands in Pulaski County 3   536
James, John
  (a) Trustee Stanford Academy 2   240
  (b) Authorized, with Henry James and William Ray to locate iron-ore lands in Pulaski County.... 3   536
  (c) Given time to return plats and certificates at (b) 4   13
Jameson, John, deceased
  (a) Sale of land authorized...................... 3   97
  (b) Additional land authorized to be sold......... 3   162
Jameson, John
  One of Commission to open road from Mt. Sterling to Prestonsburg and Cumberland Mountain 5   553
January, Peter, Sr.
  Trustee Lexington Seminary 2   108
January, Samuel
  Named as owner of a lot in Paris............. 1   648
January, Thomas
  (a) Trustee of Lexington........................ 1   577
  (b) Promoter for Lexington of Kentucky Assurance Society 4   254

JARRETT 94

	VOL.	PAGE
(c) Incorporator of Fayette Paper Manufacturing Company	5	409

Jarrett, ——
Marriage, improperly solemnized in Henderson County was legalized.................... 3 220

Jefferson County
(a) Formed November 1, 1780 from Kentucky County 1 627
(b) Nelson County carved from.................. 1 627
(c) Bullitt County carved from.................. 1 364
(d) Shelby County carved from.................. 1 629
(e) Part of it added to Bullitt County............ 4 219

Jefferson Seminary
(a) 6000 acres of land vested in John Thompson, William Croghan, Alexander S. Bullitt, James Meriwether, John Thruston, Henry Churchill, William Taylor, and Richard Clough Anderson, as Trustees for its benefit.................. 2 108
(b) Abraham Hite, James F. Moore, John Speed, Samuel Oldham, Robert Breckenridge, Gabriel J. Johnson, Fortunatus Cosby and Abner Field named as additional Trustees.......... 2 378
(c) Trustees authorized to move location to any place in Jefferson County 2 429
(d) Alexander S. Bullitt, Richard C. Anderson, Robert Breckenridge, Abraham Hite, Henry Churchill, Abner Fields, Gabriel J. Johnson, Samuel Oldham, John Bates, Thomas Barbour, Jonathan Taylor and David L. Ward named Trustees 3 207
(e) Name changed to Estill Academy.............. 5 509

Jefferson, Town of
(a) Established December 13, 1794 as New-Town on lands of James Francis Moore, with Abner Field, Basil Prather, Isaac Hornbeck, Lewis Field and James Standiford, Trustees....... 1 233
(b) Adverse claims to site of adjusted............ 1 261
(c) John Murphy, William Shannon, Philip Tilhart, Robert McCowen, Adam Hoke, James Denny and John Stuckley, named Trustees........ 2 380
(d) Claim of heirs of Peter Shepherd to title to site quieted 5 353

Jennings, Jonathan
One of Commissioners for Gallatin County to open road from Newcastle to mouth of Licking 3 365

JESSAMINE COUNTY

	VOL.	PAGE
Jessamine County		
(a) Formed February 1, 1799 from Fayette County	2	213
(b) Fayette County line surveyed	2	297
Jett, James		
Peggy Jett authorized to sue him in Franklin County for divorce	3	516
Jett, Peggy		
See James Jett		
Jimms, John		
Trustee of Versailles	1	355
Jinkins, Thomas		
Named in Nicholas-Fleming County boundary	5	366
Johns, William		
Trustee Newton Academy	3	409
Johnson, Benjamin		
Trustee of Louisville (1789)	3	547
Johnston, Benjamin		
Trustee of Williamsville	1	118
Johnson, Cave		
Trustee of Versailles	1	63
Trustee of Port William	1	232
Inspection site in Campbell County	2	140
Johnson, David, deceased		
(a) Sale of lands authorized	5	315
(b) Further sale of lands authorized	5	511
Johnston, Gabriel J.		
Trustee Jefferson Seminary	2	378
Johnson, Gabriel J.		
(a) Trustee Jefferson Academy	3	207
(b) Lands vested in him and others as Trustees for Jefferson Academy	3	490
Johnston, James		
One of Commission to locate County Seat of Union County	4	213
Johnson, John (see Johnston)		
(a) Trustee Town of Washington	1	199
(b) Trustee Franklin Academy	1	296
(c) Trustee Franklin Academy	3	255
Johnston, John (see Johnson)		
Trustee Town of Washington	2	393
Johnson, John C., deceased		
Sale of lots in Lexington authorized	5	508
Johnson, John I.		
Promoter at Georgetown of Lexington and Louisville Turnpike Road Company	5	520
Johnston, Richard		
Trustee Georgetown Library	2	376

JOHNSON 96

	VOL.	PAGE
Johnson, Robert		
(a) Delegate from Scott County to second Constitutional Convention (1799)	1	58
(b) Trustee of Georgetown (1790)	3	570
(c) Trustee Transylvania Seminary (1783)	3	572
(d) One of Commission to open road from Lindsey's Station in Scott County to the Ohio	5	272
(e) One of Commission to locate Kentucky-Virginia boundary	2	276
Johnson, Robert, deceased		
Sale of lands authorized	5	334
Johnston, Robert		
(a) Trustee Rittenhouse Academy	2	240
(b) Named in boundary of Town of Washington (1790)	3	556
(c) Trustee of Frankfort (1786)	3	557
Johnson, Samuel		
Inspection site in Fayette County	1	606
Johnston, Samuel		
Inspection site at Ferry on Kentucky River	2	173
Johnston, Thomas		
(a) Trustee Shelby Library Company	4	89
(b) Voting place at house in Wayne County	5	36
Johnston, Capt. Thomas		
Named in Pulaski-Wayne County boundary	2	392
Johnston, Thomas, deceased		
Heirs allowed pay for a beef and gun he furnished the Wabash expedition	3	450
Johnson, William		
(a) Town of Williamsville, at mouth of Salt River, established on his lands	1	118
(b) His securities as Sheriff of Shelby County given time to settle	5	463
Johnson, William, Sr.		
Named in boundary of election precinct in Christian County	5	80
Johnston, William Garrett		
Trustee Georgetown Library	2	376
Jones, Daniel M.		
(a) Trustee Allen Seminary	5	433
(b) Trustee of Scottville	5	483
Jones, Elizabeth		
Authorized to sue for divorce	2	54
Jones, Fielding		
Given time to settle as Sheriff of Henderson County	5	203

	VOL.	PAGE
Jones, Humphrey		
Promoter in Madison County of Madison Hemp Company	3	533
Jones, John		
Trustee Lancaster Academy	2	242
Jones, Jonas		
One of Commission to open road from Lindsey's Station in Scott County to the Ohio	5	272
Jones, Joshua		
(a) Granted 1000 acres for bloomery	2	425
(b) Given time to locate land at (a)	2	487
(c) Given further time to locate land at (a)	3	207
Jones, Lowry		
One of Commissioners for Shelby County to survey Shelby-Henry County line	5	103
Jones, Richard		
Trustee of Winchester	1	340
Jones, Roberts and		
Inspection site at mouth of Marrowbone Creek	3	514
Jones, Samuel Paul, deceased		
Trustees named to administer trust in his will for benefit of church in Bardstown	5	100
Jones, Thomas		
(a) Trustee of Paris	1	188
(b) Promoter for Paris of Maysville and Lexington Turnpike Road Company	5	536
Jones, Thomas, Sr.		
(a) Trustee Bourbon Academy	2	237
(b) Trustee Bourbon Academy	2	242
Jones, Walter		
(a) Trustee Logan Academy	3	206
(b) Trustee Newton Academy	3	277
Jones, Walter E.		
Trustee Newton Academy	3	409
Jordan, John		
(a) Promoter for Fayette County of Kentucky River Navigation Company	2	448
(b) Promoter for Lexington of Ohio Canal Company	3	221
Jordan, John, Jr.		
Incorporator of Ohio Canal Company	3	260
Jouet, John		
Trustee Town of New Market (1786)	3	560
Jouit, John		
Trustee of Danville (1787)	3	562

	VOL.	PAGE

Jouitt, John
  (a) Trustee Woodford Academy 3   181
  (b) Named in boundary of election precinct in
      Montgomery County 4   173
  (c) Named in Montgomery-Bath County boundary 4   215
  (d) One of Commission to lease road from Fleming
      County to the Big Sandy 4   236

Jouitte, John
  Trustee Woodford Academy 2   243

Judy, John
  Co-founder of Mt. Sterling 1   125

Kalfrus, Henry
  Named in boundary of election precinct in
    Jefferson County 5   308

Kay, John
  Allowed to withdraw money paid for Green
    River land under mistake 3   509

Keith, James
  Patent allowed for 90 acres Muhlenberg County 5   69

Kelkott, Samuel
  Named in boundary of election precinct in
    Christian County 4   225

Keller, George
  One of Commission to open Nolinn Creek in
    Hardin County to navigation 4   221

Kelly, Benjamin
  (a) Voting place at house in Ohio County 4   416
  (b) Act (a) repealed 5   474

Kelley, David
  Voting place at house in Ohio County 5   474

Kelley, Griffin
  One of Commission to build bridge over North
    Elkhorn in Scott County 4   88

Kelly, Nathan
  Trustee of Newport 1   281

Kelly, William
  (a) Trustee Bourbon Academy 2   237
  (b) Trustee Bourbon Academy 2   242
  (c) One of Commission to open road from Paris or
      Mt. Sterling to the Big Sandy 3   4
  (d) Trustee Paris Library 3   455

Kelly, William L.
  Judge Circuit Court Ninth District 3   507

Kelsoe, Charles
  Given time to settle as Sheriff of Harrison
    County 4   174

Kemper, James (see Camper)

	VOL.	PAGE
Kencaid, James (see James Kinkead)		
Named in Madison-Knox County boundary....	3	182
Kendell, William (see William Kindell)		
Trustee of Beallsborough (1787)	3	564
Kennedy, Archibald		
Kennedysville, in Green County, established on his lands	1	341
Kennedy, James		
Allowed to resign as administrator of William Kennedy, deceased	3	163
Kennedy, John		
(a) Trustee of Boonesborough (1779)	3	538
(b) Trustee of Beallsborough (1787)	3	564
Kennedy, John, deceased		
Sale of lands in Nelson County authorized....	3	164
Kennedy, Joseph		
(a) Trustee Madison Academy	2	241
(b) Commissioner for Campbell County to open road from Newcastle to Mouth of Licking..	3	365
(c) Trustee of Covington	5	283
Kennedy, Thomas		
(a) Trustee of Boonesborough (1787)	3	539
(b) Trustee of Newport	1	281
(c) Trustee Newport Academy	2	240
(d) Promoter for Garrard County of Kentucky River Navigation Company	2	448
(e) Inspection site in Campbell County	3	513
(f) Owner of town site of Covington	5	283
Kennedy, William		
(a) Trustee of Harrodsburg (1785)	3	552
(b) Trustee of Danville (1787)	3	562
(c) Trustee Newport Academy	2	240
Kennedy, William, deceased		
(a) His Administrator, James Kennedy, was allowed to resign	3	163
(b) Division and sale of lands in Campbell County authorized	5	566
Kennedysville (Green County)		
Established December 21, 1795 on lands of Archibald Kennedy, with Thomas Hall, Joshua Armstrong, Thomas Morris, Martin Frazier, John Thurman, James Spilman, Adam Mitchell and Samuel Duncan as Trustees	1	341
Kenton, John		
Newtown, in Mason County, established on his lands	1	285

KENTON 100

	VOL.	PAGE
Kenton, Simon (see Simon Canton)		
(a) Claimant of part of site of Town of Washington	1	201
(b) Same as (a)............................	2	396
(c) Inspection site in Mason County............	2	140
(d) Named in boundary of Town of Washington	3	556

Kenton, William
    Trustee of Newtown in Mason County 1   285

Kentucky Academy
    (a) Incorporated December 12, 1794 with David Rice, Caleb Wallace, Jacob Froman, Samuel Shannon, Terah Tamplin, John Miller, James Crawford, Robert Finley, Andrew McCalla, William Ward, James Thompson, James Camper, John Caldwell, William Henry, Robert Marshall, Notly Conn, James Blythe and Cary Allen as Trustees............... 1   228
    (b) Granted 6000 acres of land on Green River.. 2   107
    (c) Merged with Kentucky Academy under name Transylvania University.................. 2   234

Kentucky County
    Formed December 1, 1776 from Fincastle County 1   626

Kentucky Gazette
    See Newspapers

Kentucky Hotel (Lexington)
    A Commission to meet at (1812)............ 4   318

Kentucky Insurance Company
    Incorporated at Lexington December 16, 1802 3   25

Kentucky Mutual Assurance Society
    Incorporated, January 29, 1811, the promoters being Alexander Parker, Henry Purviance, Thomas January, and Thomas J. Barr, of Lexington, John Instone and Daniel Weisiger, at Frankfort, John Gwathmey and Thomas Prather, at Louisville, James Smiley, and William P. Duval, at Bardstown, Richard Dallam and Amos Edwards, at Russellville, David Bell, Daniel McIlvoy and Richard Davenport, at Danville, Benjamin Bayles and Adam Beatty, at Washington, John Hickman and Valentine Peers, at Paris, and Thomas C. Howard and William Irvine, at Richmond 4   253

Kentucky River Company
    Incorporated December 19, 1801 for the purpose of improving and extending the navigation of Kentucky River, the promoters being

KENTUCKY SEMINARY

	VOL.	PAGE

Christopher Greenup, Burnett Pemberton and Thomas Todd in Franklin County; Robert Alexander, Thomas Bullock and William Steele in Woodford County; James Trotter, John Jordan and Thomas Wallace in Fayette County; David Bullock, Robert Clarke, Jr., and Dillard Collins in Clarke County; John Patrick, James Barnett and John Wilkinson in Madison County; John Harrison, Thomas Kennedy and Abner Baker in Garrard County; Gabriel Slaughter, James Birney and James Moore in Mercer County; William Price, George Walker and Benjamin Bradshaw in Jessamine County; William Henry, David Flournoy and Bartlett Collins in Scott County; Isaac Shelby, William Logan and William Whitley in Lincoln County 2   448

(b) Daniel Garrard, John Bates and Beverly Broddas named commissioners to open South Fork of Kentucky River to navigation........... 4   94

(c) Green Clay, Thomas C. Howard, John W. Hunt, Lewis Sanders, William N. Lane, Beverly Broaddus, Jepthah Dudley, Charles Buck, John Rochester, Beriah Megoffin and John Hann appointed commissioners to raise by lottery a fund to open Kentucky River to navigation from Garrards Lick on Goose Creek to its mouth...................... 4   210

(d) Green Clay, John Jackson, Robert Burnside, William N. Lane, Jepthah Dudley, Stephen Trigg, Samuel McCoun, Charles Wilkins, Lewis Sanders, John Hanna and Beverly Broadus appointed commissioners in lieu of those named at (c)...................... 4   318

(e) John W. Hunt, Lewis Sanders, Abner Legrand, Samuel Maccoun and James Morrison appointed commissioners in lieu of those at (c) and (d)................................. 5   12

(f) Henry Clark, John Gilbert and John Murphy appointed commissioners to open Red Bird Fork to navigation....................... 5   149

Kentucky Seminary (Franklin County)
(a) Incorporated December 17, 1800 with Bennett Pemberton, Thomas Todd, William Murry, George Madison, Baker Ewing, Otho Beatty, Isaac E. Gano, James Blair, Daniel Weisiger,

KENNY 102

	VOL.	PAGE
William Trigg, John M. Scott, Anthony Crockett, Thomas Tunstall, John Logan, Isham Talbot, Joseph H. Daviess and William Hunter as Trustees..................	2	388
(b) John Brown, Daniel Weisiger, William Hunter, Achilles Sneed, James Blair, William Trigg and Christopher Greenup appointed Trustees	4	319

Kenney, James (see James Kinney)
(a) Trustee Bourbon Academy..................	2	242
(b) Commissioner for Bourbon County to open South and Stoners Forks of Licking to navigation	3	193

Kerby, Jesse
One of Commission to open Drake Creek in Warren County to navigation.............	4	361

Kerchevall, John
(a) Suits by Commonwealth against him in Mason and Montgomery Counties to recover money fraudulently obtained from the Treasury were authorized...........................	4	74
(b) Fees allowed witnesses on trial..............	4	188

Kerley, William
Commissioner of the Madison Road..........	4	55

Kesler, Daniel
(a) Authorized to locate 200 acres of land and erect a grist mill on Russells Creek..............	3	465
(b) Quantity of land at (a) reduced to 49 acres..	4	6

Kester, William, Sr.
Title confirmed to 557 acres in Shelby County purchased from Adam Shepherd...........	5	299

Ketcham, John
Trustee Shelby Library Company............	4	90

Killam, Asa
Patent granted to land on which he had resided since 1788.........................	5	310

Kincaid, Andrew
Trustee Fleming Academy..................	2	241

Kincaid, Archibald
Promoter at Versailles of Lexington and Louisville Turnpike Road Company..............	5	519

Kincaid, James (see Kencaid)
Relieved of consequences of errors as proprietor of head-right claims.................	4	38

Kincaid, John
Sale to him and Joseph Kincaid of part of public square in Versailles confirmed..........	4	206

KINCAID

	VOL.	PAGE
Kincaid, Joseph		
(a) Sale to him and John Kincaid of part of public square in Versailles confirmed	4	206
(b) Incorporator of Versailles Library Company	4	356
Kincheloe, Lewis		
Inspection site in Muhlenberg County	2	383
Kindell, William (see Kendell)		
Inspection site in Nelson County	2	384
King, Abraham		
Gallatin-Ohio Steamboat Company to organize at his house in Gallatin County	5	345
King, Elizabeth		
Authorized to sue Robert King for divorce	2	187
King, James		
Trustee Pendleton Academy	5	174
King, Robert		
(a) Elizabeth King authorized to sue him for divorce	2	187
(b) Incorporator and promoter of Gallatin-Ohio Steamboat Company	5	343
Kinkead, James (see Kencaid)		
House near Rockcastle River on Wilderness Road	3	511
Kinney, James (see James Kenney)		
Trustee Bourbon Academy	2	237
Kirby, Samuel		
Trustee of Louisville	3	547
Kirk, Robert		
Inspection site in Livingston County	2	391
Kirkpatrick, James		
Given time to build on lot in Harrodsburg	5	7
Kirkpatrick, Moses		
Inspection site in Cumberland County	3	124
Kirtley, Jeremiah		
Trustee Boone Academy	5	76
Kirtley, Pleasant		
Trustee of Campbellsville	5	430
Kishner, David		
Voting place at house in Christian County	4	225
Knapp, Joshua		
Commissioners to lease road from Fleming County to the Big Sandy directed to meet at his house	4	238
Knight, John		
Trustee of Shelbyville	1	151
Knighten, Jesse		
Donated 98 acres of land in Muhlenberg County	4	394

	VOL.	PAGE
Knobler, John		
Trustee Bethel Academy...................	2	174
Knox County		
(a) Formed June, 1800 from Lincoln County......	2	298
(b) Part of Madison County added to..........	3	182
(c) Clay County, in part, carved from..........	3	338
(d) Rockcastle County, in part, carved from......	4	91
Kyle, Thomas		
Trustee Washington Academy...............	2	242
Lacassagne, Michael		
Trustee of Louisville......................	3	547
Lacey, Benjamin		
Named in boundary of election precinct in Christian County.........................	4	329
Lacey, William		
An over-payment for head-right land refunded	4	87
Lackey, Alexander		
One of Commission to open road from Mt. Sterling to Prestonburg and thence to Cumberland Mountain........................	5	553
Lad, Benjamin		
Named in boundary of election precinct in Christian County.........................	5	80
Laman, John		
Voting place at house in Ohio County........	4	416
Lamb, Samuel		
Trustee Harrison Academy.................	2	241
Lamb, William		
(a) Trustee Town of Washington (1786).........	3	555
(b) Same as (a) (1790)......................	3	556
Lancaster		
Established February 10, 1798 on lands of William Buford.........................	2	172
Lancaster Academy		
Incorporated December 22, 1798 with Benjamin Perkins, John Harrison, James Thompson, John Bryant, Samuel Gill, Henry Pawling, Benjamin Letcher, William Bledsoe, John Jones, John Boyle, Jr., and William Campbell as Trustees........................	2	242
Lancaster, John		
Trustee Washington Academy...............	2	242
Lancaster Library Company		
Incorporated December 18, 1804 by John Boyle, Jr., Peter Bembridge, Benjamin Letcher, Samuel McKee, William Owsley, Jr., William M. Bledsoe, Abner Baker,		

	VOL.	PAGE
Stephen Perkins, John Bryant, Achilles Ballinger, John Yantes, Isaac Alderson, William Buford and Alexander Wright	3	208
Lancaster, Susannah		
Price of small tract of land remitted	5	149
Landers, John		
Trustee of Winchester	1	340
Landreth, David		
Authorized to sue Delilah Landreth in Logan County for divorce	3	179
Landreth, Delilah		
See David Landreth		
Lane, James H.		
Named in Montgomery-Bath County boundary	4	215
Lane, William N.		
(a) Trustee Winchester Library Company	4	195
(b) One of Commission to raise by lottery a fund to open Kentucky River to navigation	4	210
(c) Same as (b)	4	318
Langby, Jeremiah		
Trustee Greenville Academy	4	113
Langford, Stephen (see Lankford)		
Justices of Rockcastle County to meet at house	4	92
Langhorn, Morris		
Promoter at Maysville of Maysville and Lexington Turnpike Road Company	5	536
Langhorne, Maurice		
Some warrants collected by him as Deputy Sheriff of Bourbon County were ordered paid	2	485
Lanier, James		
(a) Authorized to erect mill dam on South Fork of Licking	2	359
(b) Mill seat sold to Alvin Montjoy	3	172
(c) Trustee of Hopewell (Paris) (1789)	3	568
Lankford, Stephen (see Langford)		
Named in Lincoln-Pulaski County boundary	2	189
Lapsley, Samuel		
Trustee of Harrodsburg (1785)	3	552
Larue, Jacob		
Trustee Hardin Academy	2	243
Laurence, James		
Granted reward for arrest of Hugh Ross	1	358
Lawes, Thomas		
Voting place at house in Jefferson County	5	334
Lawless, Benjamin		
One of Commission to open Big Barren River to navigation	4	116

LAWRENCE 106

| | VOL. | PAGE |

Lawrence, Joseph
    Allowed pay for guarding families moving through Cumberland Gap in 1786 3   407
Lawrence, Samuel
    Promoter at Middletown of Lexington and Louisville Turnpike Road Company 5   519
Leadworks (near Millersburg)
    Lottery for benefit of authorized 2   491
Leaman, John
  (a) Justices of Daviess County to meet at his house   5   160
  (b) One of Commission to locate County Seat of Daviess County 5   160
Leavel, Lewis
    Trustee Lebanon Academy 5   323
Leavy, William
  (a) Director Vineyard Society of Lexington 2   268
  (b) Incorporator of Lexington White Lead Manufacturing Company 5   204
Lebanon
    Established January 31, 1815 on lands of William Purdie, Robert H. Fogle, David Graham, George Mercer, Richard Foreste, and Benedict Spalding, Jr., with David Clark, Edward M. Elder, David Graham, Clement Parsons, Robert H. Fogle, Stephen Purdie, Benedict Spalding, Jr., and James McElroy, as Trustees 5   191
Lebanon Academy (Christian County)
  (a) Incorporated December 17, 1810 with Fines Ewing, Ephriam McClean, Samuel Moore, Young Ewing, Daniel Benham, Robert Coleman and David Barty, as Trustees 4   193
  (b) Lewis Leavel, Elijah Garth, John Davis, Abraham McKinney and James Berry named as additional Trustees 5   323
Lee, Hancock
    Inspection site at Leestown in Fayette County..   3   580
Lee, Henry
  (a) Trustee of Washington (1786) 3   555
  (b) Trustee of Washington (1790) 3   556
  (c) Trustee of Charlestown (1787) 3   562
  (d) Trustee of Maysville (1787) 3   565
Lee, John
    Reward paid for his apprehension for felony...   5   385
Lee, John N.
    Granted reward for apprehending a fugitive from justice 4   148

	VOL.	PAGE
Lee, Peter		
Promoter for Town of Washington of Ohio Canal Company	3	221
Lee, Willis A.		
Clerk of Kentucky Senate (1814)	5	270
Lees, Benjamin		
Inspection site in Logan County	2	278
Lees Lick		
(a) Road from to Crab Orchard improved	2	162
(b) Road from to intersect Wilderness Road opened	3	53
Legate, Samuel		
Trustee Henderson Library Company	5	460
Legrand, Abner		
One of Commission to raise by lottery a fund to open Kentucky River to navigation	5	12
Leiper, John		
Granted reward for capture of Micajah Harp	2	365
Letcher, Archibald S.		
Trustee of Crab Orchard	5	351
Letcher, Benjamin		
(a) Trustee Lancaster Academy	2	242
(b) Trustee Lancaster Library Company	3	208
Leuther, John, Sr.		
Commissioner for Campbell County to open road from Newcastle to mouth of Licking	3	365
Lewis, Aaron		
Trustee of Boonesborough	3	539
Lewis Academy		
Incorporated January 31, 1809 with Winslow Parker, Robert Robb, Aaron Stratton, William Walker, John Radford, James Barclay and Rowland Thomas, Trustees	4	17
Lewis, Colonel		
A Chickasaw Indian—granted relief	1	696
Lewis County		
(a) Formed April 1, 1807 from Mason County	3	339
(b) William P. Fleming, Cornelius Hall, David Ballengall, William Woodward and William Lowry named commissioners to locate County Seat	3	340
Lewis, George		
(a) Trustee of Washington	1	199
(b) Founder of Lewisbourgh	1	295
(c) Trustee Franklin Academy	1	296
Lewis, John		
(a) Trustee Bullitt Academy	2	243
(b) Inspection site on Jessamine Creek	1	370

LEWIS 108

	VOL.	PAGE
(c) Inspection site on Jessamine Creek	2	279
(d) Balance of State price of land remitted	3	171

Lewis, Samuel
One of Commission to clear Kentucky River at
Frankfort to navigation 5 390

Lewis, Thomas
(a) Trustee Transylvania University.............. 2 234
(b) Acts as commissioner to replace Fayette County
Burnt Records confirmed................... 3 154

Lewis, William
(a) Trustee Town of New Market (1786).......... 3 560
(b) Given time to settle as Sheriff of Jessamine
County 3 94

Lewisbourgh (Mason County)
Established December 17, 1795 on lands of
George Lewis, with Thomas Young, Jesse
Hoard, Alexander K. Marshall, William Triplett, William Derrett and Duval Payne as
Trustees 1 295

Lexington
(a) Established May, 1782 on 640 acres of unappropriated land and 70 acres, part of a survey for
John Floyd, with John Todd, Robert Patterson,
William Mitchell, Andrew Steel, William Henderson, William McCownald and William Steel
as Trustees 3 549
(b) Part of public square set apart for a house of
divine worship (1789)..................... 3 550

Lexington Library Association
Incorporated November 29, 1800 by Thomas
Hart Sr., James Morrison, John Bradford,
James Trotter, John A. Seitz, Robert Patterson, John McDowell, Robert Barr, William
McBean, James McCown, Caleb Wallace, Fielding L. Turner, Samuel Postlethwait and
Thomas Barr 2 375

Lexington and Louisville Turnpike Road Company
Incorporated February 4, 1817 by John W.
Hunt, Charles Wilkins, Charles Humphreys
and John Telford, of Lexington; John Brown,
James W. Hawkins, William Starling and
Richard Taylor, Jr., of Frankfort; Adam
Steele, Isaac Watkins, William Logan and
Samuel Dupuy, of Shelbyville; Samuel Lawrence and Benjamin Head, at Middletown;
Cuthbert Bullitt, Richard Steele, John Edwards and Samuel Churchill at Louisville;

	VOL.	PAGE
John McKinney, Jr., John Mitchum, Archibald Kincaid and David Crawford, at Versailles; and Elijah Craig, Samuel Shepard, Job Stevenson and John I. Johnson at Georgetown	5	519
Lexington Manufacturing Company Incorporated February 4, 1815 by Charles Wilkins, George Trotter, Jr., Samuel Trotter, James Prentiss, John T. Mason, Jr., and James D. Wolf, to manufacture woolen and cotton goods	5	251
Lexington Medical Society Lottery for its benefit authorized	3	159
Lexington Seminary 6000 acres Green River lands vested in Adam Rankin, Peter January, Sr., David Logan, William Robinson, David McGee, Richard Steele and James Scott, as Trustees for its benefit	2	108
Lexington White Lead Manufacturing Company Incorporated February 3, 1815 by Samuel Trotter, George Trotter, Jr., William Leavy, Joseph H. Hawkins, Littleberry Hawkins, and Frederick Ridgely; Richard Higgins, John Tilford and George Trotter, Jr., being authorized to accept stock subscriptions	5	204
Liberty Academy (Casey County) Incorporated January 18, 1810 with Moses Rice, John Depau, Archibald Northcut, Job Sweney, William Scott, John Campbell and James Swegit, Trustees	4	114

Libraries—see

Danville	Mt. Sterling
Frankfort	Newcastle
Georgetown	Paris
Henderson	Shelby—see Washingtonian
Hopkinsville	Stanford
Lancaster	Versailles
Lexington	Washingtonian
Louisville	Winchester

	VOL.	PAGE
Licking Iron Company Incorporated February 4, 1817	5	552
Licking River (a) Declared navigable to Slate Creek	1	227
(b) South and Stoners Forks declared navigable, and Benjamin Harrison, John Wall and Isaac Riddle named commissioners to open South		

		VOL.	PAGE
	Fork, and Samuel Clay, Benjamin Bedford, John Allen and Laban Shipp to open Stoners Fork	1	192
(c)	Milldams on Main Licking regulated	2	314
(d)	Milldams on South Fork regulated	2	315
(e)	Fish dams on Main Licking prohibited	3	8
(f)	Milldams on South and Stoners Forks regulated	3	32
(g)	James Kenny, Henry Clay, Jr., Jacob Spears, and Joseph L. Stephens, of Bourbon County, and Thomas Holt, John Wall and John Smith, of Harrison County, named commissioners to clear South and Stoners Forks to navigation	3	193
(h)	Milldams on Main Licking below mouth of Fleming Creek prohibited	5	585

Lincoln County

(a)	Formed November 1, 1780 from Kentucky County	1	626
(b)	Mercer County carved from	1	627
(c)	Madison County carved from	1	627
(d)	Logan County carved from	1	630
(e)	Green County, in part, carved from	1	631
(f)	Garrard County, in part, carved from	1	384
(g)	Pulaski County, in part, carved from	2	189
(h)	Knox County carved from	2	298
(i)	Part of added to Garrard County	2	461
(j)	Casey County carved from	3	325
(k)	Part of Casey County returned to	3	474
(l)	Part of added to Mercer County	4	86
(m)	Rockcastle County, in part, carved from	4	91
(n)	George Murrell and John Blain of Lincoln County and Major John Woolford of Casey County named commissioners to survey Lincoln-Casey County line	5	105

Lincoln, Mordecai

Appointed surveyor of road from Springfield toward Frankfort	3	22

Lindsey, Thomas

Trustee of Newport	1	281

Linsey, Caleb

Error in patent corrected	5	367

Littell, James

Granted change of venue from Pendleton to Clarke County on trial for murder	3	515

Littell, William

(a)	Compensation allowed for services as Judge Advocate at trial of the Adjutant General	3	491

	VOL.	PAGE
(c) Granted access to all enrolled bills in office of Secretary of State	5	75
Little, James		
(a) Trustee of Hopewell (Paris)	3	568
(b) Trustee of Falmouth	1	181
(c) His sureties as Sheriff of Bourbon County required to settle	5	45
Littlepage, Eppes		
Inspection site in Muhlenberg County	3	24
Livingston County		
(a) Formed May, 1799 from Christian County	2	198
(b) Caldwell County carved from	4	22
Lockwood, Samuel		
Trustee Pendleton Academy	5	174
Lodge, Matthew, deceased		
Attested copy of certificate of survey allowed to be filed in lieu of original	4	171
Lofton, John G.		
Claimant of site of Centreville in Livingston County	3	354
Logan Academy		
(a) William Wallace, Ninian Edwards, Reazin Davidge, Walter Jones, Reubin Ewing, Moses Steele, William Reading, John Porter, James McMahan, Maxwell Sharp, Robert Ewing, Samuel Caldwell and William S. Dallum appointed Trustees	3	206
(b) Amos Edwards, William W. Whitaker and Armstead Morehead appointed Trustees instead of Rezin Davidge, Moses Steele and William S. Dallum	3	277
(c) Merged into Newton Academy	3	409
Logan, Benjamin		
(a) Trustee Transylvania Seminary (1783)	3	571
(b) Stanford established on his lands (1786)	3	558
(c) Trustee of Stanford (1786)	3	559
(d) Delegate from Shelby County to second Constitutional convention (1799)	1	58
(e) Trustee Shelby Academy	2	241
Logan, General Benjamin (see Logan's Expedition)		
Pay allowed William Hadden and James Neville for services under him on his expedition against the Shawnees in 1786	3	344
Logan County		
(a) Formed September 1, 1792 from Lincoln County	1	630
(b) Christian County carved from	1	365
(c) Warren County carved from	1	369

LOGAN 112

	VOL.	PAGE
(d) Muhlenberg County, in part, carved from	2	205
(e) Butler County, in part, carved from	4	110
(f) Part of added to Butler County	5	70

Logan, David
(a) Trustee Lexington Seminary ... 2 ... 108
(b) Trustee Stanford Library Company ... 5 ... 455

Logan's Expedition against the Shawnees
Pension granted William Rout on account of services on, in 1786 ... 2 ... 485

Logan, Hugh
Trustee Stanford Academy ... 2 ... 240

Logan, James
Trustee Shelby Academy ... 2 ... 241

Logan, John
(a) Trustee of Stanford (1786) ... 3 ... 559
(b) Delegate from Franklin County to second Constitutional Convention (1799) ... 1 ... 58
(c) Trustee of Frankfort ... 1 ... 247
(d) One of Commission to erect a jail at Frankfort ... 1 ... 263
(e) His addition included in Frankfort ... 1 ... 641
(f) Trustee Kentucky Seminary ... 2 ... 389
(g) Trustee Washingtonian Library ... 4 ... 354
(h) Justices of Knox County to meet at his house ... 2 ... 298

Logan, John, deceased
(a) Suit by State authorized to ascertain the amount due on a settlement of his accounts as State Treasurer ... 3 ... 492
(b) Property to be sold under execution in suit by Commonwealth ... 4 ... 59
(c) Late State Treasurer—the Attorney General was directed to institute suit against his heirs ... 5 ... 47

Logan, Joseph
Trustee Bracken Academy ... 2 ... 242

Logan Vineyard Society
Incorporated December 24, 1803 by William S. Dallum, William W. Whitaker, James Wilson, Amos Edwards and Samuel Caldwell ... 3 ... 139

Logan, William
(a) Trustee of Harrodsburg (1785) ... 3 ... 552
(b) Delegate from Lincoln County to second Constitutional Convention (1799) ... 1 ... 58
(c) Promoter for Lincoln County of Kentucky River Navigation Company ... 2 ... 448
(d) Trustee Stanford Academy ... 3 ... 334
(e) Trustee Glasgow Academy ... 4 ... 85
(f) Promoter at Shelbyville of Lexington and Louisville Turnpike Road Company ... 5 ... 519

	VOL.	PAGE
(g) Named in boundary of election precinct in Bracken County	3	487

Loney, Amos
| Attested copy of survey allowed filed in lieu of certificate of survey | 4 | 192 |

Long, Nimrod
| One of Commission to open Mud River in Logan County to navigation | 4 | 338 |

Long, Thomas
| Allowed pay for services as provost marshal.... | 3 | 491 |

Long, William B.
| Incorporator of Versailles Library Company.... | 4 | 356 |

Loofbourrow, Thomas V.
| Promoter of Frankfort Bridge Company | 4 | 138 |

Louisville
(a) Established May 1780 on lands belonging to John Connolly, with John Todd, Jr., Stephen Trigg, George Slaughter, John Floyd, William Pope, George Merriwether, Andrew Hynes and Marsham Brashiers, Trustees	3	540
(b) John Campbell asserted title to townsite (1783)	3	542
(c) Claims of John Campbell and John Connolly to townsite adjusted	3	542
(d) Same as (c)	3	543
(e) Same as (c)	3	545
(f) Richard Clough Anderson, William Taylor, Robert Breckenridge, David Meriwether, John Clarke, Alexander Scott Bullitt and James Francis Moore named commissioners to collect from the Trustees the proceeds of sales of lots and to sell the remaining lots and to settle the claims of John Campbell and Joseph Simon on account of a mortgage to them of the townsite by John Connolly (1786)	3	545
(g) Buckner Thruston, James Wilkinson, Michael Lacassagne, Alexander Scott Bullitt, Benjamin Sebastian, John Felty, Jacob Reager, James Patton, Samuel Kirby, Benjamin Erickson, and Benjamin Johnson appointed Trustees (1789)	3	547
(h) James Francis Moore, Abraham Hite, Abner Martin, Donne Basil Prather, and David Standeford named commissioners for sale of lots as at (f) (1790)	3	547
(i) Campbell Town established (1785)	3	554

LOUISVILLE LIBRARY CO. 114

	VOL.	PAGE

Louisville Hospital
  Incorporated February 5, 1817 by Robert Breckenridge, Levi Tyler, Thomas Bullitt, Thomas Prather, David Fetter, Richard Ferguson, John Croghan, Peter B. Ormsby, James H. Overstreet, William S. Vernon, Paul Skidmore and Dennis Fitzhugh............ 5 574

Louisville Library Company
  Incorporated February 8, 1816 by Mann Butler, William C. Galt, Brooke Hill, Hezekiah Hawley and William Tompkins................. 5 359

Love, James
  Trustee of Hartford...................... 3 443

Love, Joseph
  (a) Authorized to locate 2000 acres of land in Pulaski County for iron works............ 4 257
  (b) Benjamin Fisher, assignee, given time to locate lands at (a)........................... 5 463

Love, William
  (a) Trustee Newton Academy.................... 2 241
  (b) Trustee Grayson Seminary................... 5 325

Lowry, William
  One of Commission to locate County Seat for Lewis County 3 340

Lusk, James
  Inspection site in Livingston County.......... 3 24

Lutheran High Dutch Congregation
  Sale of lands for benefit of Franklinian School in Mercer County authorized.............. 3 458

Lyle, John
  Trustee Winchester Academy............... 2 217

Lynch, Charles
  Trustees named to sell lands for his benefit.... 1 219

Lyne, Edmund
  (a) Trustee Town of Washington (1786)........ 3 555
  (b) Trustee Town of Washington (1790).......... 3 556
  (c) Lands named in boundary of Washington.... 3 556

Maberry, ——
  Inspection site in Christian County.......... 3 124

Macbean, William (see McBean)
  Promoter of Madison Hemp Company........ 3 532

Maccoun, David
  Promoter of Madison Hemp Company.......... 3 532

Maccoun, James (see McCown)
  (a) Promoter of Madison Hemp Company........ 3 532
  (b) One of Commission to build bridge over North Elkhorn in Scott County................. 4 88

	VOL.	PAGE
Maccoun, Samuel (see McCoun)		
One of commission to raise by lottery a fund to open Kentucky River to navigation	5	12
Macey, Alexander		
One of Commission to open Kentucky River at Frankfort to navigation	5	390
Machir, John		
(a) Trustee Franklin Academy	1	296
(b) Promoter at Town of Washington, of Ohio Canal Company	3	221
(c) Trustee Franklin Academy	3	255
(d) Promoter at Town of Washington of Bank of Kentucky	3	390
(e) Trustee of Charlestown (1787)	3	562
Madison Academy		
(a) Incorporated December 22, 1798 with Hickerson Grubbs, Robert Caldwell, Green Clay, Christopher Irwin, Archibald Wood, James Speed, Matthew Huston, Joseph Kennedy, James Barnet, Robert Rhodes, John Millar and John Patrick, Trustees	2	241
(b) Robert Rodes, Archibald Woods, William Irvine, John Patrick and James Barnett appointed Trustees	3	278
(c) John Patrick, Moses M. Price, Anthony W. Rollins, Archibald Woods and Curtis Fields appointed Trustees	5	133
Madison County		
(a) Formed August 1, 1785 from Lincoln County	1	627
(b) Garrard County, in part, carved from	1	384
(c) Part added to Garrard County	2	270
(d) Part added to Knox County	3	182
(e) Clay County, in part, carved from	3	338
(f) Part added to Floyd County	3	339
(g) Estill County, in part, carved from	3	441
(h) Part of Estill County added to	3	473
(i) Rockcastle County, in part, carved from	4	91
(j) Parts of Clay and Rockcastle Counties added to	4	406
Madison, Gabriel		
Trustee of New Market (1786)	3	560
Madison, Gabriel, deceased		
(a) Inspection site on lands in Ohio County	3	324
(b) Hartford established on his lands	3	443
Madison, George		
(a) Trustee Town of Preston	1	347
(b) Trustee Kentucky Seminary	2	389

MADISON SPINNING CO. 116

	VOL.	PAGE
(c) One of Commission to settle accounts at the penitentiary	5	296
(d) One of Commission to open Kentucky River at Frankfort to navigation	5	390

Madison Hemp and Flax Spinning Company
Incorporated February 24, 1808 by William Macbean, Henry Clay, Robert Frazier, James Maccoun and David Maccoun 3   532

Madison, Rev. James
Allowed to re-survey 10,000 acres on Big Sandy 3   346

Madison, Rowland, deceased
(a) Former Surveyor of Warren County. The present Surveyor was authorized to record plats and certificates made by him 2   287
(b) His securities authorized to collect the surveyors fees due him 2   360

Magary, Hugh
Trustee Town of Warwick (1787) 3   564

Magoffin, Beriah
One of Commission to raise by lottery a fund to open Kentucky River to navigation 4   210

Mahan, James
Granted patent to Green River land 5   18

Manchester Academy
Incorporated January 31, 1809 with Winslow Parker, Robert Robb, Aaron Stratton, William Walker, John Radford, James Barclay and Rowland Thomas, Trustees 4   17

Manifee, Richard
See Menifee

Manns Lick (Jefferson County)
(a) Named in location of New Town 1   233
(b) Road from to mouth of Big Barren opened.... 2   191

Mangham, John K.
Authorized to patent land on which he lived.. 4   248

Marble, Peter F.
Ordered to alter mill dam on Main Licking so as not to obstruct navigation 5   374

Marrs, William
Registry of a survey in his favor authorized.. 5   553

Marshall, Alexander
Trustee Franklin Academy 1   296

Marshall, Alexander K.
Trustee of Lewisbourgh..................... 1   295

	VOL.	PAGE
Marshall, Robert		
(a) Trustee Kentucky Academy	1	228
(b) Trustee Transylvania University	2	234
Marshall, Thomas		
(a) Trustee Franklin Academy	1	296
(b) Trustee Franklin Academy	3	255
(c) Trustee of Frankfort (1786)	3	557
(d) Trustee Transylvania Seminary (1788)	3	572
Marshall, Thomas, deceased		
Sale of lands authorized	5	4
Marshall, Thomas, Jr.		
Delegate from Mason County to second Constitutional Convention (1799)	1	58
Marstison, Richard (see Masterson)		
Justices of Gallatin County to meet at his house	2	204
Martin, Abner		
One of Commissioners to sell lots in Louisville (1790)	3	547
Martin, David, deceased		
Sale of lands authorized	2	486
Martin, Edward		
Named in Allen-Warren County boundary	5	348
Martin, Henry		
Balance of State price of land remitted	5	482
Martin, James		
Given time to certify delinquent list as Deputy Sheriff of Shelby County	3	345
Martin, John		
Trustee of Winchester	1	340
Martin, General Joseph		
Commissioner for Virginia to locate boundary line	2	276
Mason County		
(a) Formed May 1, 1788 from Bourbon County	1	628
(b) Campbell County, in part, carved from	1	632
(c) Bracken County carved from	1	366
(d) Fleming County carved from	2	175
(e) Floyd County, in part, carved from	2	282
(f) Nicholas County, in part, carved from	2	366
(g) Greenup County carved from	3	117
(h) Lewis County carved from	3	339
Mason, Edward		
Named in Rockcastle County boundary	4	92
Mason, John T., Jr.		
Incorporator of Lexington Manufacturing Company	5	251

MASON   118

	VOL.	PAGE
Mason, Nicholas		
Allowed pay for a tour of duty	5	190
Mason, Polly, et al.		
She and Elizabeth Barnett granted 400 acres as heirs of Abraham Holt	5	22
Masons		
(a) Lottery for Lexington Lodge No. 25 authorized.	1	577
(b) Gabriel Tandy, Thomas Bodley, Daniel Bradford, John Tilford, and Dr. William Richardson named managers to raise by lottery $30,000 to build a Grand Masonic Hall in Lexington....	5	181
(c) Franklin Lodge No. 28 authorized to hold lodge in Court House at Danville	5	481
Massie, David		
Promoter at Town of Washington of Maysville and Lexington Turnpike Road Company....	5	536
Masterson, Richard (see Marstison)		
(a) Trustee Town of Port William	1	340
(b) Trustee Bethel Academy	2	174
Matson, James		
(a) Trustee Bourbon Academy	2	238
(b) Trustee Bourbon Academy	2	242
Maxwell, David		
Voting place at house in Warren County	5	16
May-Bannister & Company		
Their line named in boundary of election precinct in Breckenridge County	4	328
May, Daniel		
Promoter for Newport of Ohio Canal Company..	3	221
May's Entry Books		
Copied and compared	3	530
May, Gabriel		
Inspection site in Shelby County	2	278
May, John		
(a) Lands named in boundary of Town of Washington	3	556
(b) Maysville established on his lands	3	565
(c) Trustee Transylvania Seminary	3	571
(d) Inspection site in Mason County	2	140
(e) Owensboro established on his lands	5	501
(f) Inspection site in Bourbon (Mason) County....	3	582
May, John, deceased		
Commissioners named to divide lands held by him and Lewis Craig and Philemon Thomas, allotting his share to Mary May and John May, his infant heirs	1	113

	VOL.	PAGE

May, John, Jr.
See John May, deceased
May, Mary
See John May, deceased
May, Robert
   Named in boundary of election precinct in Green
     county 5   317
Mayo, Daniel
   Trustee Newport Academy................... 2   240
Mayo, William, Jr.
   Inspection site in Madison County............ 2   213
Maysville
   Established in 1787 on lands of John May and
     Simon Canton (Kenton) with Daniel Boone,
     Henry Lee, Arthur Fox, Jacob Boone, Thomas
     Brooks and George Miford, Trustees......... 3   565
Maysville and Lexington Turnpike Road Company
   Incorporated February 4, 1817 by John Sumrall,
     Johnson Armstrong, and Morris Langhorn of
     Maysville; James A. Paxton, David Massie and
     John Chambers, of Washington; Hugh Brent,
     Thomas Jones, Valentine Piers and Washington Ward, of Paris; Lewis Sanders,
     Thomas Bodley, James Prentiss and Bushrod Boswell, of Lexington; James McClelland and Daniel Talbot, of Millersburg;
     James Morris and John Shotwell, Sr. of Mays
     Lick; and Maurice Morris of Carlisle........ 5   535
Meacham, Joseph
   Named in boundary of election precinct in Christian County 4   329
Means, Thomas
   Error in charge for head right land corrected.. 4   199
Mearce, James
   Mill on Gasper River named in boundary of election precinct in Logan County.............. 3   345
Meek, David
   State price of head right land remitted........ 4   323
Megowan, James S.
   Suit by State against him in Mason and Montgomery Counties authorized to recover money
     fraudulently obtained by him from the
     Treasury 4   74
Meigs, John
   Parthenia Meigs authorized to sue him in Clarke
     County for divorce...................... 3   509

MEIGS 120

	VOL.	PAGE

Meigs, Parthenia
  See John Meigs
Menifee, Richard
  One of Commission to open road from Paris or
    Mt. Sterling to the Big Sandy............. 3   4
Mennonists
  (a) Marriages of to be registered................ 2   66
  (b) Exempted from military service............. 3   216
Mercer County
  (a) Formed August 1, 1785 from Lincoln County... 1   627
  (b) Franklin County, in part, carved from........ 1   632
  (c) Garrard County, in part, carved from........ 1   384
  (d) Part of Lincoln County added to............ 4   86
Mercer, George
  Co-founder of Lebanon..................... 5   191
Merewether, Nicholas (see Meriwether, Merriwether)
  Trustee Shelby Academy.................... 2   241
Meriwether, David
  One of Commission to sell lots in Louisville..... 3   545
Meriwether, George (see Merriwether)
  Trustee Transylvania Seminary 3   571
Meriwether, James
  Trustee Jefferson Seminary.................. 2   108
Merrimee, William, deceased
  Sale of lands authorized.................... 3   491
Merriwether, George (see Meriwether)
  Trustee of Louisville....................... 3   540
Merriwether, Major
  Empowered to appoint surveyors (1783)....... 1   442
Metcalf, John
  (a) Trustee Bethel Academy.................... 2   174
  (b) Given credit on settlement as surety for ——
    Morrow, Sheriff of Bourbon County......... 3   95
Metcalfe, John
  (a) Trustee Bourbon Academy.................. 2   237
  (b) Trustee Bourbon Academy.................. 2   242
Metcalfe, Norris
  Granted change of venue.................... 5   202
Metcalfe, Thomas
  (a) Granted change of venue.................... 5   202
  (b) Named in Nicholas-Harrison County boundary.. 5   366
Meteer, William
  Trustee of Mt. Sterling..................... 1   125
Middletown (Jefferson County)
  (a) Election of Trustees provided for............. 2   275
  (b) Election of Trustees confirmed............... 2   458

	VOL.	PAGE

Miford, George
   Trustee of Maysville........................ 3   565
Milford (Madison County)
  (a) Established in 1789 on lands of Samuel Estill and John Estill, deceased, with Green Clay, John Miller, William Irvine, Archibald Woods, James Barnett, George Adams, Michael McNeeley, James French and Robert Rhodes, Trustees................................. 3   567
  (b) Samuel Estill, James McCollister, Robert Caldwell and Benjamin Holliday, appointed Trustees 1   225
  (c) Road from (described as Madison Court-house) to intersect Wilderness Road, authorized..... 1   687
  (d) County Seat of Madison County, removed from 2   165
Miligan, John
   Costs of trial of allowed................... 1   239
Millar, John
   Trustee Madison Academy................... 2   241
Miller, David
   Inspection site in Livingston County.......... 2   457
Miller, David, deceased
   Plat and certificate of survey registered....... 5   513
Miller, Hugh, Sr.
   Trustee Harrison Academy.................. 2   241
Miller, Isaac
   Incorporator of Cynthiana Manufacturing Company 5   378
Miller, Jacob
  (a) Named in boundary of election precinct in Hardin County 4   202
  (b) One of Commission to open Nolinn Creek in Hardin County to navigation............... 4   221
Miller, James
   John Carter, charged with his murder, escaped jail and was apprehended................. 4   148
Miller, John
  (a) Trustee Town of Milford (1789).............. 3   567
  (b) Trustee Kentucky Academy................. 1   228
Miller, Samuel A.
  (a) Trustee Hopkinsville Library Company........ 5   361
  (b) One of Commission to sell part of public square in Hopkinsville 5   511
Millersburg
  (a) Lottery authorized to promote lead works near.. 2   491
  (b) Act (a) repealed........................... 3   98

MILLS   122

	VOL.	PAGE
Mills, Benjamin		
Trustee Paris Library......................	3	455
Mills, Jesse		
Named in boundary of election precinct in Green County	5	317
Mills, Thomas		
Inspection site in Mason County.............	2	280
Minor, George D.		
One of Commission to open Big Barren River to navigation	4	116
Minor, Nicholas		
Delegate from Nelson County to second Constitutional Convention (1799)	1	58
Minter, Jane, deceased, and		
Minter, Joseph, deceased		
Sale of land authorized	5	4
Mitchell, Adam		
Trustee of Kennedysville	1	342
Mitchell, David		
Inspection site in Woodford County	1	370
Mitchell, Ignatius		
Charlestown established on his lands	3	562
Mitchell, James		
Named in Adair-Green County boundary	2	430
Mitchell, John A.		
Allowed pay for repairs to State House—also one of Commission to make further repairs...	3	509
Mitchell, Joseph, deceased		
Sale of lands authorized	1	219
Mitchell, Thomas		
One of Commissioners for Shelby County to survey the Shelby-Henry County line.......	5	330
Mitchell, William		
(a) Voting place at house in Bourbon County	2	385
(b) Trustee of Lexington (1782)	3	549
Mitchell, William, deceased		
Lands authorized conveyed to Cornelius Shuck	4	241
Mitchell, Willis, Sr.		
(a) Justices of Allen County to meet at his house	5	157
(b) Voting place at his house in Allen County	5	157
Mitchison, John		
Credit allowed on settlement as surety for an insolvent sheriff	5	578
Mitchum, John		
Promoter at Versailles of Lexington and Louisville Turnpike Road Company	5	519

	VOL.	PAGE
Mitchuson, William		
Trustee Caledonia Academy	5	3
Mock, Daniel		
Trustee of Springfield	1	176
Moderel, Robert (see Modrel)		
Trustee Somerset Academy	3	37
Modrel, Robert		
(a) Commissioner to build section of road from Danville to Tellico, beginning at Smith Ferry on Cumberland River	3	275
(b) Allowed compensation for services at (a)	3	364
Monks		
Exempted from military service	3	216
Monrow, Alexander		
Trustee Pendleton Academy	5	174
Monroe, Benjamin		
Trustee of Stanford	5	166
Monroe, John		
(a) Judge Circuit Court Third District	3	507
(b) Trustee Glasgow Academy	4	85
Monroe, William		
Trustee of Falmouth	1	181
Montague, Thomas		
Trustee of Port William	1	232
Montford, John, deceased		
Sale of lands authorized	5	42
Montgomery Academy		
(a) Incorporated December 22, 1798, with Enoch Smith, James Pogue, Jilson Payne, Bennett Clark, Joseph Hume, William Payne, Abijah Brooks, James Ward, William Robinson and James McIllany, Trustees	2	241
(b) Joseph How, Moses Bledsoe, James French, John Young and James Crawford named additional Trustees	3	438
Montgomery County		
(a) Formed March 1, 1797 from Clarke County	1	366
(b) Floyd County, in part, carved from	2	282
(c) Bath County carved from	4	215
(d) Part of added to Estill County	5	327
Montgomery, James		
(a) Inspection site in Wayne County	3	24
(b) Inspection site in Pulaski County	3	243
Montgomery, John		
Trustee New Athens Academy	2	242
Montgomery, Nathan		
Trustee New Athens Academy	2	242

MONTGOMERY 124

	VOL.	PAGE
Montgomery, Thomas		
(a) Surveyor of Lincoln County	2	192
(b) Authorized to sell lands of William Montgomery, deceased	2	236
(c) Same as (b)	2	359
(d) Inspection site in Wayne County	3	24
(e) Trustee Stanford Academy	3	334
Montgomery, William		
(a) Trustee of Stanford	3	559
(b) Trustee of Stanford	1	240
(c) Allowed reward for arrest of Hugh Ross	1	358
(d) Costs of trial allowed	1	239
(e) Granted change of venue from Hardin to Bullitt County on trial for larceny	5	538
Montgomery, William, deceased		
(a) Sale of lands by Thomas Montgomery authorized	2	236
(b) Same as (a)	2	359
Montjoy, Alvin		
Given time to complete mill seat on South Licking	3	172
Moore, Ephraim		
Named in boundary of election precinct in Knox County	5	426
Moore, George, deceased		
Lands taken into bounds of Bowling Green	5	192
Moore, James		
(a) Promoter for Mercer County of Kentucky River Navigation Company	2	448
(b) Trustee Washingtonian Library	4	354
Moore, Dr. James		
Part of lands added to Shelbyville	5	255
Moore, James F.		
Trustee Jefferson Seminary	2	378
Moore, James Francis		
(a) One of Commission to sell and adjust claims respecting lots in Louisville	3	542
(b) Same as (a)	3	547
(c) Founder of New Town	1	233
(d) Title to site of New Town quieted	1	261
Moore, John		
Trustee New Athens Seminary	3	302
Moore, Lewis		
(a) Trustee Franklin Academy	1	296
(b) Trustee Town of Washington	2	393
Moore, Robert		
Made an addition to Bowling Green	5	192

	VOL.	PAGE

Moore, Samuel
  (a) Trustee Stanford Academy 2   240
  (b) Trustee Lebanon Academy 4   193
Moore, Thomas
  Given credit on settlement as keeper of turnpike on Wilderness Road for money of which he was robbed 3   162
Moore, William
  Incorporator of Cynthiana Manufacturing Company 5   378
Moore, Zachariah
  Trustee Town of Salisberry 3   369
Morehead, Armstead
  (a) Trustee Bullitt Academy 2   243
  (b) Promoter at Russellville of Ohio Canal Company 3   221
  (c) Trustee Newton Academy 3   277
  (d) Trustee Logan Academy 3   277
  (e) Trustee Newton Academy 3   409
  (f) Promoter at Russellville of Bank of Kentucky 3   391
Morehead, Charles
  (a) Inspection site in Nelson County 2   280
  (b) One of Commission to open Beech Fork of Salt River to navigation 2   312
Morehead, Presley
  One of Commission to open Mud River to navigation 4   115
Moren, John
  Relieved of consequences of irregularities with respect to head right lands 4   13
Morgan, Charles
  Trustee Newport Academy 2   240
Morgan, Brig. Gen. Daniel
  Empowered to appoint surveyors (1783) 1   442
Morgan, Jesse, deceased
  Sale of land authorized 2   53
Morgan, William, deceased
  Sale of lands authorized 5   474
Morris, James
  (a) One of Commission to raise by lottery a fund to improve road from Maysville to Town of Washington 4   279
  (b) Promoter at Mayslick of Maysville and Lexington Turnpike Road Company 5   536
Morris, Maurice
  Promoter at Carlisle of Maysville and Lexington Turnpike Road Company 5   536

	VOL.	PAGE

Morris, Richard
  Relieved of effects of some errors in respect to
    headright claims 4   340
Morris, Thomas
  Trustee of Kennedysville 1   342
Morris, William
  Named as terminus on Kanawah River of the
    Greenbrier Road 3   4
Morrison, Isaac
  (a) Trustee of Beallsborough 3   564
  (b) Trustee of Bairdstown 3   566
  (c) Trustee Salem Academy 3   580
Morrison, James .
  (a) Trustee of Beallsborough 3   564
  (b) Trustee of Bairdstown 3   566
  (c) Trustee Salem Academy 3   580
  (d) Trustee of Lexington 1   577
  (e) Trustee Lexington Library Association 2   375
  (f) One of Commission to raise by lottery a fund to
    open Kentucky River to navigation 5   12
Morrison, Robert
  Trustee Fleming Academy.................... 2   241
Morrow, William
  (a) Given time to settle as Sheriff of Bourbon County   2   485
  (b) Credit allowed surety on his bond as Sheriff.... 3   95
  (c) Commission allowed Richard Turner for levying
    an execution against Morrow in favor of the
    Commonwealth 3   97
  (d) Time given Robert Buckner to settle as his
    surety 3   163
Morton, George W.
  Given time to return delinquent list as Sheriff
    of Fayette County........................ 5   498
Morton, Richard
  Mistakes in proceedings relative to headright
    lands were corrected...................... 4   157
Morton, Major Thomas
  Re-imbursed for repairs to arms at arsenal..... 2   354
Morton, William
  Trustee Transylvania University.............. 2   234
Mosby, ——
  Inspection site in Madison County............. 3   323
Mosby, John
  Trustee Transylvania Seminary............... 3   572
Mosby, Robert
  (a) Trustee of Harrodsburg...................... 3   552
  (b) Trustee Town of New Market................ 3   560

	VOL.	PAGE

Mosely, Robert
  (a) Justices of Ohio County to meet at his house.. 2   209
  (b) Trustee of Hartford 3   443
Moseley, Thomas
  (a) Trustee of Hartford........................ 3   443
  (b) Incorporator of Mt. Sterling Library Company.. 5   177
Moss, Frederick, deceased
  Sale of lands authorized.................... 1   359
Moss', Hilliard's and
  Inspection site at mill in Green County........ 3   322
Mount Sterling
  Established December 17, 1792 on lands of Enoch Smith, Hugh Forbis, John Judy and Samuel Spurgin, with Enoch Smith, Samuel Dowery, William Meteer, Cornelius Ringo, Aaron Hall, Robert Walker and Simon Adams, Trustees.. 1   125
Mount Sterling Library Company
  Incorporated January 26, 1815 by Thomas Moseley, David Barrow, George Howard, Micajah Harrison, and William C. Hayden........... 5   177
Mud River Fork of Green River
  (a) Declared navigable January 18, 1810 and James Duncan, Presley Morehead, Peter Hansberry, John Browning and Urbin Ewing named commissioners to clear it for navigation......... 4   115
  (b) Thomas Stubblefield and Nimrod Long named additional commissioners to clear it for navigation 4   338
Muhlenberg County
  (a) Formed May 15, 1798 from Logan and Christian Counties 2   205
  (b) Christian County line changed.............. 2   378
Muhlenberg, Maj. Gen. Peter
  Empowered to appoint surveyors (1783)...... 1   442
Mullin, John
  Authorized to locate 600 acres of land as heir of his father, a Revolutionary Soldier....... 2   426
Munsell, Luke
  Granted loan of $6000 with which to publish a map of Kentucky 5   566
Munsey, Jeremiah
  Given credit for six tours of duty............ 5   272
Murphy, John
  (a) Trustee Town of Jefferson................... 2   380
  (b) One of Commission to open Red Bird Fork of Kentucky River to navigation............. 5   149

Murray, William
  (a) One of Commission to erect a jail at Frankfort.. 1   263
  (b) His addition included in Frankfort........... 1   641
  (c) Trustee Kentucky Seminary 2   389
Murrell, George
  One of Commissioners for Lincoln County to
    survey Lincoln-Casey County line.......... 5   103
Murrell, Lt. George and Men
  Allowed pay for services guarding the Lincoln
    County frontier in 1787................... 3   256
Murrell, Samuel
  Trustee Glasgow Academy 4   85
Muter, Colonel
  Empowered to appoint surveyors (1783)...... 1   442
Muter, George
  (a) Trustee of Danville 3   562
  (b) Granted pension of $300 per annum in consideration of services as former Chief Justice
    of the State............................. 3   363
  (c) Pension Act repealed 4   16
Myers, Jacob
  (a) Voting place at house in Grayson County...... 4   242
  (b) Voting place at house in Grayson County.... 5   36
Myers, Jacob, deceased
  Commissioners named to settle with creditors.. 3   98
Myers, Jacob and Company
  Authorized to locate 2000 acres of land in Lincoln County, from which to procure timber
    for iron-works 2   174
McAfee, John, deceased
  Sale of lands authorized.................... 5   471
McAfee, Samuel
  Trustee Town of Warwick................. 3   564
McBean, William (see Macbean)
  (a) Trustee Lexington Library Association....... 2   375
  (b) Inspection site in Madison County........... 3   451
McBee, Silas
  Released from consequences of irregular proceedings with respect to head right lands.. 4   13
McBride, Daniel
  Trustee Henderson Academy 5   72
McBride, Lapsley, and
McBride, William
  Granted 2800 acres of land in consideration of services of their father, who as Commissioner of Kentucky County had opened the road from Holstein to Crab Orchard and

	VOL.	PAGE
who had been killed at the battle of Blue Licks	4	330
McBryers, William		
Given credit on settlement as Sheriff of Franklin County	5	165
McCahan, John		
Named in boundary to an addition to Shelbyville	5	256
McCalla, Andrew		
(a) Trustee Kentucky Academy	1	228
(b) Trustee Transylvania University	2	234
McCastlin, Andrew		
Authorized to locate lands in Wayne County containing salt water	4	374
McChord, James		
Error in settlement certificate corrected	5	367
McClain, Hector		
One of Commission to conduct a lottery	5	570
McClean, Alney		
Trustee Greenville Academy	4	113
McClean, Ephraim		
Trustee Lebanon Academy	4	193
McClean, Samuel		
One of Commission to raise by lottery a fund to open Salt River to navigation	4	249
McCleland, Daniel		
Trustee Shelby Academy	2	241
McClelland, James		
Promoter at Millersburg of Maysville and Lexington Turnpike Road Company	5	536
McClintock, Daniel, deceased		
His Executor, Joseph McClintock, allowed to resign	3	94
McClintock, Joseph		
Allowed to resign as Executor of Daniel McClintock, deceased	3	94
McClung, William		
Judge Circuit Court First District	3	507
McClure, James		
Trustee of Newport	1	281
McCollister, Aeneas		
Trustee Newton Academy	2	241
McCollister, Hannah		
James McCollister authorized to sue her in Madison County for divorce	3	466

	VOL.	PAGE

McCollister, James
  (a) See Hannah McCollister
  (b) Trustee Town of Milford 1   226
McCombs, John
  Price of small tract of land remitted......... 5   458
McConnell (see McCownald)
McCormack, ——
  Named in Cumberland-Barren County boundary   3   103
McCormack, James
  Trustees of Paris authorized to convey him a lot   5   397
McCormick, Joseph
  Named in Lincoln-Casey County boundary.... 3   326
McCoun Ferry
  Inspection site in Mercer County............. 3   332
McCoun, James
  Balance due on head right claim remitted.... 4   319
McCoun, Lawrence
  Price of land remitted 5   56
McCoun, Samuel (see Maccoun)
  (a) Inspection at his ferry in Mercer County...... 3   332
  (b) One of Commission to raise by lottery a fund
      to open Kentucky River to navigation...... 4   318
McCowen, Robert
  Trustee Town of Jefferson................... 2   380
McCown, James (see Maccoun)
  Trustee Lexington Library Association....... 2   375
McCownald, William
  Trustee of Lexington 3   549
McCullough, Joseph
  Trustee Town of Washington................ 1   199
McCully, George, deceased
  Sale of land authorized..................... 2   488
McDouglas, Alexander
  Named in boundary of election precinct in Hardin County............................. 5   473
McDowell, Dr.
  Named in boundary of public square in Danville 5   480
McDowell, Ephraim
  (a) Trustee Danville Library.................... 2   376
  (b) Trustee of Danville......................... 4   39
  (c) Trustee Danville Academy.................. 5   480
McDowell, John
  (a) Delegate from Fayette County to second Constitutional Convention (1799).............. 1   58
  (b) Trustee Transylvania University............. 2   234
  (c) Trustee Lexington Library Association........ 2   375

	VOL.	PAGE
(d) Named in boundary of election precinct in Hardin County	4	225
(e) One of Commission to build bridge over Floyds Fork of Salt River	5	22 |//END

McDowell, Samuel
(a) President Constitutional Convention (1792).. 1   38
(b) Trustee Transylvania University.............. 2   234
(c) Judge Circuit Court Tenth District........... 3   507

McDowell, Samuel, Sr.
(a) Trustee of Danville......................... 3   562
(b) Trustee Transylvania Seminary.............. 3   572

McDowell, William
(a) Trustee of Danville......................... 3   562
(b) Trustee Danville Library.................... 2   376
(c) Co-founder of Falmouth..................... 1   181
(d) Reference made to (c)...................... 5   583

McElhany, James
Named Commissioner to sell lands of John Elliott, deceased......................... 4   9

McElroy, Hugh
Trustee of Springfield....................... 1   176

McElroy, James
Trustee of Lebanon......................... 5   191

McFarland, Major Alexander
Named in Pulaski County boundary.......... 2   392

McFarlan, John
One of Commission to locate County Seat for Daviess County............................ 5   160

McFerren, John
Trustee Glasgow Academy................... 4   85

McFerrin, John
Allowed to withdraw over-payment in settlement as Sheriff of Barren County.......... 5   463

McGary, Daniel
Named Commissioner to sell lands of John Elliott, deceased......................... 4   9

McGary, Hugh
See Magary

McGary, Robert
Justices of Hopkins County to meet at house.. 3   347

McGary, William R.
One of Commission to locate County seat for Union County............................. 4   213

McGaughey, Arthur
Voting place at house in Hardin County...... 4   202

McGee, David
Trustee Lexington Seminary................. 2   108

	VOL.	PAGE
McGehee, Samuel		
Allowed $15.00 for a beef taken by Capt. Ray on the Wabash Expedition	2	484
McGill, John		
Price of head right land remitted	4	159
McGonegle, Leah		
Price of 50 acres of land remitted	5	347
McGowan, Robert		
One of Commission to open road in Madison County	1	231
McGrady, Israel		
(a) Trustee Newton Academy	2	241
(b) Resigned and successor appointed	3	277
(c) Given time to settle as Sheriff of Logan County	3	164
McHenry, Barnabas		
(a) Trustee Bethel Academy	2	174
(b) Trustee Washington Academy	2	242
(c) Trustee Washington Academy	5	15
McIllany, James		
Trustee Montgomery Academy	2	241
McIlvain, Hugh		
Trustee of Lexington Masonic Lodge	1	557
McIlvoy, Daniel		
(a) Trustee of Danville	4	39
(b) Promoter at Danville of Kentucky Assurance Society	4	254
McIntire, Alexander		
(a) Named in boundary of election precinct in Montgomery County	4	173
(b) Named in Montgomery-Bath County boundary	4	215
McIntire, John		
(a) One of Commission to open a road from Fleming County to the Big Sandy	3	167
(b) One of Commission to erect a turnpike on the road at (a)	4	154
(c) One of Commission to lease the road at (a)	4	236
(d) Incorporator of Gallatin-Ohio Steamboat Company	5	343
McKee, Alexander		
(a) His lots in Harrodsburg ordered sold to pay a debt due John Campbell and Joseph Simon	3	546
(b) Lands escheated as a British subject, and	3	571
(c) Vested in Trustees Transylvania Seminary	3	572
McKee, Samuel		
Trustee Lancaster Library Company	3	208
McKenny, Robert		
Trustee of Winchester	1	340

	VOL.	PAGE
McKenzie, Robert		
(a) Lands escheated as a British subject, and....	3	571
(b) Vested in Trustees Transylvania Seminary....	3	572
McKinley, Doctor, deceased		
Fee due him for attending a soldier, ordered paid to his widow, Hanna	2	484
McKinley, Hanna		
See Doctor McKinley		
McKinley, James		
Named in boundary of Town of Washington....	3	556
McKinley, Polly		
Marriage to John Burch by James Atwood, Justice of the Peace, without authority in the Justice, was legalized	2	364
McKinley, Samuel		
Trustee Newcastle Library Company	4	17
McKinney, Abraham		
Trustee Lebanon Academy	5	323
McKinney, John		
Given time to settle as Sheriff of Bourbon County	2	364
McKinney, John, Jr.		
(a) Incorporator of Versailles Library Company...	4	356
(b) Promoter at Versailles of Lexington and Louisville Turnpike Road Company	5	519
McKnight, Andrew		
Commissioner for Woodford County to open road from Buckley's Ferry to Bardstown....	3	463
McLardy, Alexander		
Allowed to withdraw a survey and patent....	2	220
McLaughlin, James H.		
(a) Trustee Hopkinsville Library Company.......	5	361
(b) One of Commission to sell part of public square in Hopkinsville	5	511
McLean		
See McClean		
McMahan, James		
Trustee Logan Academy	3	206
McManus, Mary		
Authorized to sell lots in Town of Washington for support of her children	3	161
McMillan, William		
One of Commission to locate County Seat for Bath County	4	215
McMillion, Samuel		
Commissioner for Harrison County to open road from Georgetown to Augusta	3	201

	VOL.	PAGE
McMullin, Samuel		
Trustee Harrison Academy...................	2	241
McNair, John		
Lexington Library Association to meet at his house	2	376
McNeal, John		
Inspection site at Jeffersonville on Big Barren	3	324
McNeeley, Michael		
Trustee Town of Milford.....................	3	567
McNeff, John T.		
Polly McNeff authorized to sue him in Washington County for divorce.....................	3	174
McNeff, Polly		
See John T. McNeff		
McPhearson, Alexander		
Commissioner for Boone County to open road from Newcastle to mouth of Licking......	3	365
McRoberts, George		
Trustee Stanford Academy...................	3	334
Nagle, Maurice, deceased		
(a) Sale of lands authorized.....................	2	52
(b) New Commissioners named to sell lands......	2	359
Nall, John		
One of Commission to open Beech Fork to navigation	2	312
Naylor, James		
Trustee Pendleton Academy	5	175
Neal, William (see Neale, Neill)		
Trustee Newcastle Library Company	4	35
Neale, William (see Neal, Neill)		
One of Commission to open road from Newcastle to mouth of Licking	5	131
Neat, Rudolph		
Authorized to erect mill on Green River	5	481
Neele, William, deceased		
Heirs given time to pay for land in Logan County	3	190
Neill, William (see Neal, Neale)		
(a) One of Commissioners for Henry County to survey Henry-Shelby County line	5	103
(b) Same as (a)	5	330
Nelson County		
Formed January 1, 1785 from Jefferson County	1	627
Green County, in part, carved from............	1	631
Hardin County carved from	1	631
Bullitt County carved from	1	364
Washington County carved from	1	628

	VOL.	PAGE

Nelson, John
Inspection at his warehouse discontinued and he was allowed to remove the tobacco 5   196

Neville, James
Allowed pay for services with Logan's Expedition in 1786 3   344

New Athens Academy (Greensburg)
(a) Established December 22, 1798, with William Casey, Robert Haskins, Elias Barbee, Jonathan Conard, William Buckner, Jonathan Patterson, Nathan Montgomery, John W. Sample, James Young, Daniel Trabue, John Montgomery, and David Sims, Trustees..... 2   242
(b) Incorporated December 24, 1805, with Rev. David Rice, A. M. Wakefield, James Allen, Robert Allen, Samuel Brents, James H. Rice, William Barret, Daniel Brown, John Moore, Thomas K. Slaughter, and Daniel White, Trustees 3   302

New Castle Library Company
Incorporated February 1, 1809, by William Butler, Rowland Thomas, Isham Henderson, John Stites, Jr., Robert Teter, Samuel McKinley, William Neal, Thomas S. Wingate and Joel Jackson 4   35

Newell, James
Register authorized to correct some irregularities as to his settlement right.............. 5   71

Newell, Samuel
(a) Inspection site in Pulaski County............ 3   24
(b) He and William Bush authorized to survey 1000 acres of mountain land on which they had discovered iron ore 3   163

New Market
Established in 1786 on lands of John Curd in Mercer County at mouth of Dick's River with John Jouet, Gabriel Madison, James Hoard, Samuel Prior, Alexander Robertson, Robert Mosby, James Overton, Harry Innes, Joseph Crocket and William Lewis, Trustees...... 3   559

Newport
(a) Established December 14, 1795 on lands of James Taylor in accordance with a plat made by John Roberts, Deputy Surveyor of Campbell County, with Thomas Kennedy, Washington Berry, Henry Brasher, Thomas Lind-

NEWPORT ACADEMY

	VOL.	PAGE
sey, Nathan Kelly, James McClure and Daniel Duggan, Trustees	1	280
(b) Purchase of land in by United States for arsenal purposes confirmed	3	142

Newport Academy
Established December 22, 1798 with William Kenndy, Washington Berry, Charles Morgan, John Grant, Thomas Kennedy, Thomas Sanford, Thomas Carneel, Richard Southgate, Daniel Mayo, John Crittenden, Robert Stubbs and James Taylor, Trustees......... 2 240

Newspapers
See Appendix

Newton Academy
(a) Established December 22, 1798 to be located in either Logan, Warren or Christian County, with Samuel Hopkins, Charles Davis, William Campbell, Robert Ewing, John Curd, Israel McGrady, Amos Balsh, Young Ewing, David Caldwell, William Prince, William Love, Finis Cox, Burwell Jackson, Aeneas McCollister, Samuel Hardin, John Bailey, Daniel Brown, and John Caldwell, Trustees 2 241
(b) Located at Russellville and Ninian Edwards, Armstead Morehead, William Reading and Walter Jones appointed Trustees in the stead of John Caldwell, deceased, Amos Balch and John Bailey, removed, and Israel McGready, resigned 3 277
(c) Logan Seminary merged into it under name Newton Academy, with Walter E. Jones, Joseph Hamilton, Armstead Morehead, Urbin Ewing, Samuel Wilson, Thomas V. Swearingen, John Curd, Samuel Caldwell, William Reading and William Johns, Trustees...... 3 409

Newton, William
State price of head right land remitted........ 5 22

New Town (Jefferson County)
(a) Established December 13, 1794 on lands of James Francis Moore, with Abner Field, Basil Prather, Isaac Hornbeck, Lewis Field and James Standiford, Trustees 1 233
(b) Title to townsite quieted................. 1 261
(c) See Jefferson, Town of

Newtown (Mason County)
Established in 1795 on lands of John Kenton in (then) Mason County with David Broad-

NICHOLAS COUNTY

	VOL.	PAGE
rick, John Getridge, William Baker, Joshua Baker, John Clarke, Edmund Collins and William Kenton, Trustees	1	285
(b) Election of Trustees provided for, the Town being described as in Nicholas County	4	8

Nicholas County
(a) Formed June 1, 1800 from Bourbon and Mason	2	366
(b) Commissioners appointed to locate County Seat	5	329
(c) Part of added to Fleming County	5	365
(d) Part of added to Harrison County	5	365
(e) Further part of added to Harrison County	5	452
(f) Part of Bourbon County added to	5	452
(g) County Court authorized to convey the public grounds at Ellisville	5	563

Nicholas, George
Trustee Transylvania University 2   234

Niel, Thomas
Named in boundary of election precinct in Logan County 5   140

Niess, David, deceased
Sale of land authorized 5   563

Noel, George, and
Noel, Taylor
Allowed to redeem land forfeited for nonpayment of taxes 5   437

Northcut, Archibald
(a) Authorized to build grist mill on Green River	4	30
(b) Trustee Liberty Academy	5	22

Norton, George
Named in boundary of public square in Danville 5   480

Norvell, Joshua
One of Commission to build bridge over Floyds Fork of Salt River................. 5   22

Nourse, Charles
One of Commission to conduct a lottery........ 5   570

Nourse, James, deceased
Sale of lands authorized..................... 2   363

O'Bannon, John
(a) Trustee of Versailles	1	355
(b) Trustee Woodford Academy	2	243
(c) Trustee Woodford Academy	3	181
(d) Authorized to erect grist mill on public spring in Versailles	3	191

Ogden, Masterson
Trustee Washingtonian Library 4   354

Ohio Canal Company
                                                                                                VOL.   PAGE

(a) Incorporated December 19, 1804 by Thomas Prather, George Wilson, Peter B. Ormsby, and James Hunter, of Louisville; Alexander Parker, John Jordan, and John Bradford, at Lexington; James Smiley, Thomas Speed and William R. Hinds, at Bardstown; James Birney and Barnabas Hughes, at Danville; John Rowan, Nicholas Clarke and William Trigg, at Frankfort; John Machir, and Peter Lee at Town of Washington; Ninian Edwards and Armstead Morehead at Russellville; Thomas Hughes and Hugh Brent at Paris; Adam Steele, and Wingfield Bullock, at Shelbyville; Daniel May and Edmund Taylor at Newport; Martin D. Hardin and John Patrick at Richmond; John Reed, James Hughes and Jesse Head at Springfield; Martin Hawkins and Josiah Pitts at Georgetown; Micajah Harrison and James Crawford at Mt. Sterling; Samuel Hopkins and Thomas Posey at Henderson; George Webb and Robert Clark, Jr., at Winchester, and John Faris and John Stockdon at Flemingsburg, the purpose of the company being to open a canal at the Falls of the Ohio............ 3   221

(b) A second corporation was created December 20, 1805, the incorporators being James Berthoud, Thomas Prather, George Wilson, Peter B. Ormsby, James Hunter, John Bradford, Alexander Parker, John Jordan, Jr., Adam Steele, Wingfield Bullock and Worden Pope 3   259

Ohio County
(a) Formed July 1, 1799 from Hardin County..... 2   208
(b) Part of added to Henderson County.......... 4   10
(c) Butler County, in part, carved from.......... 4   110
(d) Grayson County, in part, carved from........ 4   129
(e) Daviess County carved from................. 5   159
(f) Daviess County line defined................. 5   299

Oldham, John
    Trustee Town of Irvine..................... 4   339

Oldham, John P.
    Trustee Breckenridge Seminary 5   401

Oldham, Samuel
(a) Trustee Jefferson Seminary 2   378
(b) Trustee Jefferson Seminary 3   207

	VOL.	PAGE
(c) Trustee Jefferson Seminary	3	490
Oneal, Ludowick, deceased		
Patent issued to his devisees	5	513
Orchards, Isaac		
Trustee of Paris	1	188
Orear, William		
One of Commission to open road from Fleming County to the Big Sandy	3	167
Ormsby, Peter B.		
(a) Promoter at Louisville of Ohio Canal Company	3	221
(b) Promoter at Louisville of Ohio Canal Company	3	260
(c) Promoter at Louisville of Bank of Kentucky	3	391
(d) Incorporator Louisville Hospital Company	5	574
Ormsby, Stephen		
Judge Circuit Court Fifth District	3	507
Orr, Alexander D.		
(a) Trustee Town of Washington (1790)	3	556
(b) Trustee Franklin Academy	1	296
Ousley, William		
Refunded cost of repairs to Wilderness Road	3	376
Outlaws, ——		
Road to from Pulaski opened	3	95
Outlaws Salt Works		
Named in boundary of Clay County	3	338
Outton, Thomas		
Granted change of venue from Fayette to Clarke County on trial for perjury	4	358
Overstreet, James H.		
Incorporator Louisville Hospital Company	5	574
Overton, James		
Trustee Town of New Market (1786)	3	560
Overton, Samuel		
Trustee Washington Academy	2	242
Owens, Abraham (Colonel)		
(a) Delegate from Shelby County to second Constitutional Convention (1799)	1	58
(b) Trustee of Shelbyville	1	151
Owens, Col. Abraham, deceased		
(a) Part of his lands added to Shelbyville	5	255
(b) Part of his lands added to Shelbyville	5	571
(c) Owensborough named for Col. Abraham Owens, who fell at Tippecanoe	5	508
Owen, Brackett, deceased		
Part of his lands vested in Trustees of Shelbyville for benefit of his representatives	3	96

OWENS 140

	VOL.	PAGE
Owens, John		
Rebecca Owens authorized to sue him in Lincoln County for divorce	1	694
Owen, John Cockey (see John C. Owing)		
Inspection site in Nelson County	3	583
Owens, Rebecca		
See John Owens		
Owens, William		
Trustee Robertson Academy	5	125
Owensborough		
Name of Town of Rossborough changed to in honor of Col. Abraham Owens, who fell at Tippecanoe	5	508
Owing, John C. (see John Cockey Owen)		
(a) Trustee of Bairdstown (1788)	3	566
(b) Inspection site in Nelson County	2	139
Owsley, Anthony		
Pay as Commissioner of the Wilderness Road allowed	4	55
Owsley, Daniel		
Trustee of Crab Orchard	5	351
Owsley, Thomas		
(a) Named in Lincoln-Garrard County boundary	2	461
(b) Trustee of Crab Orchard	5	351
Owsley, William		
Trustee Stanford Academy	2	240
Owsley, William, Jr.		
Trustee Lancaster Library Company	3	208
Oxford, Sarah		
Authorized to sue William Oxford for divorce	2	173
Oxford, William		
See Sarah Oxford		
Parepoint, Francis		
Trustee of Beallsborough	3	564
Paris		
(a) Established in 1789 as "Hopewell" on lands of Lawrence Sprotsman, with Notley Conn, Charles Smith, Jr., John Edwards, James Garrard, Edward Waller, Thomas West, John Lanier, James Little and James Duncan, Trustees	3	567
(b) Title to town site quieted (1790) and name changed to Paris	3	569
(c) Claim of John Allen to townsite settled	1	111
(d) Horatio Hall, John Allen, Thomas Jones, John Smith, William E. Webb, Samuel Harris and		

	VOL.	PAGE
Isaac Orchards appointed Trustees	1	188
(e) Proceeds of sales of lots ordered paid to John Protzman	1	356
(f) Protzman's plat ordered reproduced	1	646
Paris Hydraulic Company		
Incorporated February 10, 1816	5	393
Paris Library Company		
Incorporated February 11, 1808 by William Garrard Jr., Robert Trimble, William Kelly, Samuel Hanson and Benjamin Mills	3	455
Parish, William, deceased		
Sale of lands authorized	5	42
Parker, Alexander		
(a) Trustee of Lexington	1	577
(b) Trustee Transylvania University	2	234
(c) Director Vineyard Society of Lexington	2	268
(d) Promoter at Lexington of Ohio Canal Company	3	221
(e) Promoter at Lexington of Bank of Kentucky	3	390
(f) Promoter at Lexington of Madison Hemp Company	3	533
(g) Promoter at Lexington of Kentucky Assurance Society	4	254
Parker, Richard		
(a) Inspection site in Washington County	2	140
(b) Inspection site in Nelson County	3	583
Parker, Robert, deceased		
Sale of lands authorized	2	362
Parker, Rowland T.		
Commissioner for Lewis County to survey road from Paris to mouth o. Big Sandy	3	461
Parker, Samuel		
One of Commissioners for Barren County to open part of Big Barren River in Barren and Warren Counties to navigation	4	198
Parker, Winslow		
(a) Trustee Franklin Academy	1	296
(b) Trustee Lewis Academy	4	17
Parks, Andrew		
State price of land remitted in consideration of former military services	4	317
Parkes, James		
Commissioner for Fleming County to survey road from Paris to mouth of Big Sandy	3	461
Parsons, Clement		
Trustee Town of Lebanon	5	191

PATRICK 142

	VOL.	PAGE
Patrick, John		
(a) Trustee Madison Academy	2	241
(b) Trustee Madison Academy	3	278
(c) Trustee Madison Academy	5	133
(d) Promoter for Madison County of Kentucky River Navigation Company	2	448
(e) Promoter at Richmond of Ohio Canal Company	3	221
Patterson, Jonathan		
Trustee New Athens Academy	2	242
Patterson, Nathaniel		
Trustee Bracken Academy	2	242
Patterson, Robert		
(a) Trustee of Lexington	3	549
(b) Trustee of Lexington	1	577
(c) Director Vineyard Society, of Lexington	2	268
(d) Trustee Lexington Library Association	2	375
Patterson, Robert, deceased		
Heirs authorized to survey 3000 acres on Green River to which he was entitled when murdered in Virginia	3	97
Pattie, John		
Trustee Bracken Academy	2	242
Patton, James		
Trustee of Louisville	3	547
Patton, John D.		
(a) Trustee Hopkinsville Library Company	5	361
(b) Trustee Christian Academy	5	450
Patton, Margaret		
Authorized to locate 21 acres Bourbon County	5	189
Paul, John		
Trustee Hardin Academy	2	242
Pauling, Henry		
Trustee of Stanford	3	559
Pawling, Henry		
Trustee Lancaster Academy	2	242
Payne, Alfred		
(a) Trustee ... n Seminary	5	433
(b) Trustee 'i a of Scottville	5	483
Payne, Deacon		
Price of land remitted	3	191
Payne, Duval		
(a) Trustee of Lewisbourgh, Mason County	1	295
(b) One of Commission to locate County Seat for Greenup County	3	117
(c) One of Commission o locate County Seat for Bath County	4	215

	VOL.	PAGE
Payne, Henry		
Acts as commissioner to replace Fayette County Burnt Records confirmed	3	154
Payne, Jilson		
(a) Tax Commissioner of Clarke County	1	188
(b) Trustee Montgomery Academy	2	241
(c) Delegate from Montgomery County to second Constitutional Convention (1799)	1	58
Payne, John		
(a) Trustee Rittenhouse Academy	2	240
(b) Trustee Georgetown Library	2	376
Payne, William		
Trustee Montgomery Academy	2	241
Paxton, James A.		
Promoter at Town of Washington of Maysville and Lexington Turnpike Road Company	5	536
Paxton, Joseph		
Trustee Stanford Library	5	455
Paythress, Rev. Francis		
Trustee Bethel Academy	2	174
Peak, Presley		
Named in boundary of election precinct in Boone County	3	488
Pearce, John D.		
Donated 800 acres for his support	5	585
Pearle, John		
Named in boundary of Rockcastle County	4	92
Pearl, William		
(a) Authorized to locate land in Knox County adjoining his present lands	4	325
(b) Given further time to locate lands	5	102
Peers, Valentine (see Piers)		
Promoter at Paris of Kentucky Assurance Society	4	254
Pelham, Charles		
Claimant of part of townsite of Versailles	1	226
Pemberton, Bennett		
(a) One of Commission to open road from Frankfort to Cincinnati	1	185
(b) Trustee Kentucky Seminary	2	389
(c) Promoter for Franklin County of Kentucky River Navigation Company	2	448
Pendegrast, Garrit		
Mary Pendegrast authorized to sue him in Jefferson County for divorce	3	515
Pendegrast, Mary		
See Garrit Pendegrast		

PENDLETON ACADEMY   144

	VOL.	PAGE

Pendleton Academy
    Incorporated January 26, 1815 with James King, Alexander Monrow, Samuel Lockwood, Stephen Thrasher, James Naylor and James Wilson, Trustees 5   174

Pendleton County
    Formed May 10, 1799 from Bracken and Campbell Counties 2   197

Pendleton, James T.
    One of Commission to conduct a lottery 5   570

Pennington, Jacob, deceased
    Error in credit on Green River land corrected 3   168

Pennybaker, Frederick
    Trustee of Shepherdsville 1   183

Penrod, John, deceased
    Died on Hopkins campaign,—balance due on 200 acres of land was remitted............. 5   69

Perkins, Benjamin
    Trustee Lancaster Academy 2   242

Perkins Mill
    Made head of navigation on Dick's River.... 5   390

Perkins, Stephen
    Trustee Lancaster Library Company......... 3   208

Perryville (Mercer County)
    Established January 17, 1817 on lands of Edward Bullock, and William Hall, with Richard Hope, Thomas Crawford, Sr., Archibald Bilbo, Nimrod Greenwood, James Warren, George H. Briscoe and Thomas J. Crawford, Trustees 5   454

Petersburg Steam Mill Company
    Incorporated February 3, 1817 5   514

Peyton, Daniel
    One of Commission to open road from Mt. Sterling to Prestonburg and thence to Cumberland Mountain 5   553

Peyton, Timothy, deceased
    Sale of land authorized.................... 1   114

Phelps, Guy
    One of Commission to erect bridge over Floyds Fork of Salt River....................... 5   22

Philips, John
    One of Commission to open Beech Fork of Salt River to navigation 2   312

Philips, Philip
    (a) Trustee of Bairdstown (1788)................ 3   566
    (b) Trustee Salem Academy (1788)............. 3   580

	VOL.	PAGE
Phillips, William E.		
Claimant of site of Centreville in Livingston County	3	354
Pickett, George		
Compromise allowed on settlement as surety for James Little, Sheriff of Bourbon County	5	45
Pickett, Wilson, deceased		
Sale of lands authorized	5	565
Pickins, James		
Pay as spy allowed	2	358
Piers, Valentine (see Peers)		
Promoter at Paris of Maysville and Lexington Turnpike Road Company	5	536
Piersey, George		
Trustee Shelby Library Company	4	90
Pigman, Ignatius		
Trustee Hartford Academy	2	242
Pitman, Thomas		
(a) Surety for William Pitman	2	362
(b) Named in boundary of election precinct in Mercer County	5	437
Pitman, William, deceased		
Lands authorized sold for benefit of Thomas Pitman, his security	2	362
Pitts, Josiah		
(a) Trustee Georgetown Library	2	376
(b) Promoter at Georgetown of Ohio Canal Company	3	221
(c) Inspection site at Georgetown	3	323
Plummer, Robert		
Trustee Gallatin Academy	5	13
Poage, John		
Trustee Greenup Academy	4	128
Poague, John		
Authorized to locate 1000 acres on Cumberland River to include a salt spring	4	325
Pogue, James		
Trustee Montgomery Academy	2	241
Pomroy, George A. K.		
Named in boundary of election precinct in Jefferson County	5	308
Pope, Benjamin		
Trustee Bullitt Academy	2	243
Pope, John		
(a) Trustee Shelby Academy	2	241
(b) Authorized to build bridge over Kentucky River at Frankfort	3	280

POPE

	VOL.	PAGE
(c) Act (b) amended	4	58
(d) Given further time to build bridge	3	491
(e) Thomas Tunstall authorized to build bridge at Frankfort on same terms as granted John Pope	3	306
(f) John Brown authorized to build bridge at Frankfort on same terms as granted John Pope	4	350

Pope, William
(a) Trustee of Williamsville	1	118
(b) Trustee of Louisville	3	540

Pope, Worden
Incorporator of Ohio Canal Company	3	260

Porter, David A.
Trustee Allen Seminary	5	433

Porter, Ephraim
Assignee of Jonathan Rossell of a survey on Green River	3	509

Porter, John
Trustee Logan Academy	3	206

Porter, Oliver
Authorized to sue for divorce	5	138

Porter, Robert
Given time to settle as Sheriff of Madison County	4	323

Port William (at mouth of Kentucky River)
(a) Established December 13, 1794 on lands of Benjamin Craig and James Hawkins with Cave Johnson, Thomas Montague, and Jeremiah Craig, Trustees	1	232
(b) Simon Adams, Richard Masterson, John Van Pelt and William Haden appointed additional Trustees	1	340
(c) Plat of Town confirmed and Garland Bullock, Presley Gray and John Davies appointed Trustees	2	337
(d) Made County Seat of Gallatin County	3	98
(e) Location of Courthouse in fixed	3	248

Posey, Thomas
(a) Promoter at Henderson of Ohio Canal Company	3	221
(b) Operated ferry on the Ohio in Campbell County	3	413
(c) Inspection site in Campbell County	3	513

Postlethwait, John
(a) Vineyard Society to meet at his house in Lexington	2	268

		VOL.	PAGE
(b)	Main Street, in Lexington, to be paved in front of his house	2	368
(c)	Promoter at Lexington of Madison Hemp Company	3	533
(d)	Lexington White Lead Manufacturing Company to organize at his house in Lexington	5	205
(e)	Lexington Manufacturing Company to organize at his house in Lexington	5	252

Postlethwait, Samuel
Trustee Lexington Library Association 2 375

Pottinger, Samuel
Trustee of Beallsborough 3 564

Powell, Levin
Trustee of Boonesborough (1779) 3 538

Powell, William
Voting place at his house in Livingston County 4 327

Prather, Basil
Trustee of New Town 1 233

Prather, Donne Basil
One of Commission to sell and adjust claims respecting lots in Louisville 3 547

Prather, Richard
Delegate from Nelson County to second Constitutional Convention (1799) 1 58

Prather, Thomas
(a) Promoter at Louisville of Ohio Canal Company 3 221
(b) Promoter at Louisville of Ohio Canal Company 3 260
(c) Promoter at Louisville of Bank of Kentucky 3 391
(d) Promoter at Louisville of Kentucky Assurance Society 4 254
(e) Incorporator Louisville Hospital 5 574

Prentiss, James
(a) Incorporator Lexington Manufacturing Company 5 251
(b) Promoter at Lexington of Maysville and Lexington Turnpike Road Company 5 536

Presbyterian Congregation of Lexington
Authorized to sell church lot and buy another 3 251

Preston (Shelby County)
Established December 21, 1795 on lands of John Smith and Francis Preston, with John Smith, George Madison, William Trigg and Abraham Cavens, Trustees 1 347

Preston, Francis
  (a) Co-founder of Town of Preston.............. 1   347
  (b) Inspection site at Prestonville in Gallatin County 2   456
Prewitt, Isham
  Named in boundary of election precinct in Mercer County 5   438
Price, Abraham
  Authorized to sue Sally Ann Price in Pulaski or Wayne County for divorce............. 3   160
Price, James C., deceased
  (a) Sale of land authorized..................... 5   105
  (b) Sale of land authorized..................... 5   356
Price, John
  Delegate from Jessamine County to second Constitutional Convention (1799).............. 1   58
Price, Sally Ann
  See Abraham Price
Price, Moses M.
  Trustee Madison Academy................... 5   133
Price, William
  Promoter for Jessamine County of Kentucky River Navigation Company................ 2   448
Price, Zachariah
  Allowed to return warrant for Green River land and take out another..................... 3   96
Prichard, Elizabeth
  Price of land remitted....................... 5   367
Prince, William
  Trustee Newton Academy.................... 2   241
Pringle, Alexander
  Polly Pringle authorized to sue him, in Henry County for divorce....................... 3   490
Pringle, Polly
  See Alexander Pringle
Prior, Samuel
  Trustee Town of New Market................ 3   560
Protzman, John (see Sprotzman)
  (a) Title to site of Hopewell (Paris) quieted....... 1   356
  (b) Cross street in Paris, adjoining his lot, changed 1   648
  (c) Title to site of Paris finally quieted.......... 5   106
Protzman, Lawrence (see Sprotzman)
  (a) Founder of Hopewell (Paris)................ 1   356
  (b) His plat of Paris ordered renewed............ 1   647
Pryor, Jack
  Co-founder and Trustee Town of Bedford...... 5   350

	VOL.	PAGE

Pugh, John
    Promoter Gallatin-Ohio Steamboat Company.... 5   343
Pulaski County
    (a) Formed June 1, 1799 from Lincoln and Green Counties 2   189
    (b) Wayne County, in part, carved from.......... 2   392
    (c) Rockcastle County, in part, carved from...... 4   91
    (d) Part of Wayne County added to............. 5   562
    (e) Part of added to Wayne County............. 5   362
Pulliam, Levy
    Assignor to Thomas Griffin of certificate for 400 acres of land............................. 5   331
Purdie, Stephen
    Trustee Town of Lebanon................... 5   191
Purdie, William
    Founder of Town of Lebanon................ 5   191
Purtle, Michael (see Pustle)
    Justices of Livingston County to meet at his house 2   199
Purtle, Peter
    Allowed to withdraw survey on Green River.... 3   158
Purviance, David
    (a) Trustee Bourbon Academy.................. 2   237
    (b) Trustee Bourbon Academy.................. 2   242
Purviance, Henry
    (a) Promoter for Lexington of Bank of Kentucky... 3   390
    (b) Promoter at Lexington of Kentucky Assurance Society 4   254
Pustle, Mr. Senior (see Michael Purtle)
    Justices of Livingston County to meet at his house 2   92
Putman, James
    (a) Voting place at house in Bracken County...... 3   487
    (b) Act (a) repealed......................... 4   241
Quakers
    (a) Marriages of to be registered................ 2   66
    (b) Exempted from military service.............. 3   216
Quarles, Henry
    Inspection site in Lincoln County............. 3   332
Quarles, Tunstall
    (a) Trustee Woodford Academy................. 2   243
    (b) Appointed Commissioner to build a section of the road from Danville to Tellico........... 3   275
    (c) Pay as Commissioner at (b) allowed.......... 3   364
Query's Mill
    Made head of navigation on Floyd's Fork of Salt River 3   475

QUIGLEY 150

	VOL.	PAGE
Quigley, William		
Trustee Town of Carthage in Union County...	5	83
Quinton, William		
State price of headright land remitted.........	5	328
Quirey, Charles		
Allowed credit on settlement as Sheriff of Jefferson County............................	4	60
Radford, John		
Trustee Lewis Academy.....................	4	17
Railey, Charles		
Trustee Woodford Academy.................	3	181
Rainey, Abraham, deceased		
Sale of lands in Scott County authorized.......	5	471
Raley, Mary, and children		
Donated small tract of land in Washington County	5	17
Ramsey, Jonathan		
One of Commission to locate County Seat for Union County	4	213
Randolph, John		
Inspection site in Muhlenberg County.........	3	332
Randolph, Thomas		
Refunded price of headright land lost by prior claim	4	323
Rankin, Adam		
(a) Trustee Lexington Seminary..................	2	108
(b) Main Street, in Lexington, in front of his lot, to be paved..............................	2	368
(c) Trustee Henderson Academy..................	5	72
(d) Trustee Henderson Library Company..........	5	460
Rankin, Robert		
(a) Trustee Town of Washington (1786)..........	3	555
(b) Trustee Town of Washington (1790)..........	3	556
(c) Trustee Town of Charlestown (1787)..........	3	562
(d) Trustee Franklin Academy...................	1	296
Rankin, Thomas		
Authorized to sue non-resident heirs of James Ferguson for sale of lot in Cynthiana........	5	498
Ratliff, James		
Voting place at house in Floyd County.........	3	255
Ray, Captain		
Samuel McGehee allowed pay for beef taken by Captain Ray on the Wabash Expedition in 1786	2	484
Ray, James		
One of Commission to locate County Seat of Bath County	4	215

Ray, Joseph
    Inspection site in Washington County 2   383
Ray, William
    Authorized, with John and Henry James, to locate iron ore lands in Pulaski County 3   536
Rayfield, Isaac
    Balance of purchase price of land remitted 4   336
Reading, George
    (a) Given time to complete lock at mill dam on Licking River 2   313
    (b) Given further time to complete lock 2   424
    (c) Given still further time to complete lock 3   302
Reading, William
    (a) Trustee Logan Academy 3   206
    (b) Trustee Newton Academy 3   277
    (c) Trustee Newton Academy 3   409
    (d) Claimant of site of Centreville in Livingston County 3   354
Reager, Jacob
    Trustee of Louisville 3   547
Record, Spencer
    Trustee of Germantown 1   329
Reddick, William
    Given time to settle as Sheriff of Campbell County 5   308
Redding, Elijah
    Frances Redding authorized to sue him in Jessamine County for divorce 3   464
Redding, Frances
    See Elijah Redding
Red River Iron Works
    Authorized to maintain height of dam 5   564
Reed, Archibald
    Named in Campbell-Boone County boundary 4   535
Reed, Francis S.
    (a) Trustee Stanford Academy 3   334
    (b) Trustee of Stanford 5   166
Reed, James
    Named in boundary of election precinct in Logan County 3   345
Reed, John (see Reid, Ried)
    (a) Trustee Washington Academy 2   242
    (b) Trustee Washington Academy 5   15
    (c) Promoter at Springfield of Ohio Canal Company 3   221
    (d) Settlement required of him as keeper of turnpike on Wilderness Road 5   199

	VOL.	PAGE
Reed, John, deceased		
Certificates due frontier guards and assigned to him were ordered paid to his heirs	3	376
Reed, Joseph		
Error in patent corrected	4	194
Rees, Jacob		
Authorized to build mill on Big Barren River in Warren County	5	259
Reeves, Benjamin H.		
Trustee Christian Academy	5	450
Reeves, Thomas		
Claimant of part of townsite of Versailles	1	220
Reid, Alexander, deceased		
(a) Sale of lands in Lincoln County authorized	1	356
(b) Sale of lands in Lincoln County authorized	2	178
Reid, John		
Settlement required as keeper of turnpike on Wilderness Road	4	264
Reid, John C. (see Reed, Ried)		
Trustee of Bairdstown	3	566
Reives, Joseph		
Trustee Union Academy	5	80
Reno, Jesse		
Trustee Greenville Academy	4	113
Renno, Jesse		
Error in settlement as Coroner of Muhlenberg County corrected	5	54
Rentfro, Absolem		
Trustee Rockcastle Academy	4	114
Rhodes, John		
One of Commission to locate County Seat for Warren County	3	447
Rhodes, Robert (see Rodes)		
(a) Trustee Madison Academy	2	241
(b) Trustee of Boonesborough (1787)	3	539
(c) Trustee Town of Milford (1789)	3	567
Rice, Claiborne		
Trustee Greenville Academy	4	113
Rice, David		
(a) Trustee Kentucky Academy	1	228
(b) Trustee Transylvania Seminary	3	572
Rice, Rev. David		
Trustee New Athens Seminary	3	302
Rice, Fisher		
Justices of Jessamine County to meet at his house	2	214
Rice, James H.		
Trustee New Athens Seminary	3	302

	VOL.	PAGE

Rice, Mary
  Sale of lands of her deceased husband, in Garrard
    County, authorized 3   164
Rice, Moses
  Trustee Liberty Academy.................... 4   114
Rice, Moses, deceased
  Administrator given time to settle his accounts
    as Clerk of Casey County.................. 5   35
Rice, William
  Certificate for military services assigned by him
    to Philip Bush, Jr., ordered paid............ 3   408
Rice, William M.
  (a) One of Commissioners for Henry County to survey Henry-Shelby County line.............. 5   103
  (b) One of Commission to open road from Newcastle to mouth of Licking....................... 5   131
Richardson, Jesse
  Trustee Somerset Academy................... 3   37
Richardson, John C.
  Acts as Commissioner to replace Fayette County
    Burnt Records confirmed................... 3   154
Richardson, Dr. William
  One of Commission to raise by lottery a fund to
    build a Grand Masonic Hall in Lexington.... 5   181
Richeson, James
  Margaret Richeson authorized to sue him for
    divorce 1   359
Richeson, Margaret
  See James Richeson
Ridgeley, Frederick
  (a) Trustee Transylvania University.............. 2   234
  (b) Incorporator of Lexington White Lead Manufacturing Company 5   204
Riddle, Isaac
  One of Commission to open South Fork of
    Licking to navigation..................... 1   193
Riddle, George
  Allowed credit on settlement as Sheriff of
    Fleming County 3   364
Riddle, Jeremiah
  Justices of Union County to meet at his house.. 4   213
Ried, John C. (see Reed, Reid)
  Trustee of Bairdstown...................... 3   566
Rife, Abraham
  Inspection site in Adair County.............. 3   385

RIGGS 154

	VOL.	PAGE

Riggs, Andrew
   Main Street in Lexington ordered paved in front of his lot............................... 2   368
Ringo, Cornelius
   Trustee of Mt. Sterling.................... 1   125
Rinicks, Henry
   Justices of Barren County to meet at his house 2   223
Ritchie, James
   Claimant of site of Centreville in Livingston County 3   354
Ritchy's Landing
   Inspection site in Livingston County........... 2   457
Rittenhouse Academy (Scott County)
   Incorporated December 22, 1798 with Robert Johnson, Bartlett Collins, John Hawkins, John Hunter, Elijah Craig, Toliver Craig, William Henry, John Payne, Samuel Shepherd, William Warren and Abraham Buford, Trustees...... 2   240
Rively, William
   Given time to complete bridge in Montgomery County on road from Mt. Sterling to the Big Sandy 3   512
Roan, Captain
   Empowered to appoint surveyors (1783)....... 1   442
Robards, James S. H.
   Pay allowed as Janitor for Court of Appeals.... 2   182
Robb, Hugh W.
   Trustee Union Academy.................... 5   80
Robb, Robert
   Trustee Lewis Academy..................... 4   17
Robbitt, William
   Named in boundary of election precinct in Christian County 5   80
Roberts, Benjamin
   (a) Trustee Shelby Academy 2   242
   (b) Trustee of Frankfort....................... 3   557
Roberts, James
   Trustee of Frankfort...................... 1   247
Roberts, John
   Deputy Surveyor of Campbell County......... 1   280
Roberts, Major John
   Named in boundary of election precinct in Christian County 4   225
Roberts and Jones
   Inspection site on Marrowbone Creek.......... 3   514
Roberts, Joseph
   Voting place at house in Clay County......... 5   472

	VOL.	PAGE

Roberts, Peter D.
    Director Vineyard Society, of Lexington 2   268
Roberts, William, deceased
    Division of his lands in Fleming County between his devisees confirmed 5   187
Robertson Academy (Adair County)
    Incorporated January 31, 1814 at Columbia with William Casey, Christopher Tompkins, William Owens, William Caldwell, and Nathan Gaither, Trustees 5   125
Robertson, Alexander
    Trustee Town of New Market................ 3   560
Robertson, Jesse S.
    Named in boundary of election precinct in Livingston County 5   462
Robertson, Joseph
    Trustee of Campbellsville................... 5   430
Robertson, Polly
    Balance due on headright land remitted........ 5   385
Robertson, Thomas, deceased
    Balance due on headright land remitted........ 5   385
Robins, Vincent
    Certificate for spy service by him ordered paid to Philip Bush, Jr., as assignee............. 3   408
Robinson, Jacob
    Sarah Robinson authorized to sue him in Livingston County for divorce................... 3   516
Robinson, Jeremiah
    Trustee of Cynthiana...................... 1   179
Robinson, John
    Inspection site in Cumberland County........ 3   24
Robinson, John, deceased
    Patent granted his heirs...................... 4   412
Robinson, Sarah
    See Jacob Robinson
Robinson, William
    (a) Trustee Lexington Seminary................ 2   108
    (b) Trustee Montgomery Academy............... 2   241
Robsammon, Jacob, deceased
    Title of John Fowler to lands in Campbell County, formerly owned by Robsammon, perfected 4   253
Rochester, John
    (a) Trustee Danville Library.................... 2   376
    (b) Trustee Danville Seminary.................. 3   381
    (c) Trustee Town of Danville................... 4   39

		VOL.	PAGE
(d) One of Commission to raise by lottery a fund to open Kentucky River to navigation		4	210
Rochester, Nathaniel			
Director Wilderness Road		4	265
Rockcastle Academy			
Incorporated January 18, 1810 with James Dysert, William Cason, William Smith, Absolem Rentfro, John Burdett, Henry P. Buford and John Dysert, Trustees		4	114
Rockcastle County			
(a) Formed April 1, 1810 from Lincoln, Pulaski, Madison and Knox Counties		4	91
(b) Part of added to Madison County		4	406
Rodes, Robert (see Rhodes)			
(a) Commissioner to open road in Madison County		1	231
(b) Trustee Madison Academy		3	278
Rodgers, William (see William C. Rogers)			
Impeachment proceedings against him mentioned		4	127
Roe, William			
Trustee Franklin Academy		1	296
Rogers, Captain			
Empowered to appoint surveyors (1783)		1	442
Rogers, John			
Trustee Town of Washington		1	199
Rogers, Nathaniel			
Delegate from Bourbon County to second Constitutional Convention (1799)		1	57
Rogers, Polly			
Authorized to sue Robert Rogers for divorce		2	362
Rogers, Robert			
See Polly Rogers			
Rogers, William			
(a) Appointed to audit claim of Peter Stiger		2	355
(b) Costs of his suit against Peter Stidger allowed		2	486
(c) Warrant for costs ordered issued		3	193
(d) One of Commission to build bridge over Rough Creek at Hartford		4	88
Rogers, William C. (see William Rodgers)			
Witness fees allowed in impeachment proceedings against him		4	91
Roling, Stephen			
Trustee Hardin Academy		2	242
Rollings, Pemberton			
Trustee of Boonesborough		3	538
Rollins, Anthony W.			
Trustee Madison Academy		5	133

	VOL.	PAGE

Roman, William
Incorporator of Fayette Paper Manufacturing
Company 5   409
Roper, William P.
(a) Commissioner for Fleming County to survey road
from Paris to mouth of the Big Sandy....... 3   461
(b) One of Commission to erect turnpike on road at
(a) 4   154
(c) One of Commission to lease road at (a)........ 4   236
Rose, Samuel
Promoter at Hartford of Bank of Kentucky.... 3   391
Ross, David
Rossborough, later Owensborough, located on his
lands 5   501
Ross, Hugh
Arrested for felony......................... 1   358
Ross, James
Co-respondent in divorce proceedings by Daniel
Stilwell against Delilah Stilwell............. 3   512
Rossborough, Town of
Name changed to Owensborough in honor of
Col. Abraham Owens who fell at Tippecanoe.. 5   508
Rossell, Jonathan
Error in Green River survey corrected......... 3   509
Rountree, Mary (see Rowntree)
Pay due her deceased husband allowed her..... 5   337
Rouse, Jacob
Trustee Boone Academy..................... 5   76
Rout, William
(a) Granted pension for services as Captain in
Logan's Expedition against the Shawnees in
1786 2   485
(b) His plat of Flemingsburg confirmed.......... 5   188
Rowan, John
(a) Delegate from Nelson County to second Constitutional Convention (1799).................. 1   58
(b) Promoter at Frankfort of Ohio Canal Company 3   221
(c) Trustee Salem Academy..................... 5   7
Rowntree, Samuel
Inspection site in Warren County............. 2   140
Ruby, Asa, deceased
(a) Heirs given time to pay for land............. 3   161
(b) Same as (a)............................... 3   179
Ruddle, Isaac
Inspection site in Bourbon County (1787)...... 3   582
Rue, Richard
Justices of Henry County to meet at his house 2   201

	VOL.	PAGE
Russell, Edward		
A certificate for a small sum due him was ordered paid	3	170
Russell, Hendley		
Granted duplicate for lost warrant for pay as Jailer of Logan County	3	93
Russell, John C.		
Trustee Greenville Academy	4	113
Russell, Polly		
Authorized to sue William Russell for divorce	2	362
Russell, William		
See Polly Russell		
Rutter, William		
Trustee of Campbellsville	5	430
Ryan, James		
Mill on Beech Fork of Salt River excluded from operation of a navigation act	3	82
Salem Academy (Nelson County)		
(a) Incorporated in 1788 with John Caldwell, Andrew Hynes, Isaac Morrison, Tarah Templin, Matthew Walton, John Steele, Philip Philips, Walter Beall, George Harrison, James Baird, Joseph Barnet, James Morrison, James Allen, Cuthbert Harrison and William Taylor, Trustees	3	579
(b) Granted 6000 acres Green River land	2	107
(c) Walter Brashear, Burr Harrison, Thomas Speed, John Rowan and William P. Duvall appointed Trustees	5	7
Salisberry, Town of (Campbell County)		
Established December 22, 1806 on land of Squire Grant with Bartlett Graves, Zachariah Moore, John Winston, Frank Spelman, Nicholas Gherry, William Stephens and Benjamin Allen, Trustees	3	369
Salsbury, Thomas		
Title to land in Muhlenberg County quieted	4	241
Salt Licks		
(a) Salt works to be fenced	2	188
(b) Act (a) repealed	2	379
Sample, John W.		
Trustee New Athens Academy	2	242
Sampson, William, deceased		
Each of his ten children granted 100 acres of land in consideration of his services under Gov. Shelby in the expedition to Canada	5	408

	VOL.	PAGE

Sams, James
  Named in boundary of election precinct in Grayson County 5 35
Samuels, Robert
  Allowed pay for spy service in 1794 .... 3 354
Sanders, John
  Trustee Town of Wilmington 1 175
Sanders, Lewis
  (a) One of Commission to raise by lottery a fund to open Kentucky River to navigation 4 210
  (b) Same as (a) 4 318
  (c) Same as (a) 5 12
  (d) Title of State released as to escheated land he had purchased 4 325
  (e) Promoter at Lexington of Maysville and Lexington Turnpike Road Company 5 536
Sanders, Nathaniel (see Saunders)
  (a) Commissioner to open road from Frankfort to Cincinnati 1 185
  (b) Commission for Gallatin County to open road from Newcastle to mouth of Licking 3 365
  (c) Voting place at house in Gallatin County 4 107
Sanders, Robert
  Trustee Georgetown Library 2 376
Sanders, Thomas
  Trustee Bullitt Academy 3 478
Sandford, Alfred
  Trustee of Covington 5 283
Sandford, Thomas (see Sanfort)
  Delegate from Campbell County to second Constitutional Convention (1799) 1 57
Sanduskies Cabin
  Named in Pulaski County boundary 2 392
Sanfort, Thomas (see Sandford)
  Trustee Newport Academy 2 240
Sappington, John
  Trustee of Boonesborough (1787) 3 540
Saunders, Joseph
  Trustee Bullitt Academy 2 243
Saunders, Nathaniel (see Sanders)
  Inspection site in Gallatin County 3 513
Sargent, Johnston
  Errors in proceedings relative to headright claims were corrected 4 157
Sawyer, Benjamin
  Granted patent for 200 acres as assignee of Lewis Collins 5 70

SCOTT 160

	VOL.	PAGE
Scott, Charles		
(a) Inspection site in Fayette County (1787)	3	582
(b) Inspection site in Woodford County	2	140
Scott, Major General Charles		
Empowered to appoint surveyors (1783)	1	442
Scott County		
(a) Formed September 1, 1792 from Woodford	1	629
(b) Harrison County, in part, carved from	1	631
(c) Campbell County, in part, carved from	1	632
Scott, James		
Trustee Lexington Seminary	2	108
Scott, John M.		
Trustee Kentucky Seminary	2	389
Scott, John M., deceased		
Died in office as Sheriff of Franklin County. Time was given his representatives to settle his accounts	5	83
Scott, Moses		
Trustee Boone Academy	5	76
Scott, Thomas		
(a) His plat of Winchester confirmed	2	458
(b) Fee allowed for plat of Winchester	3	144
(c) Auditor directed to issue him a warrant	4	192
(d) One of Commission to extend Short Street in Winchester to Water Street	4	379
Scott, William		
(a) Promoter at Paris of Bank of Kentucky	3	390
(b) Trustees of Paris authorized to convey him a part of the public square	5	397
(c) Trustee Liberty Academy (Casey County)	4	114
Scottville (Allen County)		
Thomas Gatton, John Buckannan, Daniel M. Jones, Alfred Payne and Samuel Garrison appointed Trustees	5	483
Searcy, Charles, deceased		
Sale of lands authorized	5	316
Searcy, Edmund		
One of Commission to open road from Newcastle to mouth of Licking	5	131
Searcy, Samuel		
Sale of lands held jointly with heirs of Charles Searcy, deceased, was authorized	5	316
Sebastian, Benjamin		
Trustee of Louisville (1789)	3	547
Sebree, Uriel		
Trustee of Covington	5	283

	VOL.	PAGE

Seitz, John A.
  (a) Director Vineyard Society, of Lexington 2   268
  (b) Trustee Lexington Library Association 2   375
  (c) Acts as Commissioner to replace Fayette County
        Burnt Records confirmed 3   154

Shackett, Benjamin
  (a) Voting place at house in Hardin County 4   226
  (b) Act (a) repealed 5   181

Shackleford, Benjamin
  Trustee Hopkinsville Library Company 5   361

Shackleford, Samuel
  Trustee Stanford Academy 3   334

Shanks, Archibald
  Trustee of Crab Orchard 5   351

Shanks, James
  His survey of Shepherdsville confirmed 4   212

Shannon, Samuel
  Trustee Kentucky Academy 1   228

Shannon, Samuel, deceased
  Commissioners named to settle disputes concerning his lands 5   272

Shannon, William
  (a) Shelbyville located on his lands 1   151
  (b) Trustee Town of Jefferson 2   380

Sharp, Armstead
  Conducted to several Courts under guard to testify for Commonwealth 1   274

Sharp, Benjamin
  Trustee Shelby Library Company 4   89

Sharp, Fidelio
  Trustee Caledonia Academy 5   3

Sharp, Maxwell
  Trustee Logan Academy 3   206

Shaw, Aner
  State price of headright land remitted 5   22

Shelby Academy
  Incorporated December 22, 1798 with Joseph Hornsby, Benjamin Logan, Bland W. Ballard, Benjamin Roberts, Thomas Given, Simon Adams, James Logan, John Allen, Joseph Winlock, John Pope, Nicholas Merewether, Daniel McCleland and Aquila Whitaker, Trustees 2   241

Shelby County
  (a) Formed September 1, 1792 from Jefferson County 1   629
  (b) Franklin County, in part, carved from 1   632
  (c) Henry County carved from 2   200

SHELBY 162

	VOL.	PAGE
(d) Gallatin County, in part, carved from	2	203
(e) Andrew Holmes, William Taylor, David Standiford and Lowry Jones, of Shelby County, and William Neill, John Calloway, William M. Rice and Edmund Bartlett, of Henry County, named commissioners to survey the Henry-Shelby County line	5	103
(f) Thomas Mitchell, David Standiford and Andrew Holmes, of Shelby County; and James Bartlett, John Calloway and William Neil, of Henry County, named commissioners in lieu of those at (e)	5	330

Shelby, Isaac

(a) Governor authorized to appoint his successor as Sheriff of Lincoln County	1	113
(b) One of Commission to locate penitentiary	2	15
(c) Promoter for Lincoln County of Kentucky River Navigation Company	2	448
(d) Trustee of Stanford (1786)	3	559
(e) Trustee Transylvania Seminary (1783)	3	572
(f) Lands granted heirs of William Sampson for services under him in his expedition into Canada	5	408

Shelby Library Company

Incorporated January 4, 1810 with Thomas Johnston, Edward Talbot, Benjamin Sharp, William Adams, George Piersey, John Ketcham, Joseph Bondurant, James Ford and David Demaree, Trustees	4	89

Shelbyville

(a) Established December 20, 1792 with David Standiford, Joseph Winlock, John Knight, Abraham Owens, and Thomas J. Gwinn, Trustees	1	151
(b) Trustees vested with title to part of lands of Brackett Owens, deceased	3	96
(c) Lands of Col. Abraham Owen and of Dr. James S. Moore, added to	5	255
(d) Lands of Col. Abraham Owen and of David Shipman added to	5	571

Shelton, Jeremiah

Price of land remitted	3	164

Shepard, Samuel (see Shepherd)

Promoter at Georgetown of Lexington and Louisville Turnpike Road Company	5	520

Shepherd, Adam

(a) Shepherdsville established on his lands	1	183
(b) Inspection site in Bullitt County	2	279

	VOL. PAGE
(c) Unpatented land was sold by him to William Kester, to whom title was released...........	5 299
Shepherd, Peter, deceased	
Title to site of Town of Jefferson quieted.....	5 353
Shepherd, Samuel (see Shepard)	
(a) Trustee Rittenhouse Academy................	2 240
(b) Trustee Georgetown Library.................	2 376
Shepherdsville	
(a) Established December 11, 1793 on lands of Adam Shepherd with Nacy Brashears, Samuel Crow, Michael Troutman, Frederick Pennybaker, Benjamin Stansberry, Joseph Brooks and John Essery, Trustees..........................	1 183
(b) Survey of town by James Shanks confirmed....	4 212
Shields, Polly	
Authorized to locate small tract of land in Mercer County	5 135
Shipman, David, deceased	
Part of his lands added to Shelbyville..........	5 571
Shipp, Laban	
One of Commission to open Stoner Fork of Licking to navigation	1 193
Shoan, Patrick	
State's right to escheated settlement and preemption released	4 51
Short, Samuel	
His title as assignee of Robert Hooker to land in Hopkins County confirmed................	4 105
Shotwell, John, Sr.	
Promoter at Mayslick of Maysville and Lexington Turnpike Road Company..................	5 536
Shuck, Cornelius	
Lands of William Mitchell, deceased, to be conveyed to him..........................	4 241
Sibert, Peter	
Authorized to erect mill on Beech Fork in Nelson County	5 563
Simms, Martin	
Authorized to work a salt lick on public land....	2 485
Simon, Joseph	
(a) Mortgagee of Townsite of Louisville...........	3 542
(b) Claim under mortgage at (a) adjusted.........	3 543
(c) Payment of mortgage at (a) to be made out of proceeds of sales of lots in Louisville.........	3 546
Simpson, David, deceased	
Heirs given time to pay for land..............	5 369

	VOL.	PAGE

Simpson, James
   Trustee Winchester Library Company......... 4   195
Simpson, Thomas
   New survey and patent of headright claim granted 5   458
Simrall, James
   Trustee Washingtonian Library............... 4   354
Simrall, William F., deceased
   Sale of lands in Beargrass authorized.......... 4   325
Sims, David
   Trustee New Athens Academy................ 2   242
Singleton, Matthew
   Balance of price of land remitted............. 4   195
Skidmore, Paul
   Incorporator of Louisville Hospital............ 5   574
Skiles, Jacob (see Skyles)
   One of Commission to open Big Barren River to navigation 4   116
Skiles, William
   One of Commission to open Drake Creek in Warren County to navigation................... 4   361
Skyles, Jacob (see Skiles)
   Payment of his costs in his prosecution before the Legislature, in which he was acquitted, ordered paid 4   150
Slaughter, Gabriel
   (a) Trustee Harrodsburg Academy............... 2   240
   (b) Promoter for Mercer County of Kentucky River Navigation Company................ 2   448
Slaughter, George
   (a) Trustee of Williamsville 1   118
   (b) Trustee of Louisville (1780)................. 3   540
Slaughter, Thomas K.
   Trustee New Athens Seminary............... 3   302
Slavey, Richard
   (a) Authorized to locate 1000 acres in Wayne County to include a salt spring................... 4   257
   (b) Given time at (a)........................... 5   138
   (c) Given further time at (a).................... 5   428
Sleet, Weedon
   Voting place at house in Boone County........ 3   488
Sloan, Patrick
   See Shoan
Sloe, Thomas (see Sloo)
   Trustee Town of Washington (1790).......... 3   556

	VOL.	PAGE
Sloo, Thomas (see Sloe)		
(a) Trustee Franklin Academy	1	296
(b) One of Commission to locate County Seat for Greenup County	3	117
Sloss, Joseph		
(a) Named in boundary of election precinct in Logan County	5	140
(b) Named in boundary of election precinct in Warren County	5	473
Smart, John		
Inspection site in South Frankfort	3	439
Smiley, Esther		
Authorized, with commissioners, to sell lands of her insane husband	5	458
Smiley, James		
(a) Promoter at Bairdstown of Ohio Canal Company	3	221
(b) One of Commission to raise by lottery a fund to open Salt River to navigation	4	249
(c) Promoter at Bairdstown of Kentucky Assurance Society	4	254
Smiley, Samuel		
One of Commission to raise by lottery a fund to open Salt River to navigation	4	249
Smith, Charles		
Delegate from Bourbon County to second Constitutional Convention (1799)	1	57
Smith, Charles, Jr.		
(a) Trustee of Charlestown (1787)	3	562
(b) Trustee of Hopewell (Paris) (1789)	3	568
Smith, Christiana		
Authorized to sue Terrence Smith for divorce	2	425
Smith, Clarke and		
Inspection at iron works on Red River in Clarke County	3	324
Smith, Enoch		
(a) Co-founder and Trustee of Mt. Sterling	1	125
(b) Trustee Montgomery Academy	2	241
Smith's Ferry, on Cumberland River		
Named as station on road from Danville to Tellico	3	275
Smith, James, deceased		
Sale of lands authorized	3	99
Smith, John		
(a) Trustee of Harrodsburg (1785)	3	552
(b) Trustee of Paris	1	188
(c) Co-founder and Trustee of Preston	1	347
(d) Inspection site at Prestonville, Gallatin County	2	456

SMITH 166

	VOL.	PAGE
(e) Commissioner for Harrison County to open South and Stoner Forks of Licking to navigation....	3	193

Smith, Jonathan
(a) Commissioner to build a section of the road from Danville to Tellico to begin at Smiths Ferry on Cumberland River 3 275
(b) Allowed pay for services at (a).............. 3 364

Smith's Mill (in Bourbon County)
Made head of navigation on Stoner Fork...... 2 455

Smith, Polly
Co-respondent Hauskins vs. Hauskins.......... 3 290

Smith, Samuel
Trustee Caledonia Academy.................. 5 3

Smith, Terrence
Christiana Smith authorized to sue him for divorce 2 425

Smith, William
(a) Trustee Rockcastle Academy................. 4 114
(b) Authorized to locate 1000 acres in Knox County 4 325
(c) Given further time at (b).................... 5 102

Smith, William Bailey
Trustee Hartford Academy.................. 2 242

Smith, William P., deceased
Sale of lands authorized..................... 3 164

Smock, Henry
Trustee Washington Academy................ 2 242

Sneed, Achilles
(a) Trustee Kentucky Seminary.................. 4 319
(b) One of Commissioners for Franklin County to survey Franklin-Woodford County line...... 5 447

Snelling, Elizabeth, deceased
Appointment of Administrators in Woodford County confirmed 3 242

Somerset Academy
Incorporated December 18, 1802 with William Fox, James Hardgrove, Robert Moderel and Jesse Richardson, Trustees 3 37

South, Benjamin
(a) One of Commission to erect a turnpike on road from Fleming County to the Big Sandy...... 4 154
(b) Authorized to sell lands of his deceased brother, John South 5 356

South, John, deceased
(a) Sale of lands authorized..................... 5 15
(b) Sale of additional lands authorized............ 5 78
(c) Benjamin South authorized to make sales....... 5 356

	VOL.	PAGE
Southgate, Richard		
Trustee Newport Academy	2	240
Spalding, Benedict, Jr.		
Co-founder Town of Lebanon	5	191
Spaun, Elizabeth		
Given ten years time to pay for Green River land	2	426
Spears, Jacob		
Commissioner for Bourbon County to open South and Stoner Forks of Licking to navigation	3	193
Spears, Solomon, deceased		
Sale of lands authorized	2	487
Speed, James		
(a) Named as boundary of New Town	1	233
(b) Trustee Madison Academy	2	241
(c) Trustee Transylvania Seminary (1783)	3	572
Speed, James, Sr.		
Trustee Danville Library	2	376
Speed, James, Jr.		
Trustee Danville Library	2	376
Speed, John		
Trustee Jefferson Seminary	2	378
Speed, Thomas		
(a) Trustee Bullitt Academy	2	243
(b) Promoter for Bairdstown of Ohio Canal Company	3	221
(c) Trustee Salem Academy	5	7
Spelman, Frank (see Spillman)		
Trustee Town of Salisberry	3	369
Spiers, William		
Balance due on headright land remitted	5	384
Spillman, Frank (see Spelman)		
Allowed credit on settlement as Sheriff of Campbell County	5	437
Spilman, James		
Trustee of Kennedysville	1	342
Spires, James G.		
Allowed pay for services as adjutant of militia	3	491
Springfield (Washington County)		
(a) Established December 7, 1793 on lands of Matthew Walton with David Caldwell, Hugh McElroy, Benjamin Harding, Daniel Mock and Josiah Wilson, Trustees	1	176
(b) Additional land included therein	4	47
Sprotzman, John (see Protzman)		
Purchaser from Lawrence Sprotzman of his rights in Townsite of Paris	1	356

Sprotzman, Lawrence (see Protzman)
  (a) Town of Hopewell (Paris) established on his lands (1789) 3   568
  (b) Inspection site at Paris (1790) 3   584
  (c) Inspection site at Paris 2   140

Sproul, Alexander
  Voting place at house in Cumberland County.. 3   487

Spurgin, Samuel
  Co-founder of Mt. Sterling 1   125

Stafford's Landing
  Inspection site in Clarke County 1   135

Standeford, David
  One of Commission to sell, and adjust claims respecting lots in Louisville 3   547

Standiford, David
  (a) Trustee of Shelbyville 1   151
  (b) One of Commissioners for Shelby County to survey Shelby-Henry County line 5   103
  (c) Same as (b) 5   330

Standiford, George
  Trustee of Falmouth 1   181

Standiford, James
  Trustee of New Town 1   233

Stanford
  (a) Established in 1786 on lands of Benjamin Logan with Benjamin Logan, John Logan, William Montgomery, Henry Pauling, Isaac Shelby, Walker Baylor and Alexander Blane, Trustees 3   558
  (b) James Davidson, Francis S. Reed, Thomas Helm, Michael Davidson and Benjamin Monroe, appointed Trustees 5   166

Stanford Academy
  (a) Incorporated December 22, 1798 with Nathan Huston, Hugh Logan, Richard Gains, George Davidson, Samuel Finly, William Owsley, Samuel Moore, Jonathan Forbes and John James, Trustees 2   240
  (b) William Logan, Joseph Wilch, Thomas Montgomery, Richard Gaines, Samuel Shackleford, James T. Worthington, George McRoberts, William Davis and Francis S. Reed, appointed Trustees 3   334

Stanford Library Company
  Incorporated January 21, 1817 by David Logan, William Forbis, Joseph Paxton, Thomas Helm and Michael Davidson 5   455

	VOL.	PAGE
Stansberry, Benjamin		
Trustee of Shepherdsville	1	183
Stapp, Gholston		
Inspection site on Cumberland River	2	456
Starling, William		
Promoter at Frankfort of Lexington and Louisville Turnpike Road Company	5	519
Starrat, Thomas		
One of Commission to open Big Barren River to navigation	4	116
Steele, Adam		
(a) Promoter at Shelbyville of Ohio Canal Company	3	221
(b) Incorporator of Ohio Canal Company	3	260
(c) Promoter at Shelbyville of Bank of Kentucky	3	391
(d) Promoter at Shelbyville of Lexington and Louisville Turnpike Road Company	5	519
Steele, Andrew		
Trustee of Lexington	3	549
Steele, John		
Trustee Salem Academy	3	580
Steel's Mill		
Made terminus of navigation on Little River in Christian County	5	259
Steele, Moses		
(a) Trustee Logan Academy	3	206
(b) Removed from County—successor at (a) appointed	3	277
Steele, Richard		
(a) Trustee Lexington Seminary	2	108
(b) Promoter at Louisville of Lexington and Louisville Turnpike Road Company	5	519
Steel, Robert		
Trustee Transylvania University	2	234
Steele, William		
(a) Delegate from Woodford County to second Contitutional Convention (1799)	1	58
(b) Trustee Woodford Academy	2	241
(c) Promoter for Woodford County of Kentucky River Navigation Company	2	448
(d) Trustee Woodford Academy	3	181
(e) One of Commissioners for Woodford County to survey Woodford-Franklin County line	5	447
(f) Terminus of ferry across Kentucky River at Stone Lick (1785)	3	586
(g) Trustee of Lexington (1782)	3	549

STEIVIS 170

	VOL.	PAGE

Steivis, Reuben
    Allowed compensation for two drums furnished
        the 8th Regiment in 1793................. 4   259
Stennett, Charles
    Voting place at house in Washington County... 5   425
Stephens, James
    Trustee of Winchester..................... 1   340
Stephens, John
    State price of land remitted................ 5   490
Stephens, Joseph L.
    Commissioner for Bourbon County to open South
        and Stoner Fork of Licking to navigation.... 3   193
Stephens, Luther
    Incorporator of Fayette Paper Manufacturing
        Company 5   409
Stephens, Richard
    Inspection site in Nelson County.............. 1   370
Stephens, William
    (a) Trustee Town of Salisberry................ 3   369
    (b) Authorized to sue for divorce on special grounds 5   54
Stephenson, John
    (a) Allowed pay for spy service................ 2   358
    (b) Inspection site in Lewis County.............. 3   452
Stephenson's Cooper Shop
    Named in a boundary in Louisville............ 5   321
Sterling, William, Jr.
    One of Commission to open Kentucky River at
        Frankfort to navigation................... 5   390
Stevenson, Job
    Promoter at Georgetown of Lexington and Louisville Turnpike Road Company.............. 5   520
Stewart, James
    Inspection site in Warren County............. 2   279
Stewart, Levi
    Given time to complete bridge in Montgomery
        County on road from Mt. Sterling to the Big
        Sandy 3   512
Stewart, William, devisees
    Owners of a ferry landing in Franklin County.. 1   225
Stewart, William
    He and James Crawford and Solomon Tabor
        authorized to locate 1000 acres in Barren
        County to include a salt spring............ 5   202
Stewart, Major William
    Voting place at house in Hopkins County...... 4   328

	VOL.	PAGE
Stewart, Williby		
Named in Nicholas-Harrison County boundary..	5	366
Stidger, Peter (see Stiger)		
(a) Costs in suit against him allowed William Rogers	2	486
(b) Warrant issued for costs of William Rogers at (a)	3	193
Stiger, Peter		
Ordered to account for arms delivered to him to be repaired	2	354
Stiggall, William		
Given time to perfect patent	4	317
Stillwell, Delilah		
Daniel Stillwell authorized to sue her in Nelson County for divorce	3	512
Stillwell, Daniel		
See Delilah Stillwell		
Stites, John, Jr.		
Trustee Newcastle Library Company	4	35
Stith, Baldwin B.		
Trustee Franklin Academy	3	255
Stith, Benjamin		
Named in boundary of election precinct in Hardin County	4	225
Stith, John		
Named in boundary of election precinct in Hardin County	4	225
Stockden, George (see Stockton)		
Trustee Fleming Academy	2	241
Stockdon, John		
Promoter at Flemingsburg of Ohio Canal Company	3	222
Stockton, George (see Stockden)		
(a) Delegate from Fleming County to second Constitutional Convention (1799)	1	58
(b) Trustee Franklin Academy	1	296
(c) Founder of Flemingsburg	5	187
Stockton, George, Sr.		
(a) Commissioner for Fleming County to survey road from Paris to mouth of Big Sandy	3	461
(b) Lost plat of Flemingsburg to be replaced	4	358
Stokes, Young		
Paid wages due for clearing road to Cumberland Gap	2	164
Stone, Barton W.		
Trustee Bourbon Academy	2	240
Storey, William		
Trustee Georgetown Library	2	376

STORM 172

	VOL.	PAGE
Storm, Leonard		
Inspection site in Muhlenberg County	2	383
Stout, Benjamin		
Director Vineyard Society of Lexington	2	268
Stratton, Aaron		
Trustee Lewis Academy	4	17
Strode, John		
Trustee of Winchester	1	187
Strode, Samuel		
Named as boundary of Lewisbourgh	1	295
Strong, Mrs. ——		
Named in boundary of public square in Danville	5	480
Strother, John		
Authorized, with Samuel Gill, to survey 102,912 acres in Jefferson County	3	100
Stroud, Isaac		
Named in boundary of election precinct in Christian County	4	225
Stuart, Archibald		
Commissioner for Virginia to locate state boundary line	2	276
Stubblefield, Thomas		
One of Commission to open Mud River to navigation	4	338
Stubbs, Robert		
Trustee Newport Academy	2	240
Stuckley, John		
Trustee Town of Jefferson	2	380
Sturgus, Robert A.		
Required to report settlement made with Directors of the Wilderness Road	5	199
Sudduth, William		
(a) Delegate from Clarke County to second Constitutional Convention (1799)	1	58
(b) Trustee Winchester Academy	2	217
Sugg, Simon		
Named in boundary of election precinct in Hopkins County	4	328
Sullenger, Robert		
Inspection site in Henry County	2	457
Sullivan, James		
Trustee of Campbell Town	3	554
Sullivan, William, deceased		
Estate given a credit in settlement as Deputy Sheriff of Jefferson County	4	,60

	VOL.	PAGE

Sullivan, Wilson
  Granted change of venue from Floyd to Clarke
    County on trial for murder.................. 5   353

Summers, Agnes
  Allowed compensation for horse taken from her
    husband, John Summers, on Wabash Expedition in 1786............................. 3   94

Summers, Benjamin
  (a) Trustee Bullitt Academy..................... 2   243
  (b) Trustee Bullitt Academy..................... 3   478

Summers, Caleb
  Named in boundary of election precinct in Boone
    County................................. 3   488

Summers, John
  See Agnes Summers.

Summers, Richard
  Trustee Bullitt Academy..................... 2   243

Summers, William
  Trustee Bullitt Academy..................... 2   243

Sumrall, John
  Promoter at Maysville of Maysville and Lexington Turnpike Road Company............... 5   536

Sutton, David
  Authorized to erect grist mill at Todds Ferry on
    Kentucky River in Madison County......... 3   354

Swearingen, Thomas
  Trustee Newton Academy.................... 3   409

Swegit, James
  Trustee Liberty Academy.................... 4   114

Sweney, Job
  Trustee Liberty Academy.................... 4   114

Swigate, James
  Justices of Casey County to meet at his house... 3   326

Sypes, George
  Voting place at house in Hardin County....... 5   473

Tabor, Pardon
  Named in boundary of election precinct in Ohio
    County................................. 4   416

Tabor, Solomon
  He and James Crawford and William Stewart
    authorized to locate 1000 acres in Barren
    County to include a salt spring............ 5   202

Tabue, Daniel
  See Trabue

TADLOCK 174

	VOL.	PAGE

Tadlock, Ann
    John Tadlock authorized to sue her in Mercer County for divorce, she having deserted him and assigned as a reason that her former husband, James Harrod, was living when she married Tadlock............................ 3   196

Tadlock, John
    See Ann Tadlock

Talbot, Daniel
    Promoter at Millersburg of Maysville and Lexington Turnpike Road Company............ 5   536

Talbot, Edmund
    (a) Error in patent corrected.................... 4   212
    (b) Error in certificate and patent of headright land in Henderson County corrected............. 5   304

Talbot, Edward
    Trustee Shelby Library Company............. 4   89

Talbott, Isham
    Trustee Kentucky Seminary.................. 2   492

Tall, Jonathan
    Tax Commissioner of Wayne County.......... 2   492

Tamplin, Terah (see Templin)
    Trustee Kentucky Academy.................. 1   228

Tandy, Gabriel
    One of Commission to raise by lottery a fund to erect a Grand Masonic Hall in Lexington..... 5   181

Tarent, Carter
    Trustee Gallatin Academy................... 5   13

Taul, Micah and Company
    Authorized to locate iron ore land............. 3   531

Taylor, ——
    Named in boundary of Louisville.............. 3   540

Taylor, Benjamin
    One of Commission to open Kentucky River at Frankfort to navigation.................... 5   390

Taylor, Chapman
    Inspection site in Logan County............... 3   124

Taylor, Creed
    Commissioner for Virginia to locate boundary line 2   276

Taylor, Edmund, deceased
    (a) Sales of lands confirmed..................... 1   170
    (b) Guardian of infant heirs authorized to compromise disputes concerning lands in Campbell County 3   463

                                                                    TAYLOR
                                                              VOL.   PAGE
Taylor, Edmund
  (a) Promoter at Newport of Ohio Canal Company..   3   221
  (b) Trustee of Boonesborough (1779).............   3   538
  (c) Trustee Transylvania Seminary (1783)........   3   572
  (d) Trustee Seminary lands (1780)...............   3   571

Taylor's Ferry (Cumberland River)
  Named in boundary of election precinct in Cumberland County........................   4   328

Taylor, Francis
  (a) Trustee Franklin Academy...................   3   255
  (b) Incorporator Washington Library Company (Mason County)........................   4   273
  (c) One of Commission to raise by lottery a fund to improve the road from Maysville to the Town of Washington..........................   4   279

Taylor, George
  Sales by him of lands of Edmund Taylor, deceased, were confirmed.....................   1   170

Taylor, Harrison
  (a) Trustee Hartford Academy...................   2   242
  (b) Trustee Hartford Academy...................   3   278

Taylor, Hubbard
  Trustee Winchester Academy.................   2   217

Taylor, James
  (a) Newport established on his lands..............   1   280
  (b) Trustee Newport Academy...................   2   240
  (c) Inspection site in Newport...................   2   280

Taylor, Jonathan
  (a) Trustee Jefferson Academy...................   3   207
  (b) Inspection site in Henderson County...........   3   324
  (c) Inspection site in Hopkins County............   3   450
  (d) Trustee Union Academy.....................   5   80

Taylor, Richard
  (a) Delegate from Jefferson County to second Constitutional Convention (1799)..............   1   58
  (b) Inspection site in Shelby County..............   1   370
  (c) Inspection site in Shelby County..............   2   278
  (d) Given time to complete wall around penitentiary   2   365
  (e) Claim for pointing penitentiary walls allowed..   2   484
  (f) Allowed compensation as Sergeant at Arms of the House of Representatives...............   3   174
  (g) One of Commission to erect a State House......   5   123
  (h) One of Commission to settle accounts at the penitentiary   5   276
  (i) Trustee of Campbell Town (1785)............   3   554

TAYLOR 176

	VOL.	PAGE

Taylor, Richard, Jr.
  Promoter at Frankfort of Lexington and Louisville Turnpike Road Company.............. 5 519
Taylor, Robert
  Incorporator of Washington Library Company (Mason County)......................... 4 273
Taylor, Samuel
  (a) Delegate from Mercer County to second Constitutional Convention (1799)................. 1 58
  (b) Trustee Harrodsburg Academy............... 2 240
  (c) One of Commission to have State House repaired 3 509
  (d) Trustee of Harrodsburg (1785)............... 3 552
Taylor, Thompson
  Granted change of venue from Bullitt to Nelson County, on trial for murder................ 3 465
Taylor, William
  (a) Trustee Salem Academy (1788)............... 3 580
  (b) Trustee Jefferson Seminary................... 2 108
  (c) One of Commission to sell, and adjust claims respecting, lots in Louisville (1786)........... 3 545
  (d) One of Commissioners for Shelby County to survey Shelby-Henry County line.............. 5 103
Teague, William
  Granted a change of venue................... 5 202
Tebbs, John
  (a) Named in boundary of Town of Washington (1790) 3 556
  (b) Claimant of part of townsite of Washington.... 1 201
  (c) Rights to town site of Washington recognized... 2 396
Tegarden, George
  Trustee of Lexington 1 577
Telfair, Isaac, deceased
  Sale of lands on Dicks River authorized........ 2 221
Temple, Lieutenant Colonel
  Empowered to appoint surveyors (1783)...... 1 442
Temple, Benjamin
  Trustee Woodford Academy.................. 3 181
Templin, Tarah (see Tamplin)
  Trustee Salem Academy..................... 3 580
Teter, Robert
  Trustee Newcastle Library Company.......... 4 35
Thacker, Daniel
  Tavern named in boundary of election precinct in Campbell County...................... 3 413
Theobald, James
  (a) Voting place at house in Pendleton County..... 3 414
  (b) Voting place at house in Pendleton County..... 5 335

	VOL.	PAGE

Thomas, Edmund
  (a) Appointed to obtain original land title papers from Virginia 1   652
  (b) Given further time at (a) 2   181
Thomas, Edmund, deceased
  Estate allowed $400.00 for services—see Edmund Thomas (a) 3   245
Thomas, Elizabeth
  Richard M. Thomas authorized to sue her in Woodford County for divorce 3   446
Thomas, Isaac
  Trustee Grayson Seminary 5   325
Thomas, Jack
  Trustee Grayson Seminary 5   325
Thomas, John
  (a) His plat of Danville confirmed 2   178
  (b) Trustee Harrodsburg Academy 2   240
Thomas, John P.
  Error in settlement corrected 4   134
Thomas, Philemon
  (a) Delegate from Mason County to second Constitutional Convention (1799) 1   58
  (b) Commissioners named to partition land held jointly with Lewis Craig and John and Mary May, infant heirs of John May, deceased 1   113
  (c) Trustee Franklin Academy 1   296
  (d) Founder of Germantown 1   329
  (e) Title to site of Germantown granted 1   653
  (f) Inspection site in Boone County 2   384
  (g) One of Commission to locate County Seat of Greenup County 3   117
Thomas, Richard M.
  Authorized to sue Elizabeth Thomas in Woodford County for divorce 3   446
Thomas, Rowland
  (a) Commissioner to bring from Virginia title papers affecting lands in forks of Big Sandy 3   58
  (b) Trustee Lewis Academy 4   17
  (c) Trustee Newcastle Library Company 4   35
  (d) Trustee Henry Academy 5   134
Thompson, George
  (a) Trustee Harrodsburg Academy 2   240
  (b) Trustee of the seminary lands 3   571
Thompson, George, deceased
  Sale of lands authorized 5   510

THOMPSON 178

	VOL.	PAGE

Thompson, James
  (a) Trustee Kentucky Academy................. 1   228
  (b) Appointed Commissioner to locate military lands
      on head of Green River.................... 1   349
  (c) Named in Lincoln-Madison County boundary... 1   627
  (d) Allowed compensation for running line from
      Green River to Cumberland Mountain, see (b) 2   182
  (e) Trustee Lancaster Academy.................. 2   242
  (f) Voting place at house in Christian County..... 4   329

Thompson, John
  (a) Trustee Jefferson Seminary.................. 2   108
  (b) Trustee Georgetown Library.................. 2   376

Thompson, Rodes
  Trustee of Georgetown (1790)................. 3   570

Thrasher, John, Sr.
  Trustee of Wilmington....................... 1   175

Thrasher, Stephen
  Trustee Pendleton Academy................... 5   174

Threlkeld, Daniel
  Voting place at house in Bracken County...... 4   242

Throckmorton, John
  Inspection site in Nicholas County............ 3   243

Throckmorton, Thomas
  Named in Nicholas-Harrison County boundary. 5   366

Thruston, B.
  Delegate from Fayette County to second Constitutional Convention (1799)................. 1   58

Thruston, Buckner
  (a) Trustee Transylvania University.............. 2   234
  (b) Commissioner to locate Kentucky-Virginia state
      boundary 2   276
  (c) Trustee of Louisville (1789).................. 3   547

Thruston, Charles Minn
  Trustee of Boonesborough (1779)............. 3   538

Thruston, John
  Trustee Jefferson Seminary................... 2   108

Thurman, Benjamin
  One of Commission to open road from Knox
  Court House to Pulaski; his land also a land
  mark on said road......................... 3   464

Thurman, John
  (a) Trustee of Kennedysville..................... 1   342
  (b) Turnpike keeper on Wilderness Road.......... 2   162
  (c) Error in patent corrected.................... 3   465

Thurman, Richard
  Trustee of Greensburg....................... 1   273

	VOL.	PAGE

Thurston, Robert
Trustee Henry Academy.................... 5 134
Thweatt, Thomas
Authorized to survey 1000 acres on Green River in consideration of service in the Revolutionary War............................ 2 358
Tibbs, Diskin
Inspection site on Green River............... 3 514
Tibbs, John
See John Tebbs (c)......................... 2 396
Tilford, James
Given time to settle as Sheriff of Mercer County 3 161
Tilford, John
(a) One of Commission to raise by lottery a fund to erect a Grand Masonic Hall in Lexington.... 5 181
(b) Incorporator of Lexington White Lead Manufacturing Company....................... 5 204
(c) Promoter at Lexington of Lexington and Louisville Turnpike Road Company.............. 5 519
Tilhart, Philip
Trustee Town of Jefferson.................... 2 380
Tilton, Richard
Trustee Fleming Academy.................... 2 241
Todd, Andrew
(a) Trustee Bourbon Academy.................. 2 237
(b) Trustee Bourbon Academy.................. 2 242
Todd, Bernard
Title of Walker Daniel to 23,692 acres in Fayette County, assigned to him by Todd in 1782, was perfected 4 133
Todd, David
One of Commission to locate County Seat for Bath County............................. 4 215
Todd, James
Trustee Manchester Academy................. 4 18
Todd, John
Trustee of Lexington (1782)................. 3 549
Trustee of Seminary Lands (1780)............ 3 571
Todd, John, Jr.
Trustee of Louisville (1780)................. 3 540
Todd, Levi
(a) Trustee Seminary Lands (1780).............. 3 571
(b) Trustee Transylvania Seminary (1783)........ 3 572
(c) Trustee Transylvania University.............. 2 234
Todd, Robert, deceased
(a) Sale of lands authorized.................... 1 114
(b) Vacancy in Trustees at (a) filled............. 2 425

TODD 180

	VOL.	PAGE

Todd, Robert
  Acts as Commissioner to replace Fayette Burnt
    Records confirmed 3   154
Todd, Samuel
  Reimbursed for flour and whiskey impressed for
    the Wabash Expedition.................... 3   95
Todd, Thomas
  (a) Clerk first Constitutional Convention.......... 1   38
  (b) Trustee of Frankfort........................ 1   247
  (c) One of Commission to erect jail at Frankfort... 1   263
  (d) Trustee Kentucky Seminary.................. 2   389
  (e) Promoter for Franklin County of Kentucky
        River Navigation Company................ 2   448
Tompkins, Christopher
  Trustee Robertson Academy.................. 5   125
Tompkins, William
  (a) Permitted to withdraw a survey and plat...... 2   213
  (b) Incorporator Louisville Library Company
        (Name spelled Tomkins)................... 5   360
Toulmin, Harry
  (a) Commissioner to locate settlers on lands south
        of Green River........................... 2   290
  (b) Secretary to Governor Garrard (1798)......... 4   534
Tousey, Zerah
  Inspection site in Boone County............... 3   451
Towles, Lieutenant Colonel
  Empowered to appoint surveyors (1783)...... 1   442
Townsend, James
  Trustee Union Academy..................... 5   80
Townsend, Thomas
  Authorized to survey land in Madison on which
    he had settled........................... 4   336
Trabue, Daniel
  (a) Trustee New Athens Academy................ 2   242
  (b) Named in Adair-Green County line (as Tabue). 2   430
  (c) Refunded over-payment in settlement as Sheriff
        of Adair County........................ 4   394
Transylvania Presbytery
  To control Kentucky Academy............... 1   229
Transylvania Seminary
  (a) Created by Act of May, 1780, by which the
        escheated lands of Robert McKenzie, Henry
        Collins, and Alexander McKie, British sub-
        jects, were vested in William Fleming, William
        Christian, John Todd, Stephen Trigg, Benja-
        min Logan, John Floyd, John May, Levi Todd,
        John Cowan, George Meriwether, John Cobbs,

	VOL.	PAGE
George Thompson, and Edmund Taylor, as Trustees for a seminary...................	3	571
(b) By Act of May, 1783, Transylvania Seminary was incorporated and the lands at (a) were vested in its Trustees, who were William Fleming, William Christian, Benjamin Logan, John May, Levi Todd, John Cowan, Edmund Taylor, Thomas Marshall, Samuel McDowell, John Bowman, George Rogers Clark, John Campbell, Isaac Shelby, David Rice, John Edwards, Caleb Wallace, Walker Daniel, Isaac Cox, Robert Johnston, John Craig, John Mosby, James Speed, Christopher Greenup, John Crittenden and Willis Green..........	3	572
(c) Kentucky Academy merged with it under name of Transylvania University and James Garrard, Samuel McDowell, Cornelius Beatty, Frederick Ridgeley, Robert Marshall, George Nicholas, James Crawford, Joseph Crockett, Bartlett Collins, Andrew McCalla, William Morton, Robert Steel, John McDowell, Alexander Parker, Caleb Wallace, James Trotter, Levi Todd, James Blythe, Thomas Lewis, John Bradford and Buckner Thruston appointed Trustees	2	234

Traver's Mill
Named in boundary of election precinct in Logan County 5 140

Treacle, Stephen
(a) Trustee Town of Washington................. 1 199
(b) Trustee Town of Washington................. 2 393

Trew, Thomas
Authorized to erect a mill on Green River in Green County 3 356

Trigg, Haydon
Appointed to survey road from Greensburg to the Tennessee line........................ 3 21

Trigg, Stephen
(a) Trustee Seminary lands (1780)............... 3 571
(b) Trustee of Louisville (1780)................ 3 540
(c) One of Commission to raise by lottery a fund to open Kentucky River to navigation......... 4 318
(d) Trustee Town of Irvine.................... 4 339

Trigg, William
(a) Trustee Town of Preston................... 1 347
(b) Authorized to employ caretaker for State House 1 650
(c) Incorporator of Frankfort Bridge Company.... 2 304

TRIMBLE

	VOL.	PAGE
(d) Incorporator of Frankfort Bridge Company No. 2	4	138
(e) Trustee Kentucky Seminary	2	389
(f) One of Commission to open new channel for Kentucky River at Fish Trap Island below Frankfort	3	121
(g) Promoter at Frankfort of Ohio Canal Company	3	221
(h) Promoter at Frankfort of Bank of Kentucky	3	390
(i) Trustee Kentucky Seminary	4	319
(j) One of Commission to settle accounts at the penitentiary	5	296

Trimble, James, deceased
Authorized sale of lands to pay debt due Marquis Calmes 3   243

Trimble, Robert
Trustee Paris Library........................... 3   455

Triplett, Francis
Granted change of venue from Montgomery to Bourbon on trial for shooting Daniel Connor, but died before he could be tried........... 4   163

Triplett, William
Trustee Town of Lewisbourgh................. 1   295

Trotter, George, Jr.
(a) Incorporator of Lexington White Lead Manufacturing Company 5   204
(b) Incorporator of Lexington Manufacturing Company 5   251

Trotter, James
(a) Trustee Transylvania University.............. 2   234
(b) Trustee Lexington Library Association........ 2   375
(c) Promoter for Fayette County of Kentucky River Navigation Company 2   448
(d) One of Commission to open a road from Paris or Mt. Sterling to the Big Sandy............ 3   4
(e) Acts as Commissioner to replace Fayette Burnt Records confirmed 3   154

Trotter, Samuel
(a) Incorporator of Lexington White Lead Manufacturing Company....................... 5   204
(b) Incorporator of Lexington Manufacturing Company 5   251

Troutman, Michael
Trustee of Shepherdsville 1   183

Trumbo, ——
Inspection site in Montgomery County......... 3   123

Tully, Christiana
Given time to pay for Green River land........ 2   427

	VOL.	PAGE

Tully, Samuel
    One of Commission to build a bridge over North
        Elkhorn in Scott County.................. 4   88

Tuly, Lieut. Charles P.
    Commander on a tour of duty................ 3   408

Tuly, William
    Certificate for military services by him ordered
        paid to Philip Bush, assignee............... 3   408

Tunstall, Thomas
    (a) Trustee Kentucky Academy.................. 2   389
    (b) Authorized to build a bridge over Kentucky
        River at Frankfort 3   306

Turner, Fielding L.
    Trustee Lexington Library Association......... 2   375

Turner, James
    Inspection site in Green County............... 3   332

Turner, Richard
    Allowed commissions for levying executions
        against William Morrow.................... 3   97

Turpin, Edmund
    Allowed pay for guarding families moving
        through Cumberland Gap in 1786.......... 3   407

Turpin, Thomas
    (a) Inspection site in Woodford County........... 1   370
    (b) Inspection site in Woodford County........... 3   437

Twyman, Reuben
    Trustee Woodford Academy.................. 3   181

Tyler, John
    Justices of Butler County to meet at his house 4   111

Tyler, Levi
    Incorporator of Louisville Hospital........... 5   574

Underwood, Captain
    A Chickasaw Indian—relief of 2   365

Union Academy
    Incorporated January 19, 1814 with Robert
        Gilchrist, Jonathan Taylor, James Gray,
        James Townsend, Hugh W. Robb, and Joseph
        Reives, Trustees 5   80

Union County
    Formed May 1, 1811 from Henderson County.. 4   213

Upton, John, deceased
    Forfeiture of title by his heirs for non-payment
        of taxes was waived...................... 4   12

Vance, John
    Trustee of Falmouth....................... 1   181

Vance, Joseph (an alien)
    Escheat of his lands waived................. 3   272

VANHOOK 184

	VOL.	P
Vanhook, Archelaus		
Given time to settle as Sheriff of Nicholas County	5	4
Vanmatree, Jacob		
One of Commission to open Nolinn Creek in Hardin County to navigation...............	4	2
Vanmetre, Jacob		
Pay allowed for spy service..................	2	3
Vanmetre, Morgan		
Trustee of Cynthiana	1	1
Van Pelt, John		
Trustee Town of Port William...............	1	3
Van Pradelles, Cassandra Deye		
Granted privileges of a *feme sole*..............	3	1
Vantreese, John		
Trustee Hardin Academy....................	2	2
Vanwinkle, Abraham, and		
Vanwinkle, John		
Named in boundary of election precinct in Wayne County	5	
Vaughn, Ensign		
Allowed fee for escort of witness...............	1	2
Vawter, William		
(a) Trustee Woodford Academy.................	2	2
(b) Trustee Woodford Academy.................	3	1
Ver Bryke, Lawrence, deceased		
Sale of lands in Mercer County authorized......	3	1
Vernon, William S.		
Incorporator of Louisville Hospital............	5	5
Versailles		
(a) Established June 22, 1792 on lands of Hezekiah Briscoe, with John Watkins, Richard Young, Cave Johnson, Marquis Calmes, Richard Fox, John Cooke, and Parmenas Briscoe, Trustees.	1	
(b) John O'Bannon, John Crittenden, William Whittington and John Jimms, appointed trustees to fill vacancies...........................	1	3!
(c) Lottery authorized to drain pond.............	1	6!
(d) John O'Bannon authorized to erect a grist mill on public spring..........................	3	1!
Versailles Library Company		
Incorporated January 31, 1812 by William B. Blackburn, John McKinney, Jr., Nathaniel Hart, William B. Long and Joseph Kincaid..	4	3!
Vertner, Daniel		
(a) Trustee Town of Washington.................	2	3!
(b) Promoter at Town of Washington of Bank of Kentucky	3	3!

VINEYARD SOCIETY

	VOL.	PAGE
Vineyard Society, of Lexington		
Incorporated November 21, 1799 by Samuel Brown, John A. Seitz, Peter D. Roberts, Andrew Holmes, William Leavy, Alexander Parker, Thomas Bodley, John Bradford, Robert Patterson, Walker Baylor, Benjamin Stout and James Hughes..........................	2	268
Virginia		
(a) Appointment of Commissioners to survey boundary line authorized..........................	1	348
(b) Report of Commissioners, Archibald Stuart, General Joseph Martin and Creed Taylor, and John Coburn, Robert Johnson and Buckner Thruston, for Kentucky, adopted	2	276
Voorhies, Peter G.		
(a) Allowed pay for sundry services...............	3	489
(b) One of Commissioners for Franklin County to survey Franklin-Woodford County line......	5	447
Voris, John		
Administratrix of William Downing authorized to convey land to him.....................	1	359
Wadlington, Ferdinand (see Wardlington)		
Trustee Christian Academy..................	5	450
Wakefield, A. M.		
Trustee New Athens Seminary................	3	302
Wakefield, Allen M.		
Judge Circuit Court Eighth District...........	3	507
Wakefield, Allen M., deceased		
Acts of administratrix confirmed.............	4	163
Walker, David		
(a) Inspection site at Eddyville................	2	213
(b) Trustee to locate settlers on lands south of Green River	2	290
Walker, George		
(a) Promoter for Jessamine County of Kentucky River Navigation Company................	2	448
(b) Granted 124 acres Rockcastle County.........	5	131
Walker, Jacob W.		
Trustee Allen Seminary.....................	5	433
Walker, James		
(a) Appointed manager of Wilderness Road.......	5	197
(b) Authorized to install ferry on Wilderness Road over Rockcastle River.....................	5	313
Walker, James, deceased		
Settlement of his accounts as Manager of Wilderness Road ordered made...................	5	577

WALKER 186

	VOL.	PAGE
Walker, James, Sr.		
Justices of Adair County to meet at his house..	2	430
Walker, John		
Trustee Allen Seminary	5	433
Walker, John M.		
Trustee Caledonia Academy	5	2
Walker, John W., deceased		
Sale of lands in Madison County authorized....	4	282
Walker's Line		
Confirmed as Virginia-Carolina State boundary line (1791)	1	463
Walker, Robert		
Trustee of Mt. Sterling	1	125
Walker, Saunders		
Allowed compensation for clearing road to Cumberland Gap	2	164
Walker, William		
(a) Granted reward for capturing Thomas Hopper, who had escaped from the penitentiary	3	414
(b) Trustee Lewis Academy	4	17
(c) Charged with murder of John Coffman	4	148
Walker, William, deceased		
Sale of land in Woodford County authorized...	2	178
Wall, John		
(a) Commissioner to open South Fork of Licking to navigation	1	193
(b) Trustee Harrison Academy	2	241
(c) Commissioner for Harrison County to open South and Stoner Forks of Licking to navigation	3	193
Wall, John, Sr.		
Trustee of Cynthiana	1	179
Wallace, Caleb		
(a) Trustee of Frankfort	3	557
(b) Trustee Transylvania Seminary	3	572
(c) Delegate from Woodford County to second Constitutional Convention (1799)	1	58
(d) Trustee Kentucky Academy	1	228
(e) One of Commission to locate penitentiary	2	15
(f) Trustee Transylvania University	2	234
(g) Trustee Woodford Academy	2	243
(h) Trustee Lexington Library Association	2	375
Wallace, Robert		
Named in boundary of election precinct in Wayne County	5	35

	VOL.	PAGE
Wallace, Thomas		
Promoter for Fayette County of Kentucky River Navigation Company	2	448
Wallace, William		
(a) Trustee Logan Academy	3	206
(b) Judge Circuit Court Seventh District	3	507
Waller, Edward		
(a) Trustee Town of Washington (1786)	3	555
(b) Trustee of Hopewell (Paris) (1789)	3	568
Waller, John		
(a) Co-founder of Falmouth	1	181
(b) Reference to (a)	5	583
Waller, Pomphrett, deceased		
Sale of lands authorized	5	584
Walton, Matthew		
(a) Trustee Salem Academy (1788)	3	580
(b) Inspection site in Nelson County (1789)	3	583
(c) Springfield, in Washington County, established on his lands	1	176
(d) Inspection site in Nelson County	2	139
(e) Trustee Washington Academy	2	242
(f) Trustee Washington Academy	5	15
(g) Inspection site in Bullitt County	2	279
(h) Surveyor of road from Springfield toward Frankfort	3	22
(i) Richard Berry named in his stead at (h)	3	203
Wand, Thomas		
Authorized to erect mill dam on Green River	3	330
Ward, David L.		
(a) Trustee Jefferson Academy	3	207
(b) Trustee Jefferson Academy	3	490
Ward, Isaac		
Sale of land descended to him authorized	5	510
Ward, James		
(a) Trustee Montgomery Academy	2	241
(b) One of Commission to open road from Licking River to the Big Sandy	3	350
(c) Given credit on account of error in settlement as Sheriff of Montgomery County	3	364
Ward, John		
One of Commission to extend Short Street in Winchester, to Water Street	4	379
Ward, Mary		
(a) Authorized to re-survey 50 acres on Big Benson	5	56
(b) Donated 50 acres in Knox County	5	553
Ward, Sarah, deceased		
Sale of lands authorized	5	459

	VOL.	PAGE

Ward, Washington
   Promoter at Paris of Maysville and Lexington
      Turnpike Road Company 5   536
Ward, William
   (a) Claimant of part of site of Town of Washington 1   201
   (b) Claim at (a) recognized 2   396
   (c) Trustee Kentucky Academy 1   228
   (d) Trustee Franklin Academy 1   296
   (e) Named in boundary of Town of Washington (1790) 3   556
Ward, William, deceased
   Sale of lands authorized 5   325
Wardlington, Ferdinand (see Wadlington)
   Voting place at house in Christian County 4   225
Waring, Francis
   Commissioner for Greenup County to survey road from Paris to mouth of the Big Sandy 3   461
Waring, Francis, Sr.
   Trustee Greenup Academy 4   128
Waring, Thomas
   Trustee Franklin Academy 1   296
Warren County
   (a) Formed March 1, 1797 from Logan County 1   369
   (b) Allen County, in part, carved from 5   157
   (c) Part of Allen County added to 5   348
   (d) Barren County, in part, carved from 2   222
Warren, James
   Trustee of Perryville 5   454
Warren, Thomas
   Trustee of Charlestown 3   562
Warren, William
   Trustee Rittenhouse Academy 2   240
Warwick, Town of (Mercer County)
   Established in 1787 on lands of Walter Beall, with Hugh Magary, Thomas Allen, Benjamin Bell, Christopher Greenup, Samuel McAfee and Stephen Arnold, Trustees 3   563
Washburn, Philip
   Trustee Washington Academy 2   242
Washington, Town of (Mason County)
   (a) Established in 1790 in (then) Bourbon County, with Edmund Lyne, Henry Lee, Miles W. Conway, Arthur Fox, Robert Rankin, John Gutridge, William Lamb, Alexander D. Orr, Thomas Sloe, and Richard Corwine, Trustees 3   555

WASHINGTON ACADEMY

	VOL.	PAGE
(b) John Gutridge, Thomas Foreman, John Johnson, Edward Harris, John Rogers, George Lewis, David Brodrick, George Wood, Joseph Allen, David Davis, Joseph McCullough and Stephen Treacle appointed Trustees (1793)	1	199
(c) Edward Harris, Sr., John Johnston, Benjamin Bayles, David Davis, Daniel Vertner, William Heddleston, Samuel Baldwin, Stephen Treacle and Lewis Moore appointed Trustees (1800)	2	393

Washington Academy (Washington County)
(a) Incorporated December 22, 1798 with Felix Grundy, Matthew Walton, Benjamin Hardin, Thomas Kyle, Samuel Overton, John Helm, John Reed, Barnabas McHenry, John Lancaster, Philip Washburn, Henry Robert Able, Charles Ewing and Charles Wickliff, Trustees ... 2 ... 242
(b) Matthew Walton, John Reid, Barnabas McHenry, Elias Davidson, John Calhoon, Stephen Cocke and Paul J. Booker appointed Trustees (1813) ... 5 ... 15

Washington County
Formed September 1, 1792 from Nelson County ... 1 ... 628

Washington Library Company
Incorporated, in Town of Washington January 31, 1811 by Bazil Duke, Robert Taylor, Francis Taylor, Mann Butler, and Adam Beatty ... 4 ... 273

Washington, William Augustine
Error in patent corrected ... 3 ... 514

Washingtonian Library Company (Shelbyville)
Incorporated January 31, 1812 by John Willett, James Simrall, Wingfield Bullock, Masterson Ogden, Cuthbert Bullitt, John Logan and James Moore ... 4 ... 354

Waters, Richard Jones, deceased
Sale of lands authorized ... 5 ... 76

Watkins, Isaac
Promoter at Shelbyville of Lexington and Louisville Turnpike Road Company ... 5 ... 519

Watkins, John
(a) Trustee of Versailles and Commissioner to sell lots therein ... 1 ... 63
(b) Trustee Woodford Academy ... 2 ... 243

Watkins, Samuel
Commissioner for Franklin County to open road from Buckley's Ferry to Bairdstown ... 3 ... 463

WATSON 190

	VOL.	PAGE
Watson, Evan		
Authorized to locate 100 acres Estill County....	5	5
Watson, Joel		
Inspection site in Warren County............	2	279
Watson, Shemi		
Balance due on headright land remitted........	4	319
Watts, John		
Inspection site in Boone County.............	3	243
Waugh, Samuel M.		
Promoter at Carlisle of Maysville and Lexington Turnpike Road Company..................	5	536
Wayne County		
(a) Formed December 18, 1800 from Pulaski and Cumberland Counties	2	392
(b) Part of Adair County added to.............	3	112
(c) Part of added to Pulaski County.............	5	562
(d) Part of Pulaski County added to.............	5	562
Weagle, John		
Authorized to locate 200 acres in Madison County for tan-bark purposes....................	4	282
Weare, James (see Weir)		
Trustee Greenville Academy.................	4	113
Webb, George		
Promoter at Winchester of Ohio Canal Company	3	222
Webb, William E.		
Trustee of Paris...........................	1	188
Webber, Philip		
One of Commission to open road from Lindseys Station in Scott County to the Ohio.........	5	272
Weedon, Major General George		
Empowered to appoint surveyors (1783).......	1	442
Weir, James (see Weare)		
Allowed pay as Deputy Sheriff of Muhlenberg County	2	486
Weisiger, Daniel		
(a) One of Commission to open road from Frankfort to Cincinnati	1	185
(b) Trustee of Frankfort.......................	1	247
(c) Inspection site in Frankfort.................	2	196
(d) Incorporator of Frankfort Bridge Company....	2	304
(e) Trustee Kentucky Seminary	2	389
(f) Promoter at Frankfort of Bank of Kentucky....	3	390
(g) One of Commission to repair State House......	3	509
(h) Promoter at Frankfort of Kentucky Assurance Society	4	254
(i) Trustee Kentucky Seminary.................	4	319

	VOL.	PAGE
(j) One of Commission to erect a State House	5	123
(k) Authorized to convey lots in Frankfort	5	490

Welch, Joseph (see Welsh)
    Trustee Stanford Academy ... 3   334

Weller, John, Sr.
    Authorized to erect a mill dam on Beech Fork in Nelson County ... 2   489

Wells, Francis
    Trustee Brucken Academy ... 2   242

Welsh, Joseph (see Welch)
    (a) Director Wilderness Road ... 4   265
    (b) His addition included in Stanford ... 5   171

Welsh, Thomas
    His addition included in Stanford ... 5   171

West Point
    Inspection site in Hardin County ... 2   456

Westport (Henry County)
    Plat of by William Hogshead confirmed ... 2   408

West, Thomas
    Trustee of Hopewell (Paris) (1789) ... 3   568

Wherns, Henrietta
    Authorized to sue Jacob Wherns in Bourbon County for divorce ... 1   695

Wherns, Jacob
    See Henrietta Wherns

Whitaker, Aquilla
    Trustee Shelby Academy ... 2   241

Whitaker, William W.
    (a) Trustee Logan Vineyard Society ... 3   139
    (b) Trustee Logan Academy ... 3   277

White, Hugh
    One of Commissioners for Clay County to open road in Estill and Clay Counties ... 5   567

White, James
    (a) Inspection site in Madison County ... 2   457
    (b) One of Commissioners for Estill County to open road in Estill and Clay Counties ... 5   567

White, John
    Allowed pay for services in Logan's Campaign ... 5   74

White, William
    Error in settlement certificate, held as assignee of James McChord, corrected ... 5   367

Whitley, William
    Commissioner to open road from Danville to Tellico ... 3   204

Whitlington, Joshua
    Inspection site in Boone County ... 3   123

	VOL.	PAGE
Whitnell, Josiah		
Trustee Caledonia Academy	5	3
Whitney, Thomas		
Main Street in Lexington, in front of his lot, ordered paved	2	368
Whittington, William		
Trustee of Versailles	1	355
Wickliff, Charles		
Trustee Washington Academy	2	242
Wickliffe, Nathaniel		
One of Commission to raise by lottery a fund to open Salt River to navigation	4	249
Wickliffe, Robert		
Attorney in fact for heirs of Peter Shepherd in settlement of claim to site of Town of Jefferson	5	353
Wilcox, George		
Allowed compensation for services as Brigade Inspector of Militia	3	491
Wilderness Road		
(a) Pay allowed garrisons of blockhouses on	1	218
(b) Joseph Crockett appointed Commissioner to erect a turnpike on	1	687
(c) Robert Craig given further time to repair	2	211
(d) Turnpike on to be leased	2	266
(e) Repairs to provided for	3	210
(f) Andrew Craig, of Knox, John Burditt, of Rockcastle, and Robert Caldwell, of Madison County, appointed Managers, and directed to settle with Christopher Durbin, former turnpike keeper, and John Reid, present turnpike keeper, and with Joseph Welch, Robert Caldwell and Nathaniel Rochester, present directors thereof	4	264
Wiley, Robert		
Escaped from Mason Jail to Tennessee. Reward paid for his capture and return	3	111
Wilhelms, George		
Relieved of effects of errors in respect to headright claims	4	340
Wilking, John		
Named as boundary of election precinct in Christian County	4	329
Wilkins, Charles		
(a) Trustee Woodford Academy	2	243
(b) Promoter of Kentucky Assurance Society	4	257

	VOL.	PAGE
(c) One of Commission to raise by lottery a fund to open Kentucky River to navigation	4	318
(d) Incorporator of Lexington Manufacturing Company	5	251
(e) Promoter at Lexington of Lexington and Louisville Turnpike Road Company	5	519

Wilkinson, James
	VOL.	PAGE
(a) Trustee of Louisville (1789)	3	547
(b) Founder of Frankfort (1786)	3	557
(c) Inspection site at Frankfort (1791)	3	584

Wilkinson, John
	VOL.	PAGE
(a) Promoter for Madison County of Kentucky River Navigation Company	2	448
(b) Allowed credit on settlement as Sheriff of Madison County	4	276

Willett, John
	VOL.	PAGE
Trustee Washingtonian Library	4	354

Willett, Richard
	VOL.	PAGE
Voting place at house in Hardin County	5	181

Williams, Benjamin
	VOL.	PAGE
Balance due on headright land remitted	5	388

Williams, Charles
	VOL.	PAGE
Voting place at house in Franklin County	5	334

Williams, Hubbard
	VOL.	PAGE
Named in Harrison-Nicholas County boundary	5	453

Williams, James
	VOL.	PAGE
Price of land remitted	5	369

Williams, Jesse
	VOL.	PAGE
Inspection site in Logan County	3	514

Williams, John
	VOL.	PAGE
(a) Inspection site in Logan County	3	451
(b) Price of 200 acres of land remitted	5	159
(c) Claimant of part of townsite of Versailles	1	226

Williams, Samuel
	VOL.	PAGE
Promoter at Paris of Bank of Kentucky	3	390

Williamsville
	VOL.	PAGE
Established December 6, 1792 at mouth of Salt River on lands of William Johnston, with William Pope, Lewis Fields, Benjamin Johnston, Thomas M. Winn and George Slaughter as Trustees	1	118

Williby, John
	VOL.	PAGE
Named in boundary of election precinct in Warren County	3	174

Willingham, ——
	VOL.	PAGE
Marriage improperly solemnized, legalized	3	220

WILLS 194

	VOL.	PAGE

Wills, John
    Trustee Allen Seminary 5   433
Wilmington (Scott County)
    Established December 7, 1793 on lands of John Grant between mouths of the two Grassy Creeks with John Sanders, John Thrasher, Sr., Matthias Corwine, Joseph Floyd, John Hay, Squire Grant and William Henry, Trustees... 1   175
Wilmott, Richard
    Error in patent corrected.................... 4   51
Wilmot, Robert
    Delegate from Bourbon County to second Constitutional Convention (1799).............. 1   57
Wilson, George
    (a) Promoter at Louisville of Ohio Canal Company   3   .221
    (b) Allowed pay for forage furnished Alexander Scott Bullitt, County Lieutenant of Jefferson County, Virginia, in 1787................ 3   407
Wilson, James
    (a) Trustee Logan Vineyard Society.............. 3   139
    (b) Promoter at Russellville of Bank of Kentucky.. 3   391
    (c) Trustee Pendleton Academy................ 5   175
Wilson, James, deceased
    Lands named in Lincoln-Mercer County boundary 4   86
Wilson, Josiah
    Trustee of Springfield...................... 1   176
Wilson, Josiah, deceased
    Sale of lot in Springfield by Executors confirmed 3   446
Wilson, Nathaniel
    Trustee Franklin Academy 1   296
Wilson, Robert
    Error in patent corrected 3   465
Wilson, Samuel
    (a) Trustee Newton Academy.................... 3   409
    (b) One of Commission to locate County seat for Warren County 3   447
Wilson, Uel
    Trustee Henderson Library Company 5   460
Winchester
    (a) Established December 17, 1793 on lands of John Baker with Richard Hickman, David Bullock, Josiah Bullock, William Bush, Josiah Hart, John Elliott, Benjamin Combs, and John Strode, Trustees 1   187

	VOL.	PAGE

(b) John Martin, Robert Higgins, Robert McKenny, Richard Jones, John Landers, James Stephens, and John Ireland appointed additional Trustees 1   340
(c) Lands of Josiah Hart added to............... 1   367
(d) Thomas Scott and John Ward named Commissioners to extend Short Street to Water Street   4   379

Winchester Academy
    Incorporated December 19, 1798 with Robert Clark, Sr., Hubbard Taylor, John Lyle, Robert Clark, Jr., Richard Hickman, William Cavenaugh, Jacob Fishback, David Bullock, William Sudduth, Dillard Collins, John Irwin, Patterson Bullock and Robert Elkins, Trustees 2   217

Winchester Library Company
    Incorporated December 27, 1810 by William N. Lane, James Simpson, James Clark, Chilton Allen, and Samuel Hanson................ 4   195

Winchester Steam Mill Company
    Incorporated February 3, 1817............... 5   514

Wing, Charles F.
    (a) Trustee Greenville Academy................. 4   113
    (b) Penalty for failure to file settlement as Clerk of Muhlenberg County waived................ 5   337

Wingate, Thomas S.
    Trustee Newcastle Library Company.......... 4   35

Winlock, Joseph
    (a) Trustee of Shelbyville...................... 1   151
    (b) Trustee Shelby Academy.................... 2   241

Winn, Thomas M.
    Trustee of Williamsville.................... 1   118

Winslow, Hallet M.
    Incorporator of Fayette Paper Manufacturing Company 5   409

Winslow, William
    Trustee Gallatin Academy 5   13

Winston, John
    Trustee Town of Salisberry 3   369

Winters, Elisha
    (a) Special suit against him by Innes B. Brent in Fayette County authorized 1   113
    (b) Act (a) repealed........................... 1   172

Wolf, James D.
    Incorporator of Lexington Manufacturing Company 5   251

Wolfscale, George
(a) Authorized to locate land for use in manufacture of iron 2 488
(b) Named in boundary of election precinct in Wayne County 5 35

Wood, Abraham
Charlotte Wood authorized to sue him in Mason County for divorce 3 161

Woods, Archibald
(a) Trustee Town of Milford (1789) 3 567
(b) One of Commission to assess damages to property owners in Milford upon removal of County Seat of Madison County therefrom 2 166
(c) Trustee Madison Academy 2 241
(d) Trustee Madison Academy 3 278
(e) Trustee Madison Academy 5 133
(f) Trustee of Boonesborough (1787) 3 540

Wood, Charlotte
See Abraham Wood

Wood, George
Trustee Town of Washington 1 199

Wood, Brigadier General James
Empowered to appoint surveyors (1783) 1 442

Woods, Joseph
Error in patent corrected 5 436

Woods, Michael
Authorized to locate 50 acres of land on Rockcastle River for a millsite 2 426

Wood, William
(a) Deeds made as Trustee of Town of Washington confirmed 1 200
(b) Same as (a) 2 395
(c) Trustee Franklin Academy 1 296
(d) Named in boundary of Town of Washington (1790) 3 556
(e) Voting place at house in Gallatin County 5 183

Woodford Academy
(a) Incorporated December 22, 1798 with Caleb Wallace, Robert Alexander, George Brooke, William Vawter, William Steele, John Watkins, Marquis Calmes, Richard Young, John Jouitte, Charles Wilkins, Tunstall Quarles, John O'Bannon, and Alexander Dunlap, Trustees 2 243
(b) John Jouitt, William Steele, Marquis Calmes, Richard Young, George Brooke, William Vawter, Benjamin Temple, Harman Bowmar,

WOODFORD COUNTY

	VOL.	PAGE
Reuben Twyman, Charles Railey, Nathan Dedman, Thomas Eastland and John O'Bannon appointed Trustees (1804)	3	181

Woodford County
(a) Formed May 1, 1788 from Fayette County	1	628
(b) Scott County carved from	1	629
(c) Franklin County, in part, carved from	1	632
(d) Peter G. Voorhies and Achilles Sneed, for Franklin, and William Steele and Richard Fox for Woodford County, appointed Commissioners to survey Franklin-Woodford County line	5	447

Woodward, William
(a) Commissioner for Bracken County to open road from Georgetown to Augusta	3	201
(b) One of Commission to locate County Seat for Lewis County	3	340

Woolford, Major John
Commissioner for Casey County to survey Lincoln-Casey County line	5	105

Work, Samuel
Trustee Hartford Academy	3	278

Worthington, Edward, deceased
Escheat of his lands waived	4	51

Worthington, Elizabeth
Escheat of lands waived	4	51

Worthington, James T.
Trustee Stanford Academy	3	334

Wren, Woodson
Trustee Danville Library	2	376

Wright, Alexander
Trustee Lancaster Library Company	3	208

Wright, John
Balance of State price of 100 acres of land in Warren County remitted	5	108

Wright, Joseph
(a) Named in boundary of election precinct in Breckenridge County	4	328
(b) Named in Ohio-Daviess County boundary	5	160
(c) Named in Ohio-Daviess County boundary	5	299

Wright, William
Harrison County Court authorized to permit gates on a public road through his lands	5	481

Yancey, Joel
Trustee Glasgow Academy	4	85

Yantes, John
Trustee Lancaster Library Company	3	208

YATES 198

	VOL.	PAGE

Yates, Henry
   One of Commission to open road from Lindseys
      Station in Scott County to the Ohio......... 5   272
Yates, John
   Trustee Grayson Seminary.................. 5   325
Yates, Robert
   Trustee Grayson Seminary.................. 5   325
Yenowine, Leonard
   Named in boundary of election precinct in Jefferson County 5   308
Young, Henry
   (a) Promoter of Gallatin Ohio Steamboat Company 5   344
   (b) Co-founder Town of Bedford................ 5   350
Young, James
   (a) Trustee of Greensburg 1   341
   (b) Trustee New Athens Academy............... 2   242
   (c) Voting place at house in Montgomery County.. 4   173
   (d) Justices of Bath County to meet at his house.. 4   215
Young, John
   (a) Trustee Montgomery Academy............... 3   438
   (b) Named in Lincoln-Mercer County boundary... 4   86
Young, Josiah, deceased
   Heirs given time to pay for land............. 2   487
Young's Mill
   Named in boundary of election precinct in Green County 5   317
Young, Original
   (a) Named in boundary of election precinct in Montgomery County 4   173
   (b) Named in Montgomery-Bath County boundary 4   215
Young, Richard
   (a) Trustee of Versailles and Commissioner to sell lots therein 1   63
   (b) Trustee Woodford Academy.................. 2   243
   (c) Trustee Woodford Academy.................. 3   181
Young, Richard, deceased
   Sale of lands authorized..................... 5   382
Young, Thomas
   Trustee of Lewisbourgh-Mason County......... 1   295

APPENDIX

Newspapers.

	YEAR	VOL.	PAGE
American Republic, Frankfort	1810	4	203
American Statesman, Lexington	1811	4	316
Argus of Western America	1807	3	465
Bardstown Repository, Bardstown	1811	4	316
Commentator, The, Frankfort	1816	5	453
Dove, Town of Washington	1808	4	53
Eagle, The, Maysville	1814	5	174
Examiner, Lancaster	1809	4	126
Farmers Friend, Russellville	1808	4	53
Farmers Library	1800	2	422
Gazette of Public Printer	1798	2	5
Georgetown Patriot, Georgetown	1816	5	355
Globe, Richmond	1809	4	84
Guardian of Freedom	1798	2	228
Guardian of Liberty, Cynthiana	1816	5	453
Hemisphere, Hopkinsville	1815	5	362
Impartial Observer, Danville	1810	4	205
Impartial Observer, Harrodsburg	1815	5	266
Impartial Review, Bardstown	1806	3	343
Independent Gazette, Lexington	1803	3	161
Informant, Danville	1805	3	276–301
Kentuckian, Shelbyville	1814	5	137
Kentucky Advertiser, Winchester	1816	5	328
Kentucky Gazette, Lexington	1789	3	550–568
	1790	3	569
	1793	1	118
			179–181
			185–221
	1794	1	258
	1795	1	276–308
			335–344
	1796	1	513–525
			555–574
			575
	1797	1	665–695
	1798	2	16–80
			100–155

APPENDIX 200

	YEAR	VOL.	PAGE
Kentucky Gazette, Lexington...............			170–228
	1806	3	410
	1807	3	511
	1810	4	236
Kentucky Herald, Lexington...............	1795	1	295–344
	1796	1	513–525
			574–575
	1797	1	668
			666–695
Kentucky Herald, Bardstown..............	1811	4	415
(Not established)			
Kentucky Telegraphe.....................	1798	2	228
Lamp	1807	3	437
Light House, Danville.....................	1813	5	69
Louisville Correspondent	1812	5	2
Louisville Gazette	1807	3	494
			495–520
Luminary, Richmond	1810	4	203
	1814	5	172–199
Mirror, Russellville	1806	3	333
Mirror, Danville	1798	2	80–228
	1804	3	192
National Pulse, Harrodsburg...............	1816	5	453
Palladium	1798	2	228
Patriot, Glasgow	1814	5	84
Political Theatre, Lancaster...............	1808	4	53
Reporter	1807	3	530
Republican Auxiliary, Washington..........	1806	3	328
Republican Register, Shelbyville............	1804	3	192
Rights of Man	1798	2	170
Sovereign People, Russellville..............	1813	5	69
Telegraph, Georgetown	1811	4	316
Telescope, Bardstown	1814	5	293
Union, Washington	1814	5	84
Virginia Gazette	1789	3	568
Weekly Messenger, Washington.............	1803	3	161
Weekly Messenger, Russellville.............	1814	5	137
Western American, Bardstown.............	1803	3	161
Western Citizen	1807	3	530
Western Courier, Louisville...............	1811	4	316
Western Eagle, Hopkinsville...............	1813	5	15
Western Monitor, Lexington...............	1814	5	174
Western World, Frankfort................	1806	3	328
Winchester Advertiser....................	1814	5	137

Inspections.

1783: Vol. 3, p. 580:
Hickman's warehouse, in Lincoln County, at mouth of Hickman Creek, on lands of James Hogan;
Campbell's, in Jefferson County, at Falls of the Ohio on lands of John Campbell;
Lees, in Fayette County, at Leestown on Kentucky River, on lands of Hancock Lee.

1786: Vol. 3, p. 559:
Curd's, in Mercer County, at mouth of Dick's River, on lands of John Curd.

1787: Vol. 3, p. 582:
Harrod's Landing, in Mercer County, on lands of Walter Beall;
Hogan's, in Fayette County, at mouth of Hickman Creek, on lands of James Hogan;
Beall's, in Nelson County, at mouth of Beech Fork, on lands of Walter Beall;
Scott's, in Fayette County, at mouth of Craig's Creek, on the Kentucky River, on lands of Charles Scott;
Boones', in Madison County, at Boonesborough;
Collier's, in Madison County, on the Kentucky River, on lands of John Collier;
Limestone, in Bourbon County, on Limestone Creek, on lands of John May and Simon Canton.

1788: Vol. 3, p. 582:
Ruddle's Warehouse, in Bourbon County, on Stoner and Hinkston Forks of Licking, on lands of Isaac Ruddle.

1789: Vol. 3, p. 583:
Walton's, in Nelson County, on Salt River, on lands of Matthew Walton;
Parker's, in Nelson County, on Beech Fork, on lands of Richard Parker;
Stuart's Creek, in Nelson County, on Beech Fork, on lands of John Cockey Owen and David Baird.

1790: Vol. 3, p. 584:
Sprotsman's, in Paris, on lots of Lawrence Sprotsman.

1791: Vol. 3, p. 584:
Frankfort, on lands of James Wilkinson.

(The foregoing are Acts of Virginia and all apply to tobacco alone.)

Tobacco, Hemp and Flour.

1792: Vol. 1, p. 135:
Clark County Warehouses;
Cleveland's Landing;
Stafford's Landing.

Tobacco.

1792: Vol. 1, p. 150:
Cleveland's Landing;
Holder's Landing;
Stafford's Landing;
Bush's Landing.

1795: Vol. 1, p. 326:
Campbell's Warehouse, at Falls of the Ohio suppressed and one established in Louisville near mouth of Beargrass.

Flour and Hemp.

1795: Vol. 1, p. 330:
Frankfort;
Cleveland's Landing in Fayette County;
Stewart's Creek Warehouse on the Beech Fork;
Maysville;
Cynthiana;
Louisville;
Newport;
Warwick, at mouth of Dick's River;
Holder's Boatyard in Clarke County;
Mouth of Tates Creek in Madison County;
Scott's Warehouse in Woodford County;
Shepherdsville, in Jefferson County;
Walter Beall's warehouse, in Hardin County;
Jacob Doom's, at mouth of Hardin Creek in Washington County;
Parkers, on Beech Fork; and
Paris.

Tobacco, Flour and Hemp.

1796: Vol. 1, p. 369:
Near junction of Fair Fork and Mauldin's Fork of Red River in Logan County, on lands of John Bailey, occupied by Elijah Bailey.

Flour and Hemp.

1796: Vol. 1, p. 370:
In Woodford County, at mouth of Greer's Creek on Kentucky River, on lands of David Mitchell;
In Woodford County at Delaney's Ferry, on lands of Thomas Turpin;
In Fayette County at mouth of Hickman Creek, on lands of James Hogan;
In Fayette County at mouth of Jessamine, on lands of John Lewis;
In Shelby County at mouth of Brashear's Creek, on lands of Richard Taylor, and Thomas Carland;

Boonsborough, in Madison County;
Bedinger's Warehouse, near the Blue Licks in Bourbon County;
Riddle's Mill, in Bourbon County;
In Mason County at mouth of Bracken;
In Nelson County at mouth of Simpson Creek, on lands of Richard Stephens.

Flour and Hemp.

1797: **Vol. 1, p. 606:**
In Garrard County opposite mouth of Hickman, on lands of James Hogan;
In Garrard County at mouth of Sugar Creek, on lands of William Davis;
In Fayette County, below mouth of Hickman, on lands of Samuel Johnson.

Tobacco.

1798: **Vol. 2, pp. 139–140:**
Hickman's, in Garrard County on Kentucky River opposite mouth of Hickman Creek, on lands of James Hogan;
Curd's, in Mercer County at mouth of Dick's River, on lands of John Curd;
Harrod's Landing, on Kentucky River in Mercer County, on lands of Walter Beall;
Boone's, at Boonsborough in Madison County;
Biggerstaff's, in Madison County, on Kentucky River, on lands of Samuel Biggerstaff;
Hogan's, in Fayette County, at mouth of Hickman, on lands of James Hogan;
Cleveland's Landing, in Fayette County;
Stafford's Landing, in Fayette County;
Holder's Landing, in Clarke County;
Bush's Landing, in Clarke County;
Beall's, in Nelson County, at mouth of Beech Fork, on lands of Walter Beall;
Stewart's Creek, in Nelson County, at mouth of Stewart's Creek, on lands of John C. Owings and David Baird;
Walton's, in Nelson County at mouth of Long Lick Creek on Salt River, on lands of Matthew Walton;
Parker's, in Washington County, at mouth of Cartwright Creek, on Beech Fork, on lands of Richard Parker;
Scott's, in Woodford County, at mouth of Craig's Creek on Kentucky River, on lands of Charles Scott;
Limestone, in Mason County, on Limestone Creek, on lands of John May and Simon Kenton;
Bourbon, in Paris, on lots of Lawrence Sprotzman;

Frankfort;
Louisville, near mouth of Beargrass;
Bailey's, in Logan County, at Junction of Fair Fork and Mauldin's Fork, on lands of John Bailey;
Bedinger's, in Bourbon County, at Bedinger's warehouse, near Blue Licks;
Bracken, in Bracken County, at mouth of Bracken Creek;
Rowntree's, in Warren County, one mile below mouth of Little Barren, on lands of Samuel Rowntree;
Bullittsburgh, in Campbell County, on the Ohio River in Bullittsburgh Bottom, on lands of Cave Johnson.

Tobacco, Hemp and Flour.
1798: Vol. 2. p. 172–3:
In Madison County near mouth of Silver Creek, on lands of John Goggin;
Falmouth, in Forks of Licking.

Flour, Hemp and Tobacco.
1798: Vol. 2, p. 196:
Port-William, in Town of;
Silver Creek, in Madison County, on land of Green Clay at mouth of Silver Creek;
Quantico, in Garrard County at mouth of Sugar Creek, on lands of William Davis;
Gath, Town of, in Fleming County at mouth of Locust.

Hemp and Tobacco.
1798: Vol. 2, p. 196:
Greensburg, in Green County.

Hemp.
1798: Vol. 2, p. 196:
Lexington.

Tobacco.
1798: Vol. 2, p. 196:
Frankfort, at Daniel Weisiger's Warehouse.

Tobacco, Hemp and Flour.
1798: Vol. 2, p. 213:
Eddyville, on Cumberland River, on lands of David Walker;
Hinds', in Madison County, near mouth of Hinds Lick Creek on lands of William Mayo, Jr.

Tobacco.
1798: Vol. 2, p. 213:
Dooms', at mouth of Hardin Creek, on lands of Jacob Doom, deceased.

Tobacco, Hemp and Flour.

1799: Vol. 2, p. 278–9:

Froman's, in Woodford County, at mouth of Brushy Run, on lands of Jacob Froman;

Burksville, in Cumberland County;

Lees, in Logan County on Green River, near mouth of Big Barren, on lands of Benjamin Lees;

Bryant's Lick, in Lincoln County, on Green River;

Hart's, in Clarke County, at mouth of Four Mile Creek, on lands of Nathaniel Hart, deceased;

May's, in Shelby County, opposite mouth of Ashes Creek, on lands of Gabriel May;

Henderson's, in Henderson County at the Red Banks on the Ohio, on lands of Henderson and Company;

Berry's, in Henderson County, near mouth of Highland Creek, on lands of Benjamin Berry;

Taylor's, in Shelby County, at Taylorsville on Salt River, on land of Richard Taylor;

Westport, in Henry County, on the Ohio, on lands of Joseph Dupuy;

Swinney's, in Montgomery County, on Red River, on lands of Swinney and Collins;

Chapman's, in Warren County, on Drake Creek, on lands of Thomas Chapman;

Burwell's, in Christian County, at mouth of Little River, on lands of Nathaniel Burwell;

Shepherd's, in Bullitt County, at Shepherdsville, on lands of Adam Shepherd;

Walton's, in Bullitt County, near mouth of Long Lick Creek on Salt River, on lands of Matthew Walton;

Stewart's, in Warren County, on Big Barren River, on lands of James Stewart;

Cumpton's, in Warren County, at mouth of Bays Fork on Big Barren, on lands of Levi Cumpton;

Fowler's, in Montgomery County near mouth of Flat Creek on Licking River, on lands of John Fowler;

Jack's Creek, in Madison County, on lands of Green Clay between Elk Lick and Jack's Creek;

Newport, at mouth of Licking, on lands of James Taylor;

Landing Run, in Nelson County, on Beech Fork, on lands of Charles Morehead;

Lee's Creek, in Mason County, in Lee's Creek Bottom near the Ohio, on lands of Thomas Mills;

South Frankfort.

Flour and Hemp.

1799: Vol. 2, pp. 278–9:
Bush's Warehouse in Clarke County.
John Lewis' mill on Jessamine Creek;
Bealsburg, in Hardin County, at warehouse of Walter Beal.

Tobacco.

1799: Vol. 2, pp. 278–9:
Stone's, in Madison County, at Stone's Ferry, on lands of Green Clay.

Tobacco, Hemp, Flour and Cordage.

1799: Vol. 2, pp. 278–9:
Watson's, in Warren County, at mouth of Big Beaverdam on Green River, on lands of Joel Watson.

Tobacco, Hemp and Flour.

1799: Vol. 2, p. 287:
Cox's Creek, in Bullitt County, at mouth of Cox Creek, on land of Henry Crist.

Tobacco, Hemp and Flour.

1800: Vol. 2, pp. 383–4:
Huston's, in Breckenridge County, at mouth of Clover Creek, on lands of Joseph Huston;
Louisburg, in Muhlenberg County, in Town of Louisburg, on lands of Lewis Kincheloe;
Storms', in Muhlenberg County, on Green River, on lands of Leonard Storm;
Warwick, in Madison County, near mouth of Four Mile Creek, on lands of Robert Clark, Sr.;
Dowdal's, in Washington County, on Chaplins Fork, on lands of John Dowdal;
Ferguson's, in Washington County, at Ferguson's Mill on Beech Fork, on lands of Joshua Ferguson;
Rolling Fork, in Washington County, at mouth of Panther's Creek of Rolling Fork, on lands of Joseph Ray;
Big Bone, in Boone County, at Rock Landing near mouth of Big Bone Creek, on lands of Thomas Carneal;
Woolper's, in Boone County, in Woolper's bottom on the Ohio, on lands of Philemon Thomas;
Barnett's, in Hartford, Ohio County;
Drennon's Creek, in Henry County at mouth of Drennor Creek, on lands of Hite and Hogg.

Flour and Hemp.

1800: Vol. 2, p. 384:
Louisville—location of to be fixed by County Court.

Tobacco.

1800: Vol. 2, p. 384:
Limestone, in Maysville, on a lot of James Edwards;
Pocahuntas, in Nelson County, near Scott's Ferry on Beech Fork, on lands of William Kindall;
Campbell and Stapp, in Pulaski County, on Cumberland River, on lands of Thomas Cowen.

Tobacco, Hemp and Flour.

1800: Vol. 2, p. 391:
Currens', in Livingston County, at forks of Harrican, on lands of James Curren;
Kirkfield in Livingston County, on Mill Branch of Harrican, on lands of Robert Kirk.

Tobacco, Hemp and Flour.

1801: Vol. 2, pp. 456–7:
Cole's, in Warren County on Big Barren River at mouth of Beaver Creek, on lands of John Cole;
Funkhouser's, in Logan County, on Green River, on lands of Christopher Funkhouser;
Hays', in Harrison County at mouth of Grays Run on South Fork of Licking, on lands of James Hays;
West Point, in Hardin County, at Town of West Point;
Prestonville, in Gallatin County, at Town of Prestonville, on lands of John Smith and Francis Preston;
Campbell and Stapp, on Cumberland River, on lands of William Campbell and Gholston Stapp;
Garris', in Muhlenberg County, on lands of Benjamin Garris;
Hunsaker's, in Muhlenberg County, at mill of Jacob Hunsaker;
Hardin's, in Washington County, at mouth of Pleasant Run, on lands of Martin Hardin;
Sullenger's, in Henry County, on Kentucky River, on lands of Robert Sullenger;
White's, in Madison County, at mouth of middle fork of Station Camp Creek, on lands of James White;
Coleman's, in Livingston County, at mouth of Clay Lick Creek on Cumberland River, on lands of Francis Coleman;
Miller's, in Livingston County, at Ritchy's Landing, on lands of David Miller;
Flournoy's, in Campbell County on Licking River, on lands of Francis Flournoy;
Allen's, in Campbell County, on Main Licking, on lands of Benjamin Allen.

Flour.

1801: Vol. 2, p. 456:
Frankfort, at warehouse of Otho Beatty.

Tobacco.

1801: Vol. 2, p. 456:
Ellis', in Pendleton County, on Main Licking, on lands of Israel Ellis.

Tobacco, Hemp and Flour.

1802: Vol. 3, pp. 22-3:
Dickins', in Cumberland County, on lands of Ephraim Dickins;
Buckhannon's, in Adair County, on Cumberland River, on lands of Nathaniel Buckhannon;
Gullion's, in Gallatin County, at mouth of Eagle Creek on Kentucky River, on lands of Jeremiah Gullion;
Jackson's, in Wayne County at mouth of Indian Creek, on lands of William Jackson;
Montgomery's, in Wayne County on Cumberland River, on lands of James and Thomas Montgomery;
Newmarket, in Pulaski County, on Cumberland River, on lands of Samuel Newell;
Lusk's, in Livingston County on the Ohio River, on lands of James Lusk;
Pond River, in Muhlenberg County, on Pond River, on lands of Epps Littlepage;
Robinson's, in Cumberland County, near mouth of Willis Creek on Cumberland River, on lands of John Robinson;
Embree's, in Cumberland County, one mile above McFarlands Creek on Cumberland River, on lands of Joshua Embree.

Tobacco, Hemp and Flour.

1803: Vol. 3, p. 123-4:
Trumbo's, in Montgomery County, on Licking River near mouth of Slate, on lands of ―― Trumbo;
Clarke's, in Harrison County, near mouth of Beaver Creek on Licking River, on lands of Robert Clarke;
Willoughby Creek, in Boone County, at mouth of Willoughby Creek on the Ohio, on lands of Joshua Whitlington;
West Point, in Hardin County, at mouth of Salt River;
Taylor's, in Logan County, in forks of Wolf Lick and Muddy River, on lands of Chapman Taylor;
Maberry's, in Christian County, near junction of Cumberland River and Little River, on lands of ―― Maberry;
Kilpatrick's, in Cumberland County, at mouth of Masheck's Creek, on lands of Moses and Kilpatrick.

Beef and Pork.

1804: Vol. 3, p. 239:
Maysville, in Mason County;
Augusta, in Bracken County;

Lower Blue Licks, in Nicholas County;
Newport, in Campbell County;
Port William, in Gallatin County;
Louisville, in Jefferson County;
Breckenridge County, at mouth of Clover;
Henderson, in Henderson County;
Livingston County, at mouth of Cumberland;
Frankfort, in Franklin County;
Greensburg, in Green County;
Stewart's Creek Warehouse, on Beech Fork, in Nelson County;
Mouth of Hickman, in Jessamine County;
Curd's warehouse at mouth of Dick's River, in Mercer County;
Mouth of Sugar Creek in Garrard County;
Falmouth, in Pendleton County;
Mouth of Greasy Creek, in Adair County;
Mouth of Beaver Creek, in Harrison County;
Doom's warehouse in Washington County, on lands of Robert Clarke;
Bush's Landing, in Clarke County;
Mouth of Salt River, in Hardin County;
Beallsburg, at mouth of Beech Fork;
Mouth of Sinking, in Breckenridge County;
Jack's Creek warehouse, in Madison County;
Boonsborough, in Madison County.

Tobacco, Hemp and Flour.

1804: Vol. 3, pp. 242-3:
Greasy Creek, in Cumberland County, at mouth of Greasy Creek on Cumberland River;
Jackson's, at Jackson's Ferry on Cumberland River, in Cumberland County;
Doran's, at Doran's Mill on Rolling Fork in Washington County;
Indian Creek, in Wayne County, at mouth of Indian Creek, on land of William Jackman;
Watts, in Boone County, in Woolper's bottom;
Montgomery's, in Pulaski County, on Cumberland River, on lands of James Montgomery;
Thockmorton's, in Nicholas County, at mouth of Johnson, on lands of John Throckmorton;
Falmouth, in Pendleton County.

Flour.

1804: Vol. 3, pp. 242-3:
Davis, in Pulaski County, on Buck Creek, on lands of Baxter Davis.

Tobacco, Hemp, Flour, Beef and Pork.
1804: Vol. 3, pp. 242–3:
Forsythe's, in Logan County, on Green River, on lands of William Forsythe.

Tobacco, Hemp, Flour, Beef, Pork, Cotton and Cordage.
1804: Vol. 3, pp. 242–3:
Gallatin's, in Warren County, at mouth of Ray's Branch on Barren River, on Gallatin's survey.

Tobacco, Hemp, Flour, Beef and Pork.
1805: Vol. 3, pp. 322–4:
Hoagland's, in Gallatin County, in Hunter's bottom on the Ohio, on lands of Cornelius Hoagland;
Falling Spring, in Hardin County, on the Ohio, on lands of Solomon Brandenburgh;
Russell Creek, in Green County, on Russell Creek, at Hilliard and Moss' Mill;
Howard's, in Clarke County, at mouth of Upper Howard Creek, on land of John Howard;
Graves', in Campbell County on Main Licking at mill of Bartlett Graves;
Anderson's, in Mason County, on the Ohio at Stoke Anderson's;
Dibrill's, in Wayne County, on Cumberland River, on lands of Charles Dibrill;
Hartford, in Ohio County, on lands of the late Gabriel Madison;
Beaver Creek, in Harrison County, at mouth of Beaver Creek on Main Licking, on lands of James Coleman;
Hart's in Pulaski County, on Cumberland River, on lands of Israel Hart;
Cedar Creek, in Nelson County, at mouth of Cedar Creek, on lands of William Able;
Red River, in Clarke County, on Red River, at Clark and Smith's iron works.

Beef and Pork.
1805: Vol. 3, pp. 322–4:
Dorin's, in Washington County, on Rolling Fork, at Dorin's Mill;
Warwick, Town of, in Mercer County;
Goggins', in Madison County, at Goggins' warehouse on Silver Creek;
Lewisburg, in Muhlenberg County;
Georgetown, Scott County, on lands of Josiah Pitts;
Taylor's, in Henderson County, on Pond River, on lands of Jonathan Taylor.

Inspections heretofore established in Logan County, on Green River, Muddy River, and Red River, are made also inspections of beef and pork.

Beef, Pork, Hemp and Tobacco.

1805: **Vol. 3, pp. 322–4:**
Greensburg, in Green County.

Flour, Hemp and Tobacco.

1805: **Vol. 3, pp. 322–4:**
Drowning Creek, in Madison County, on Kentucky River, on lands of —— Mosby.

Flour, Hemp, Beef and Pork.

1805: **Vol. 3, pp. 322–4:**
Herndon's, in Knox County at mouth of Laurel Creek, on lands of Richardson Herndon.

Tobacco, Hemp, Flour, Beef, Pork and Cotton.

1805: **Vol. 3, pp. 322–4:**
Bay's Fork, in Warren County, on lands of Joseph Boone; McNeal's, at Jeffersonville on Big Barren River, on lands of John McNeal.

Tobacco, Hemp and Flour.

1806: **Vol. 3, p. 332:**
Jacks Creek, in Madison County, on lands of Green Clay;
Benson's, near Frankfort, on lands of Christopher Greenup:
Little Barren, in Green County, on lands of James Turner;
Vanceburgh, in Mason County;
Little Sandy, at mouth of Little Sandy in Greenup County;
Glover's Creek, on Big Barren River;
Green River, in Lincoln County, on lands of Henry Quarles;
McCoun's, in Mercer County, at Samuel McCoun's Ferry;
Rough Run, in Woodford County, on lands of Jeremiah Buckley;
Randolph's, in Muhlenberg County on Green River, on lands of John Randolph.

Tobacco, Hemp and Flour.

1806: **Vol. 3, p. 337:**
Newton's, in Jessamine County, near mouth of Dick's River, on lands of Newton Curd.

Tobacco, Hemp and Flour.

1806: **Vol. 3, p. 384:**
Doom's, a warehouse of Jacob Doom, deceased, at mouth of Hardin Creek, in Washington County;

Rife's, in Adair County, on Green River, on lands of Abraham Rife.

Tobacco.
1807: Vol. 3, p. 437:
Wilkins, in Woodford County at Delany's Ferry on lands of Thomas Turpin.

Tobacco, Hemp and Flour.
1807: Vol. 3, p. 439:
Smart's, in South Frankfort, on lands of John Smart.

Tobacco, Hemp and Flour.
1807: Vol. 3, pp. 450–1:
Tates Creek, in Madison County near mouth of Tates Creek, on lands of William McBean;
Haydon's, in Madison County at mouth of Muddy Creek on lands of Richard Haydon;
Tousey's, in Boone County, at a small village on the Ohio River opposite Lawrenceburg, Indiana;
Hedrick's, in Fleming County, on Main Licking, at mill of Michael Hedrick;
Green River, at mouth of Russell Creek on Green River;
Barnes', in Washington County on Rolling Fork, on lands of Joshua Barnes;
Williams', in Logan County, on Red River, on lands of John Williams;
Pond River, in Hopkins County, on lands of Jonathan Taylor;
Mill Creek, in Nelson County, on Beech Fork at mouth of Mill Creek, on lands of Christian Hahn;
Stephenson's, in Lewis County, at mouth of Sycamore Creek, on lands of John Stephenson.

Tobacco.
1807: Vol. 3, p. 450–1.
Ellis', in Pendleton County, on lands of Jezareel Ellis.

Tobacco.
1807: Vol. 3, p. 513.
Kennedy's, in Campbell County near mouth of Licking, on lands of Thomas Kennedy;
Posey's, in Campbell County, on the Ohio River, on lands of Thomas Posey.

Tobacco, Hemp and Flour.
1807: Vol. 3, p. 513:
Saunders', in Gallatin County, on Eagle Creek, on lands of Nathaniel Saunders;

Hieronimous, Clarke County, on Kentucky River, on lands of Henry Hieronimous.

Tobacco, Hemp, Flour and Pork.

1807: Vol. 3, p. 514:
Berthoud's, in Jefferson County, at Shippingsport, on lands of Nicholas Berthoud.

Hemp and Flour.

1807: Vol. 3, p. 514:
Henderson, in Henderson County, on lot of Philip Barbour.

Tobacco, Hemp and Flour.

1807: Vol. 3, p. 514:
Tibbs', on Green River at mouth of Robertson Creek on lands of Diskin Tibbs;
Williams', in Logan County, on Red River, on lands of Jesse Williams;
Beaver Creek, on Cumberland River at mouth of Beaver Creek;
Marrowbone, on Cumberland River at mouth of Marrowbone Creek, on lands of Roberts and Jones.

1808: Vol. 4, p. 13:
The several counties authorized to establish inspections.

www.ingramcontent.com/pod-product-compliance
Lightning Source LLC
Chambersburg PA
CBHW051058230426
43667CB00013B/2344